HTML5 & CSS3

FOR DUMMIES

A Wiley Brand

HTML5 & CSS3

FOR

DUMMIES®

A Wiley Brand

by David Karlins

FOR

DUMMIES®

A Wiley Brand

HTML5 & CSS3 For Dummies®

Published by: **John Wiley & Sons, Inc.,** 111 River Street, Hoboken, NJ 07030-5774, www.wiley.com

Copyright © 2014 by John Wiley & Sons, Inc., Hoboken, New Jersey

Published simultaneously in Canada

Media and software compilation copyright © 2014 by John Wiley & Sons, Inc. All rights reserved.

No part of this publication may be reproduced, stored in a retrieval system or transmitted in any form or by any means, electronic, mechanical, photocopying, recording, scanning or otherwise, except as permitted under Sections 107 or 108 of the 1976 United States Copyright Act, without the prior written permission of the Publisher. Requests to the Publisher for permission should be addressed to the Permissions Department, John Wiley & Sons, Inc., 111 River Street, Hoboken, NJ 07030, (201) 748-6011, fax (201) 748-6008, or online at http://www.wiley.com/go/permissions.

Trademarks: Wiley, For Dummies, the Dummies Man logo, Dummies.com, Making Everything Easier, and related trade dress are trademarks or registered trademarks of John Wiley & Sons, Inc. and may not be used without written permission. All other trademarks are the property of their respective owners. John Wiley & Sons, Inc. is not associated with any product or vendor mentioned in this book.

For general information on our other products and services, please contact our Customer Care Department within the U.S. at 877-762-2974, outside the U.S. at 317-572-3993, or fax 317-572-4002. For technical support, please visit www.wiley.com/techsupport.

Wiley publishes in a variety of print and electronic formats and by print-on-demand. Some material included with standard print versions of this book may not be included in e-books or in print-on-demand. If this book refers to media such as a CD or DVD that is not included in the version you purchased, you may download this material at http://booksupport.wiley.com. For more information about Wiley products, visit www.wiley.com.

Library of Congress Control Number: 2013944335

ISBN 978-1-118-58863-5 (pbk); ISBN 978-1-118-63941-2 (ebk); ISBN 978-1-118-63965-8 (ebk)

Manufactured in the United States of America

10 9 8 7 6 5 4 3 2 1

Contents at a Glance

Table of Contents

Introduction

HTML and CSS are the basic building blocks of websites. The advent of HTML5 and CSS3 represents a dynamic and powerful evolutionary stage in the development of web design. Maximizing the potential of HTML5 and CSS3 makes it possible to apply styling and formatting, present audio and video, and create animation and interactivity in ways that have never before been possible without stringing together plugins, image files, and JavaScript.

About This Book

The web is filled with useful (and some not so useful) resources with definitions, descriptions, and syntax for HTML5 and CSS3. This book presents, in a coherent manner, a survey of the HTML5 and CSS3 tools and features and how to deploy them. The book begins with a compressed course in building pages with HTML and CSS and then quickly moves into a detailed exploration of how to really get the most out of HTML5 and CSS3.

Here are a few basic technical conventions used throughout the book:

- Code (HTML5, CSS3, or small doses of JavaScript and PHP) is always indicated with monofont type. I provide numerous blocks of code that you might want to copy and paste as well as code snippets.

- Web addresses and programming code also appear in monofont. If you're reading a digital version of this book on a device connected to the Internet, note that you can click the web address to visit that website, like this: www.dummies.com.

- Overwhelmingly, the only "software" needed to apply all the features explored in this book is a code editor (free ones work just fine) and a browser to preview how pages will look. In rare occasions where I describe steps in command-based resources, commands are shown with arrow connectors (⇨) as in, *With your browser open, choose File⇨Open.*

Foolish Assumptions

This book is written for two audiences — and everyone who falls in between them. The first audience is readers just stepping into the world of web page layout and design in a serious way. You've been exposed to HTML and CSS and now want to jump in with both feet and learn the basics of web page design with the latest (and greatest) versions of HTML and CSS.

The second audience is experienced web designers who have explored pieces of the HTML5 and CSS3 puzzle and have applied some HTML5 and CSS3 tools but want (and need) to deploy a full understanding of HTML5 and CSS3.

Icons Used in This Book

tip

The Tip icon marks tips and shortcuts that you can use to make page design easier.

remember

Remember icons draw your attention to the information that's especially important to know.

technical stuff

The Technical Stuff icon marks information of a highly technical nature, and you can skip these if you aren't interested in information that ventures beyond the basics.

warning

The Warning icon tells you to watch out! It marks important information that may save you headaches or disasters.

on the web

The On the Web icon marks links to online reference material as well as all of the code listings used in this book.

Beyond the Book

I have written a lot of extra content that you won't find in this book. Go online to find the following:

- **Cheat Sheet:** The book's cheat sheet is found at www.dummies.com/cheatsheet/html5andcss3. There, I put together some basic, fundamental approaches and resources necessary to launch a web development project. I encourage you to jump to the cheat sheet early in the process of engaging with this book, and to bookmark it for future reference as kind of a super-compressed review of the basic points in this book.

- **Dummies.com online articles:** Each of the Part pages in this book (the pages that divide the book into different sections) includes a link to an article online at Dummies.com that extends the content covered in the book. You'll find links to the articles on the Part page and, where appropriate, at helpful points in the chapters, too. I think you'll find these articles helpful in extending the material covered in the book. Articles for this book are found at www.dummies.com/extras/html5andcss3.

- **Updates:** The world of web design is changing rapidly. I created this book with that in mind, providing links to resources that document changes in browser compatibility and other fast-changing material. When necessary, updates will be posted to the Downloads tab on the book's product page (www.dummies.com/extras/html5andcss3) where you can find an article that either describes any necessary updates or a link to updated content. And, in the event that I find a need to post a correction, you'll find that there as well.

- **Companion files:** All code listings used in this book are available for download from the Downloads tab on the book's companion website at www.dummies.com/extras/html5andcss3. You can copy the code and paste it into your code editor and then use it to follow along with the examples in the book.

Where to Go from Here

This book isn't linear — you can start anywhere. That said, for most of you, I recommend starting with Part I for an overview of how HTML5 and CSS3 fit together as well as how they've altered the world of web design. After that, jump around at will and grab features you need. Or, if you're using the book to acquire an overall and comprehensive understanding of HTML5 and CSS3, you might want to give the book a one-time straight-through read, and then return to specific features as you need them.

```
<header>

<nav>


<article>

<section>                    <aside>


<section>


<section>


<article>

<section>                    <aside>




                             <figure>



<section>
                             <figcapti


<footer>

<nav>
```

Part I

Page Structure and Design with HTML5 and CSS3

In this part, I walk you through a compressed course in building web pages with HTML5 for page structure and CSS3 for design, animation, and interactivity. Designers breaking out of the stifling box of content management system blogs and website builders whose HTML and CSS chops are a bit dated will find a solid grounding in building contemporary web pages. Designers in the midst of cutting-edge work will find material to fill in holes and round out their skills.

This part also provides an overview of accessibility and compatibility issues involved in building pages with HTML5 and CSS3 and surveys solutions to those issues.

Visit www.dummies.com for great Dummies content online.

Heading One Content

Links...

- [Link 1](#)

- [Link 2](#)

- [Link 3](#)

Right Columi

Right column content here

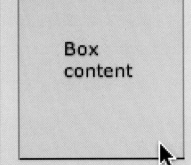

Box
content

Bo:
cor

Contact info here

Heading Here

Box
content

CHAPTER 1

Structure and Design with HTML5 and CSS3

In This Chapter

- Essential new elements of HTML5

- Dynamic new design options with CSS3

- A crash course in structuring web page content with HTML

- An introduction to contemporary CSS styling techniques

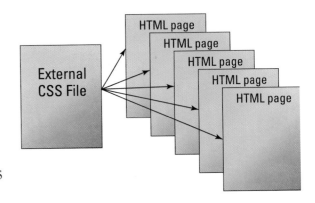

In this chapter, I pull back the lens and survey the scope and range of new web design tools provided by HTML5 and CSS3. In the remainder of this book, I'll dive deeply into specific features of both HTML5 and CSS3. But here at the beginning, it will be valuable to step back from the trees to appreciate the forest.

HTML5 is a breakthrough in structuring web page content. There are all kinds of cool new features, ranging from pop-up calendars that go with input forms (see Figure 1-1) to native video that doesn't require plugins. But the big picture is a cleaner, more logical way to organize and present content. This cleaner way to organize content is concentrated in many ways in the new semantic page elements like <article>, <header>, and <footer>. Similarly, CSS3 provides a dynamic and fun set of new styling tools — like gradient backgrounds and irregularly shaped boxes. But the sum of CSS3 is greater than the parts. CSS3 expands and stretches what designers can do with web pages in a qualitative way.

In this chapter, I give you a sweeping, bird's-eye view of HTML5 and CSS3, in part by comparing and contrasting how pages were built in the pre-HTML5/CSS3 era, and how they can and should built now. So, buckle up your seat belts and let's start on our journey.

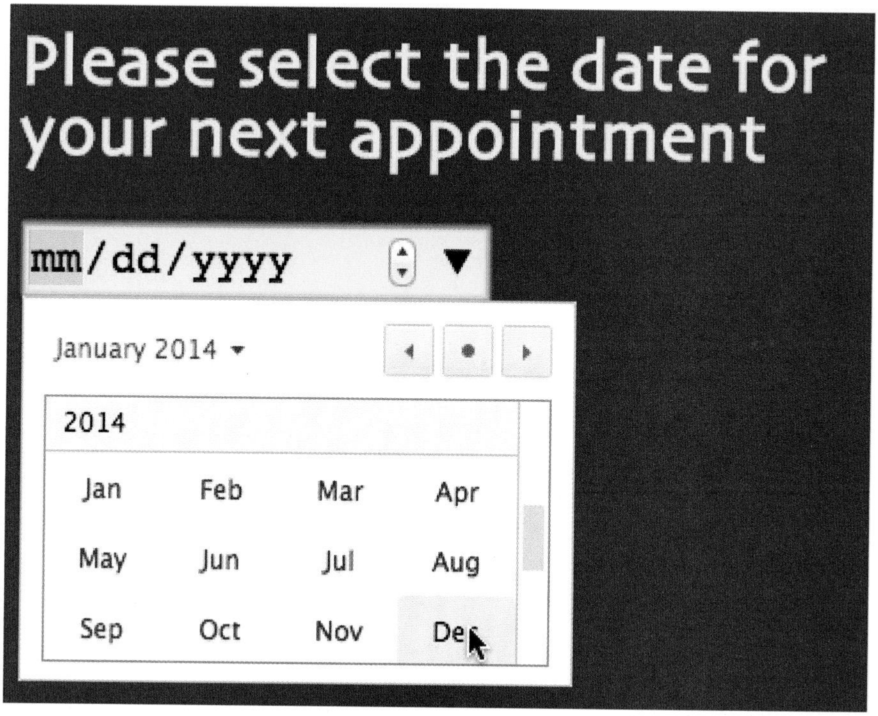

Figure 1-1

Realizing the Magic of HTML5 and CSS3

HTML5 and CSS3 open the door to designing really exciting, vibrant, and dynamic web pages. In different ways throughout this book, I will contrast new elements in HTML5 and new styling tools in CSS3 with previous versions of HTML and CSS. Here, in a compressed way, I want to quickly identify what these new features are.

Earlier versions of HTML had no systematic, universally applied set of elements for basic page content — like articles, sections, asides, and so on. HTML5 introduces a rational way to structure page content with *semantic tags* (see Figure 1-2), which describe the nature of content that they contain.

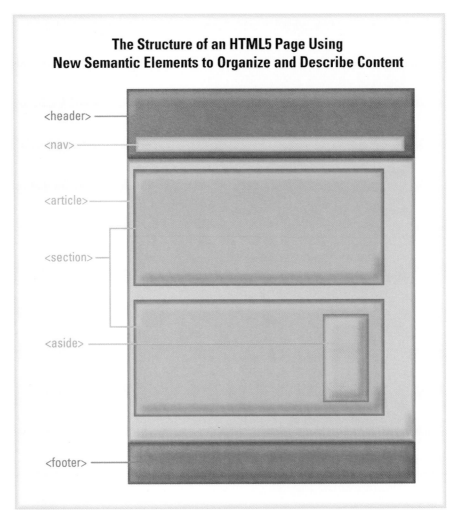

Figure 1-2

Until the advent of HTML5, plugins (like Windows Media Player or QuickTime Player) were necessary to present video. HTML5 approaches audio and video in a whole new way, freed of plugins.

| Name: | Full name go here |
| Email address | here |

Please fill out this field.

Figure 1-3

And HTML5 provides form-field prompting and validation (testing), as shown in Figure 1-3.

CSS3 hands designers a toolbox filled with tools that makes it easy to rotate, skew, scale, and overlap page elements. Web designers can now apply rounded corners to content — even turning squares into circles.

In addition, CSS3 effects make rich graphical content available without graphics. You can, for example, easily define highly complex gradient blend backgrounds (see Figure 1-4) without requiring users to download any image file.

Box
content

Box
content

Box
content

Figure 1-4

And I'm just scratching the surface here. By combining these different features, web designers can blaze new trails in creating websites that people will enjoy spending time visiting.

Not all new . . . but different

In two ways, all the exciting and dynamic design options made possible with HTML5 and CSS3 aren't exactly new.

First, almost all the features I rave about in the previous section have been available to web designers for some time. However, using them required complicated tools and/or high-level programming skills. In addition, they placed demands on computer and mobile resources that are no longer acceptable — particularly in an era when mobile viewing is such a critical dimension of reaching an audience. Here are a few examples to make the point(s):

▶ **Video:** Video has always been available (see Figure 1-5), but — as noted earlier — it required plugins like Windows Media Player, QuickTime Player, or Flash Player. These video players had to be updated regularly, they didn't support each other's formats (at least not without configuration), and they created an unpredictable viewing experience. With HTML5, users don't need to install

Figure 1-5

(or update) any media player plugins; all the software needed to view videos (or listen to audio) is built into browsers and accessed directly with HTML5 code.

 **Interactivity and animation:** Interactivity and animation (see Figure 1-6) have always been available, but they often required complex programming in Flash or JavaScript. Although HTML5 and CSS3 don't fully replicate the feature sets of Flash and JavaScript animation, they do make much of that feature set available at a far lower cost in terms of software, Flash or JavaScript coding skills on the part of designers, and download time for users.

Figure 1-6

▶ **Rich graphical backgrounds:** Rich graphical backgrounds have, until the advent of CSS3, been created by designing gradient artwork in programs like Adobe Illustrator and then saving them as web-accessible images that *tile* (repeat) in the background of a design element (like a layout box). With CSS3, these backgrounds (see Figure 1-7) can now be defined without any image files at all.

▶ **Forms:** Complex forms have required JavaScript, or server-side scripts, written in programs like Ruby or PHP. HTML5 provides prompts (see Figure 1-8) and validation tests without any scripting.

Figure 1-7

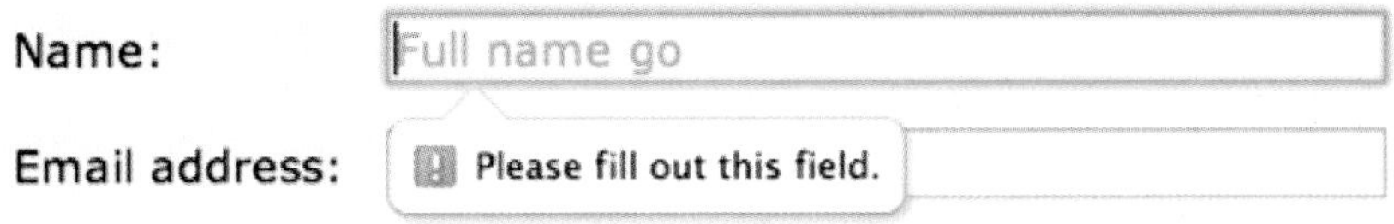

Name: [Full name go   ]

Email address: [⚠ Please fill out this field.]

Figure 1-8

My point here isn't to review the whole range of exciting new features I explore in this book, but rather to give examples of how HTML5 and CSS3 build on the history of web design. HTML5 and CSS3 make many features radically more accessible to designers — without having to resort to third-party products and plugins, as well as reducing download time for pages.

USE A CODE EDITOR!

Warning: Do *not* build HTML or CSS pages in a text editor. Doing so corrupts any code you create. For example, most text editors convert standard quotes (") into smart quotes (" ").

Plenty of very good free code editors are available. If you already have one, use it. If you don't already have a code editor, here are my recommendations. They aren't the most sophisticated code editors, but they're free, and easy to set up and work with:

- Windows: Notepad++, http://notepad-plus-plus.org).

- Mac: TextWrangler, www.barebones.com/products/textwrangler)

If you're comfortable working in another dedicated coding environment — say, Komodo Edit, Adobe Dreamweaver, Aptana Studio, or any other code editor — use that.

Second, HTML5 and CSS3 build on (and qualitatively augment) previous versions of HTML and CSS:

▶ **Simplification:** In some areas, new features in HTML5 and CSS3 replace older (which is a nice way of saying "clumsy, slower, problematic, and less-flexible") techniques. For example, HTML5 simplifies audio and video embedding. (For more on using HTML5 to embed audio and video, see Chapter 7.) And with CSS3, you can easily rotate, rescale, move, or skew boxes of content without the need for positioned background images.

▶ **New features:** In other areas, new HTML5 and CSS3 open up completely new options. For example, HTML5 mobile tools facilitate app-like, highly mobile-friendly pages. And CSS3 effects provide options for defining transparency (allowing elements to "show through" elements above them) far more powerfully than the opacity tools in earlier CSS.

HTML5: Building on HTML techniques

I can't emphasize this enough: HTML5 and CSS3 build on, and are extensions of, the most developed and current techniques for using HTML and CSS. Why am I so fixated on this? Because current techniques for HTML and CSS design are the launching pad from which you deploy HTML5 and CSS3.

HTML has evolved. The reason why this is important isn't to belabor history, but rather to understand why you build pages in a certain way — and why you *don't* build them in ways that don't provide a solid-enough foundation to present page content in an engaging way that meets the standards of today's demanding website visitor.

DO OLD BROWSERS SUPPORT HTML5?

With the exception of Internet Explorer (IE), all browsers prompt users to update frequently, so when I talk about "old browsers" I mean old versions of Internet Explorer that are installed in large corporate or institutional environments that, for reasons internal to the security and networking environments, can't be updated. All other browsers (Firefox, Chrome, Safari, Opera, and so on, in their laptop/desktop and mobile versions) essentially update automatically.

But there is, and will continue to be, a substantial installed user base for old versions of Internet Explorer. What about that community? When someone asks, "Will my old version of IE support HTML5 and CSS?," the short (and accurate) answer is yes. In fact, HTML5 pages are less problematic in old versions of IE than previous versions of HTML; the HTML5 document type declaration that identifies a page as HTML5 reduces error messages that old browsers sometimes display when they encounter minor errors in HTML coding. That said, old browsers (here, I mean Internet Explorer 8 and earlier) do not support all the new features in HTML5 and CSS3. But even in environments where support for old versions of IE is critical, this presents fewer issues than you might imagine. In most cases, new HTML5 elements and new CSS3 effects can be deployed in a way that *enhances* a visitor's experience, but are not *essential* to that experience.

Take a very basic example: Eons ago (in "web design years" that is, which is more like 10 years ago in human time), web pages were designed with tables. Tables were included in HTML by the initiators of the web to display rows and columns of data. (Tables still play that role, by the way.)

But at a certain point in the development of the web, envelope-stretching designers figured out ways to use table cells to locate content on pages. This technique ushered in a whole new era of web design that broke out of single-column, boring pages full of text and unaligned images.

remember

Here is a critical point in implementing HTML5 and CSS3: Because both these programming languages build on previous versions of HTML and CSS, the better grounded you are in basic HTML and CSS approaches and techniques, the more you'll get out of implementing HTML5 and CSS3.

Tables have been replaced in modern web design by using <div> (short for *divider*) tags combined with style rules that format <div> tags into boxes for layout.

To complete the example, unless your pages are built with <div> tags (as opposed to tables), a whole array of really fantastic new CSS3 effects, ranging from box-shadows to rounded corners to rotation, won't be deployable.

Similarly, new CSS3 design tools can't be used effectively unless your website is built with external style sheets. Older techniques of embedding styles within pages — or even older techniques of using HTML style properties (such as "align=right") to style page content — will radically reduce a designer's freedom to take full advantage of CSS3 styling.

Understanding HTML Foundations

Take a minute to see the essential, current HTML approaches and techniques on which HTML5 can soar. First, note that I said "approaches and techniques" — not "syntax and coding rules." You do *not* need anything close to an encyclopedic knowledge of HTML to build sites with HTML5!

I list a few helpful resources for HTML tutorials and syntax in the "Need More HTML Basics?" sidebar later in this chapter.

And of course, I walk you through essential HTML code and syntax in this book.

ORGANIZE SITE CONTENT IN A SINGLE FOLDER

One essential element of modern website building is that all the files for a website need to be organized in a single folder. If you're new to building modern sites, start by creating a folder on your computer to organize all your content. You can, of course, divide your root site folder into subfolders for images, video, and so on. Just remember that modern websites rely on multiple and complex linkages between files; a single page may rely on links to style sheets, links to scripts, navigation links to other pages in the site, embedded video and image files, and more.

remember

You should have a handle on a handful of very basic HTML approaches and techniques in order to make the most of HTML5. Most importantly, defining styling with external, linked CSS style sheets, not embedded styles in HTML, and designing pages with <div> elements, not tables.

Five things you need to know about HTML

I want to cut to the heart of things. There are a few basic things you need to know about HTML — in general — in order to get the most out of HTML5. The following list breaks these down:

1. HTML5 files are identified with a doctype declaration that tells browsers, "I'm an HTML file." This declaration is the first line in an HTML file (see Figure 1-9) and looks like this for HTML5:

   ```
   <!DOCTYPE HTML>
   ```

HTML5 files are identified with a doctype declaration that tells browsers "I'm an HTML file." All page content is enclosed between an open <html> tag and a close </html> tag. The <html> element is divided into the <head> and <body>.

Figure 1-9

2. All page content is enclosed between an open `<html>` tag and a close `</html>` tag (see Figure 1-9).

3. Inside the `<html>` element, page content is divided into the `<head>` element (content that doesn't display in a browser window) and a `<body>` element (content that does display in a browser window). Once again, see Figure 1-9.

4. HTML elements within the `<body>` element define visible content, including headings, paragraphs, lists, links, images, and other key content (see Figure 1-10). `<div>` tags matched with class styles (that can be used more than once on a page) or ID styles (that can only be used once on a page) are the basic building blocks of page design.

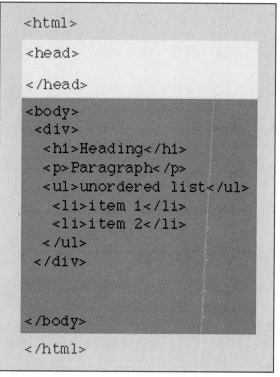

```
<html>

<head>

</head>

<body>
  <div>
    <h1>Heading</h1>
    <p>Paragraph</p>
    <ul>unordered list</ul>
      <li>item 1</li>
      <li>item 2</li>
    </ul>
  </div>


</body>

</html>
```

Figure 1-10

5. Any web pages beyond the most primitive link to external style sheet (CSS) files that determine how page content looks (see Figure 1-11).

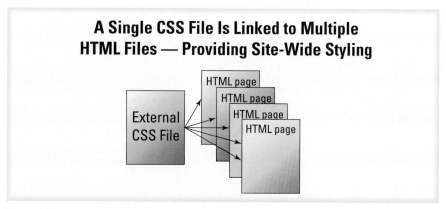

Figure 1-11

If all this is old news to you, good! You're in the right place. Bear with me while I review some basic concepts to help identify the key foundations from which you will implement radical new elements in HTML5.

If all this is new news to you, that's fine too. You'll be okay — I walk you through how all this works in a concise way in the rest of this chapter.

Getting started with a basic HTML template

One good (and quick) way to refresh/reground/ learn basic HTML5 concepts is to start with an HTML page and break down the different components. Start with a basic HTML5 template.

TAGS VERSUS ELEMENTS

What's the difference between an HTML *tag* and an HTML *element?* Not much, and sometimes the terms are used interchangeably. But it is worthwhile to identify the difference. Most HTML elements are enclosed inside an open tag (like `<body>`) and a close tag (like `</body>`). There are also some single-tag elements (like the `<br>` tag that forces a line break). In short, most elements are bookended by an open and close tag.

You can copy the code in Listing 1-1 and paste it into your code editor, or just kick back, grab a snack, and keep this page handy in your book or e-reader. I spend the next few sections walking through Listing 1-1 more or less line-by-line, and ultimately come out the other end with an understanding of the essentials of HTML.

on the web

All the code listings used in this book are available for download from the Downloads tab on the book's companion website at `www.dummies.com/extras/ html5andcss3`.

GOING LIVE

A full examination of how to contract for (and work with) remote web host providers is beyond the scope of this book. (You'll find an in-depth exploration of that challenge in *Building Websites All-in-One For Dummies,* 3rd Edition.) However, if you want to work through this book experimenting with a real, live, online site, you need two things:

- A remote hosting service: If you want to try a free one, head over to `www.000webhost.com` and sign up for this no-cost, ad-free service.

- An FTP program: You use this to transfer files from your computer to your remote site. (Your remote host will supply you with the information you need to log into your remote site.) You can download the free FileZilla FTP application from `https://filezilla-project.org/download. php`.

If you download Listing 1-1, save it as `template.html` so you can use it as you work through the remainder of this chapter.

Listing 1-1: template.html

```
<!--The HTML5 doctype (document type) declaration is very
         simple->
<!DOCTYPE HTML>
<!--All page content is inside the HTML element-->
<html>
<!--Head element content is not visible in a browser window-->
<head>
<!--The UTF-8 character set supports all symbols and
         characters-->
<meta charset="UTF-8">
<title>HTML Template</title>
<!—The following line links to our style sheet file-->
<link rel="stylesheet" type="text/css" href="style.css">
</head>
<!--Content visible in the browser's window is inside the HTML
         element-->
<body>
<!--All our content is enclosed in the wrapper ID style-->
<div id="wrapper">
<h1>Heading One Content</h1>
<!--column-2 ID style is floated left and used for
         navigation-->
<div id="column-2">
<h2>Links...</h2>
<ul>
<li> <h3><a href="#">Link 1</a></h3></li>
<li> <h3><a href="#">Link 2</a></h3></li>
<li> <h3><a href="#">Link 3</a></h3></li>
</ul>
<!--column-1 ID style is floated right and used for content-->
</div>
<div id="column-1">
<h1>Right Column Heading Here </h1>
<p>Right column content here </p>
<div class="box"><p>Box content</p></div>
<div class="box"><p>Box content</p></div>
<div class="box"><p>Box content</p></div>
</div>
<!--The clear class style clears (removes) float-->
<div class="clear"></div>
<h4>Contact info here </h4>
</div>
</body>
</html>
```

Identifying HTML document structure

The essence of the HTML document in Listing 1-1 is shown in Figure 1-12 and is as follows:

▶ **The `<!DOCTYPE HTML>` document declaration:** This tells browsers, "I'm an HTML page." This works in any browser; see the sidebar "Doctype declarations new and old" for more information.

▶ **The `<html>` element:** This wraps the entire document in HTML.

▶ **The `<head>` element:** This element holds metadata associated with the page (like a description of the page or the text that appears in a browser title bar). This is information not displayed in a browser window.

▶ **The `<body>` element:** This element holds all the content displayed in a browser.

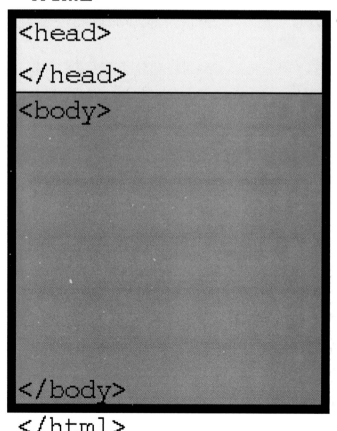

Figure 1-12

HTML documents can include **comments**. The syntax for a comment is

```
<!--this is a comment-->
```

warning

All markup, including the **head** information and the comments, are easily viewable via "view source" options in **browsers**. Avoid including anything in markup language that you do not want anyone **else** to see.

DOCTYPE DECLARATIONS NEW AND OLD

Other `doctype` declarations are used for older versions of HTML. Although not all browsers support new HTML5 elements (something I cover in detail throughout this book as I examine specific HTML5 elements), that doesn't matter when it comes to a `doctype` declaration because every browser can interpret the `<!DOCTYPE HTML>` tag to recognize that this is an HTML page.

Knowing basic element syntax

Here are a few basic rules to help understand how HTML elements are defined:

- Elements usually have open and closing tags, like `<p>` and `</p>`.
- Element parameters are defined with the open tag. For example, if a paragraph element is associated with a class style named `"hilite"`, (something I explore later in this chapter in the "Deploying class styles" section), the open tag might look like this: `<p class="hilite">`.
- Element content is usually enclosed between the open and close tags. So, a paragraph looks like this:

```
<p>Welcome to our site!</p>
```

remember

You don't have to close all elements in HTML5 — you can get away with leaving a `<p>` tag unclosed. However, it is best practice to close tags.

Working with the <head> element

The <head> element is defined after the open <hmtl> tag. Head element content includes

▶ **The charset meta tag:** A *meta tag* is a tag that defines everything in the document, and the charset meta tag defines the character set as the universally supported UTF-8.

tip

UTF-8 is an acronym for UCS Transformation Format—8-bit. It is an encoding system with the capacity to represent every symbol and character in the widest available set of alphabets including nearly every Latin-derived alphabet, along with the Greek, Cyrillic, Coptic, Armenian, Hebrew, Arabic, Syriac, and Tāna alphabets.

▶ **The <title> tag within the title element:** This tag defines the page title that appears in the title bar or tab bar of a browser.

▶ **A link to the CSS style sheet file:** This link element defines the relationship of the link to the page (stylesheet), the type of file (text/css), and the href (link to the page). (Later in this chapter, I dissect a CSS file for you.) The HTML link to a style sheet code looks like the one shown in Figure 1-13.

```
<head>
<meta charset="UTF-8">
<title>HTML Template</title>
<link rel="stylesheet" type="text/css" href="style.css">
</head>
```
Figure 1-13

Using the <body> element and <div> tags

The <body> defines content that appears in a entire browser window. However, the <body> tag isn't sufficient to define the contours of the page in which visitors will see content.

While the style associated with the <body> tag defines things like the background color for the entire web page, most designers use a separate element to define the box that contains all the page content. This is, generally, a <div> element.

remember

The <body> element holds everything you want to display in a visitor's browser.

FLUID DESIGN, RESPONSIVE DESIGN, AND THE 960 GRID

There are different approaches used to define the width of the `<div>` tag box that constrains the page content. Until the last few years, the prevailing doctrine was *fluid design.* Essentially, that meant creating pages that varied in width depending on how wide a user sized his or her browser window.

More recently, the concept of fluid design has been transcending with the concept of responsive design. *Responsive design* recognizes that the differences between laptop/desktop environments, tablets, and smart phones are so substantial that pages need to be completely redesigned for each environment, and that simply resizing page content is not sufficient.

In Chapter 9, I explore responsive design in depth and walk through new techniques in HTML5 for implementing responsive design with media queries and jQuery Mobile pages. Here, I will focus on building a desktop/laptop page.

For reasons related to aesthetics and accessibility, and to facilitate collaboration between designers in professional design workflows, the most widely applied approach to full-sized page design in professional design environments today is the 960 grid. Our model applies the *960 grid,* which in essence means constraining the page content that is displayed in full-sized browsers to 960 pixels wide.

The actual properties of the box that holds page content are defined in a linked style sheet. I provide you with a template CSS style sheet file that matches the HTML I'm creating here a bit later in this chapter in the section "Breaking Down Basic CSS." That style sheet includes an ID selector (style definition) named `"wrapper"`. For now, note that everything inside the `<body>` tag is enclosed in a `<div>` tag.

In our template model, everything inside the `<body>` tag is enveloped within the main `<div>` tag (see Figure 1-14). The `<body>` tag defines how the page background looks, but the main `<div>` element defines the box that displays all the rest of the page content appears.

```
<body>
<div id="wrapper"> ⬛ </div>
</body>
```

Figure 1-14

<DIV> TAGS: A HALLMARK OF FUNCTIONAL WEB DESIGN

Even with new page structure elements in HTML5, `<div>` tags are still a useful option that can be used together with HTML5 elements to create more semantic markup.

You might have heard that HTML5 replaces `<div>` tags for page layout. And that's understandable because HTML5 elements do replace *some* need for `<div>` tags. But the actual relationship is that HTML5 elements simplify and supplement the use of `<div>` tags, but `<div>` tags remain the essential building block for contemporary web design.

The `<div>` tag is used to created *divisions* within a page. ID and class selectors in style sheets define how those `<div>` tags look on a page. The main `<div>` tag is paired with an ID style named `"wrapper"`. Take a look at the style associated with that ID selector (`"wrapper"`) later in this chapter in the "Breaking Down Basic CSS" section, where I dissect the style sheet that goes with this page.

Using headings, lists, and links

Headings (h1, h2, and so on), lists (either numbered or bullet lists), and links are basic elements of HTML pages. While none of these elements has undergone any changes in HTML5 — compared to previous versions of HTML — I want to take a minute to review how they work.

The example page (refer to Listing 1-1) has a heading 1 (`<h1>`) element, right after the `"wrapper"` ID `<div>` tag opens. The heading 1 element content is surrounded by an open and a close tag (see Figure 1-15).

```
<div id="wrapper">
<h1>Heading One Content</h1>
<div id="left-column">
```

Figure 1-15

tip

There are six heading elements in HTML: h1 through h6. This has not changed in HTML5. By default (and in standard usage), `<h1>` elements are the most important, and `<h6>` elements are the least important. Styling for heading elements can be customized in a style sheet. And, of course, you don't need to use every one of the heading elements in web pages (our template example uses four heading elements).

A second `<div>` tag with an ID selector of `"column-2"`, holds content displayed in the left column of the page (see Figure 1-16).

Inside the left column you see

- An `<h2>` heading element
- An unordered list (`<ul>`) element
- Three list (`<li>`) elements within the unordered list
- Each `<li>` element is further defined with paragraph (`<h3>`) elements

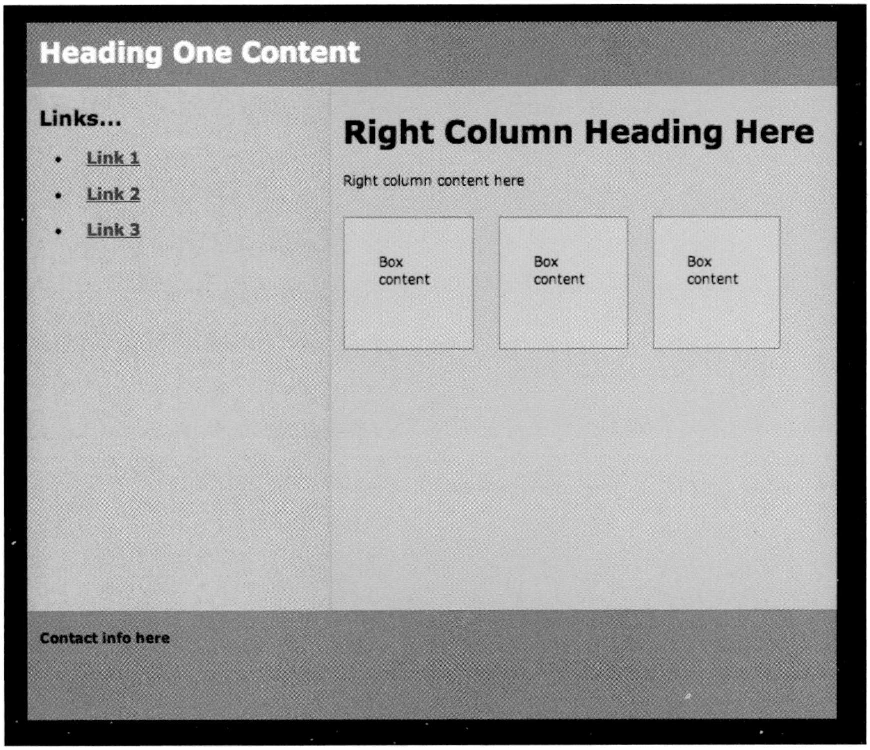

Heading One Content

Links...
- Link 1
- Link 2
- Link 3

Right Column Heading Here

Right column content here

| Box content | Box content | Box content |

Contact info here

Figure 1-16

Here are a couple of things to note in relation to this section of code:

▶ **Local trumps global:** The "cascading" in Cascading Style Sheets refers to how styling is prioritized. The rule is that the inner-most element will override any styling inherited from the outer elements. In this example, the <h3> tag, with its large type and vertical spacing, trumps the size and spacing inherited from the list elements. I like to think of this as "local trumps global."

▶ **Links:** Second, this section of code also includes links (see Figure 1-17). Link syntax opens and closes with <a> and </a> tags, and includes the link URL and the text (or image) that displays in a browser.

```
<a href="#" Link 1</a>
```
open link tag   link URL   display text   link close tag

Figure 1-17

Deploying class styles

Before wrapping up this crash course in current HTML approaches, see how class styles are deployed in the column-1 `<div>` tag (see Figure 1-18):

```
<div id="right-column">
<h1>Right Column Heading Here </h1>
<p>Right column content here </p>
<div class="box"><p>Box content</p></div>
<div class="box"><p>Box content</p></div>
<div class="box"><p>Box content</p></div>
</div>
```

Figure 1-18

 Class styles are appended to `<div>` tags (or other elements) just like ID styles, with the same syntax. The difference is that you can use a class style with multiple `<div>` tags. Comparatively, ID styles can be applied to a single element only.

 Because I want all the boxes to have identical styling, I apply the same class style to them all.

 Finally, note the class style called `"clear"` (see Figure 1-19) after the box styles. This is handy because the style sheet applies *float* to these boxes, causing them to all display in the same row instead of separate rows (which is the default for most elements).

```
<div class="clear"></div>
```

Figure 1-19

The `"clear"` class style has been defined to wipe out the float property for everything that follows so that the float is not inherited.

tip

For more exploration of using float in page design, see Chapter 5.

NEED MORE HTML BASICS?

The best resource for a basic grounding in HTML basics — beyond what I can cover here in this crash course — is *Beginning HTML5 and CSS3 For Dummies* by Ed Tittel and Jeff Noble.

Other online resources for HTML code help include:

- www.w3.org
- www.w3schools.com
- www.webplatform.org
- http://stackoverflow.com
- www.sitepoint.com

Breaking Down Basic CSS

Having crashed your way through HTML basics, it's time to tackle the basics of CSS! Listing 1-2 is a CSS file that matches the `template.html` file I dissect earlier in this chapter. Before you start, download Listing 1-2 and save it as `style.css` within the same folder on your computer that you used to save the `template.html` file.

on the web

You can download Listing 1-2 from the Downloads tab on the book's companion website (www.dummies.com/extras/html5andcss3).

I spend the next few sections working through this `style.css` file, and you can review and reinforce any skills that need strengthening by playing around with the `template.html` and `style.css` files. And of course, if you accidently trash them, you can return to the book's companion website, download them again, and start fresh.

Listing 1-2: style.css

```
@charset "UTF-8";
/* CSS Document */

/* The body tag style applies to all elements on the page */
body {
background-color: black;
font-family: Verdana, Geneva, Arial, sans-serif;
```

continued

Listing 1-2 *(continued)*

```
padding:0px;
margin:0px;
}

/* The wrapper ID style is used with a div tag to provide a 960px wide
            page */
#wrapper {
width: 960px;
height: 800px;
margin-left: auto;
margin-right: auto;
background-color: #F25F29;
}

/* The column-1 ID style is floated right */
#column-1 {
float: right;
width: 600px;
height: 600px;
background: #55D9D9;
}

/* The column-2 ID style is floated left */
#column-2 {
float: left;
width: 360px;
height:600px;
background: #F2B544;
}

/* Selector for tags separated by commas applies the style to all tags */
h1,h2,h3,h4,h5,h6,p,li {
margin-left:15px;
}

h1 {
color: white;
padding-top:15px;
}

/* Selector for tags not separated by commas applies in specific
            circumstances*/
#column-1 h1 {
padding-top:5px;
color: black;
font-size:36px;
}

/* Advanced web design relies on class or ID style boxes*/
.box {
```

```
height: 100px;
width: 100px;
float: left;
margin: 15px;
padding: 25px;
background: #A8D977;
border:2px solid gray;
}

/* The following pseudo-class applies to the box class when in a hovered
            state */
.box:hover {
background-color:#F2B544;
border-bottom:2px solid black;
}

/* This clear class style terminates float */
.clear{
clear: both;
}

}
header, footer {
background-color: F27830;
color: red;
padding-top:5px;
padding-bottom:5px;
}
```

DEFAULT BROWSER STYLING

Different browsers impose different default styles. For example, many full-sized browsers, by default, include ten pixels of padding at the top of the page in order to keep content from bumping into the top of the browser window. Mobile browsers, given their smaller viewports, might have less (or no) default margin. Another example: Many browsers have defined ways of presenting drop-down menus to maximize accessibility.

There are two basic approaches to address default browser styling. One way is for designers to do everything possible to override default styling in different browsers. Tools for doing this are found at the normalize.css site (http://necolas.github.io/normalize.css/). The other approach is to appreciate the value of different default styling for different browsers in different devices, and design pages with enough flexibility to work well in different browsers with their default styling. I explore the wide range of browsers and how they handle styling in Chapter 8.

Creating a CSS document

Defining a document type is simple in CSS — you don't have to do anything. Nice, huh? Most designer, however, open CSS documents with a UTF-8 character set declaration like this:

```
@charset "UTF-8";
```

tip

By adding a UTF-8 character set declaration, if anything in the CSS style sheet code contains characters outside the standard Western alphabet and number characters, browsers can still interpret the page.

The sample `style.css` file also opens with a comment (see Figure 1-20). Comments open with `/*` and close with `*/`. Comments are notes by the coder that do not affect the code itself, but simply help document the purpose of code.

```
@charset "UTF-8";
/* CSS Document */
```

Figure 1-20

Examining CSS style definitions

Each individual style within a style sheet is a *selector* (sometimes called a *rule*). Each selector has sets of properties *(declarations)* that consist of a property and a value (or set of values).

You can see how this works by examining the `body` style definition (see Figure 1-21):

▶ The `body` element is the selector.

▶ The four declarations for this style are `background-color`, `font-family`, `padding`, and `margin`.

```
body {
background-color: black;
font-family: Verdana, Geneva, Arial, sans-serif;
padding:0px;
margin:0px;
}
```

Figure 1-21

tip

Declarations never have spaces within them. A widely-used technique is to separate words with underscore characters (_) or dashes (–) instead of spaces.

▶ Each declaration has a property (like `background-color`) followed by a colon (`:`) and a value (like `black`).

▶ Each declaration ends with a semicolon (`;`).

That's it. With these basic rules in mind, see what you can learn from the `style.css` sample CSS code file.

I could fill the remainder of this book (or at least a few chapters) with a comprehensive list of all the available CSS properties and values, but that would be environmentally irresponsible — seriously, and a waste of space as well. When I discuss new CSS3 properties in this book, I'll walk through them in detail.

For now, I want to point out a few key CSS properties as you examine techniques in the model style sheet. In that light, focus on a few implementations of critical CSS properties that you will build on when you dive into CSS3:

ONLINE RESOURCES FOR CSS RULES

Two online resources for CSS rules are:

- W3.orgs CSS documentation: `www.w3.org/Style/CSS`

- W3Schools CSS page: `www.w3schools.com/css`

▶ ID selector names begin with #, and class selector names begin with a period (`.`).

tip

Selector names can't have spaces. As with declarations, designers typically use underscore characters (_) or dashes (-) in place of spaces.

▶ The `#column-1` and `#column-2` selectors have `float` properties, aligning them right and left (respectively), and keeping them in the same horizontal row — side by side.

▶ Color and background color values are either in standard colors (for example, `"white"`) or hexadecimal color values. You can find a wide range of online resources for getting hexadecimal values for colors, ranging from Adobe's Kuler site (`https://kuler.adobe.com`) to a nice simple chart at Total Recall (`http://html-color-codes.com`).

tip

Hexadecimal colors are the standard for defining colors (although there are other options).

▶ Pseudo-class selectors are created by placing a colon (:) after a class name, followed by a state (see Figure 1-22). For example, the .box:hover selector defines how the box looks when a user hovers over the box with a cursor or when the box is tapped in a mobile device. Pseudo-classes define link states and also define different properties for any element acted on by a user.

```
.box:hover {
background-color:#F2B544;
border-bottom:2px solid black;
}
```

Figure 1-22

States include

- :link: An unvisited link

- :visited: A visited link

- :hover: A hovered link (as in the sample page)

- :active: A style for an active element: for example, a link in the process of being opened

- :focus: An element "in focus," such as a form field in which a user has inserted a cursor

Combining style definitions

Before wrapping up this compressed overview of CSS, look at how style definitions can be combined. Style definitions for sets of selectors that are separated by commas apply to every selector in the list (see Figure 1-23).

```
h1,h2,h3,h4,h5,h6,p,li
{
margin-left:15px;
}
```

Figure 1-23

On the other hand, style definitions for sets of selectors *not* separated by commas apply only a specific set of circumstances, where the last element in the list is enclosed in every previous element in the list (see Figure 1-24). For example, the #column-1 h1 style applies only to <h1> elements that are inside a #column-1 ID element.

Note that the h1 style applies to the <h1> content differently in the right column. The color in the right column is black instead of white (see Figure 1-25), which applies to normal <h1> elements, and the sizing is different as well.

```
h1 {
color: white;
padding-top:15px;
}

#right-column h1 {
padding-top:5px;
color: black;
font-size:36px;
}
```

Figure 1-24

Heading One Content

Links...
- Link 1

Right Column Heading Here

Figure 1-25

Moving Forward with HTML5 and CSS3

Everything in in this crash course/review of basic HTML and CSS has two implications for building cutting-edge pages with HTML5 and CSS3:

▶ HTML5 and CSS3 *build on* HTML and CSS, especially current generation design techniques.

▶ You're gonna use it all!

Bearing those two points in mind (okay, maybe two ways of saying the same thing), you're ready to build pages in radically new ways that enhance web designer productivity and provide animation, interactivity, and a greatly enhanced experience for visitors.

```
article>
aside>
h1>Sidebar Heading<h1>
p>Sidebar content</p>
/aside>
h1>Article heading</h1>
p>Article content</p>
p>More content</p>
section>
h1>1st Section Heading</h1>
p>1st section content</p>
/section>
section>
h1>2nd Section Heading</h1>
p>2nd section content</p>
/section>
/article>
```

CHAPTER 2

Deploying HTML5

In This Chapter

- Advantages of HTML5

- Using the HTML5 `doctype` declaration

- Simplifying page structure

- Integrating traditional HTML elements

- HTML5 elements for JavaScript

- Using the `<canvas>` tag

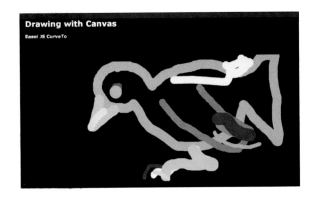

Drawing with Canvas

Easel JS CurveTo

HTML5 opens exciting new doors for web designers. HTML5 also makes life simpler for designers. "Huh?!" (I hear you.) How can a new version of the foundational markup language that underlies web pages be simpler *and* include powerful new features? The two-part short answer is

▶ HTML5 allows designers to deploy features (ranging from plugin-free video to form validation) that used to require outside tools (like media players or JavaScript).

▶ HTML5's new semantic markup tags standardize and simplify the process of organizing page content (see Figure 2-1).

In this chapter, I show you the advantages and challenges of building pages with HTML5. This chapter also provides the answers to these three existential questions:

▶ What is the point of adopting HTML5?

▶ What does it mean to adopt HTML5?

▶ What do you have to do to adopt HTML5?

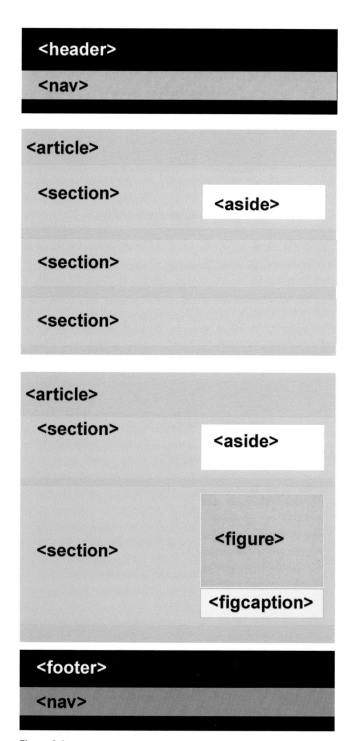

Figure 2-1

Identifying the Advantages of HTML5

Compared with previous steps in the evolution of HTML, HTML5 represents a more radical departure from past practices. HTML5 is not simply, or mainly, a set of new or *deprecated* (abandoned) tags. Although HTML5 does include an unprecedented set of new, powerful elements, it also represents a different way of building pages.

If that sounds a bit ethereal, take a minute to quickly survey some of the valuable new elements in HTML5, which

- Make it easier for you to build web pages.

- Make the web pages you build more accessible, inviting, and dynamic for visitors.

In a nutshell, three elements mark qualitative advances with HTML5 (see Figure 2-2). HTML5's breakthrough elements can be organized into the following three groupings:

- **Simplified `doc-type` delcaration:** HTML5 uses a simplified `doc-type` declaration, making it easier for you to create pages as well as making it easier for browsers to read those pages.

- **Semantic markup:** HTML5 provides standardized semantic markup that, for the first time in web history, makes it easier to organize page content in a rational way.

- **Native elements:** HTML5 provides new elements that enable animation and interactivity that used to require tools like Flash, JavaScript, server-side scripting, or browser plugins.

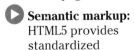

Qualitative Advances with HTML5

```
<!doctype html>

<html>
<head>
<meta charset="UTF-8">
</head>
<body>

<article>
<h1>The Making of "On Record"</h1>
</article>

<video controls>
<source src="on_record.mp4" type="video/mp4">
<source src="on_record.ogv" type="video/ogg">
</video>
```

The Making of "On Record"

Figure 2-2

tip

New HTML5 elements, like every other web design tool, are not supported completely in every browsing environment. Throughout this book, as I explore specific HTML5 features in depth, I will note when and where implementing those features might present accessibility issues in some browsing environments. Where that is the case, I'll show you solutions to address those issues.

When you understand how these three dimensions of HTML5 work — and work together — you're ready to get the most out of HTML5.

Knowing the Price of Using HTML5

In his classic song "Thunder Road," Bruce Springsteen invites Mary to hop in his car, but warns, "The door's open but the ride it ain't free."

Why bring Springsteen into the picture now? I know what you're thinking: I got a huge product placement payment from The Boss to plug his work in this book. The reason I'm using these lyrics is to issue a bit of warning of my own.

warning

If you plunge into HTML5 bit by bit, element by element, or feature by feature, you'll miss out on the value of HTML5. On the other hand, once you've got your head around the range of exciting new features in HTML5, you'll be able to deploy specific new elements more effectively and you'll be in position to unleash the full spectrum of HTML5 to build websites that are qualitatively more inviting and accessible.

Literally, of course, the ride *is* free; HTML5 doesn't cost anything. But there is a price to pay in terms of preparing yourself to get the most out of HTML5 with the least stress, wasted time, and unnecessary trauma. This chapter provides precisely the birds-eye view that will put you in position to fully deploy HTML5 with the most impact, and the least amount of stress on your end.

warning

While I'm on the subject of free, if you're coding web pages, you need a code editor. Do not use a text editor (like the one that came with your computer's operating system) to edit code. And definitely do not use a word processor like Word or Google Docs to edit code (see Figure 2-3). Text editors will corrupt code — doing things like converting regular straight quote marks (") into smartquotes (""), which will render HTML and CSS into junk.

A wide range of good, free code editors are available. I recommend TextWranger (www.barebones.com/products/textwrangler) for Macs or Notepad++ (http://notepad-plus-plus.org) for Windows.

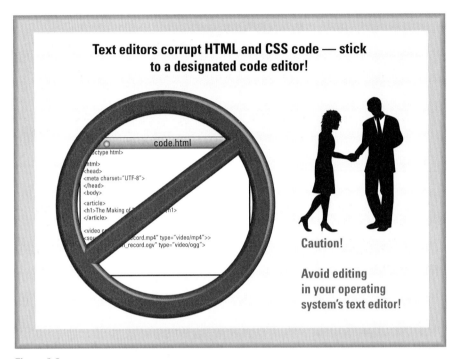

Figure 2-3

Introducing the Simplified Doctype Declaration

When a browser opens an HTML file, it relies on a doctype declaration to tell it what kind of content it's interpreting. HTML5 documents open with a very simple doctype declaration:

```
<!DOCTYPE HTML>
```

And, by the way, that doctype declaration is not case sensitive. So you could also use

```
<!doctype html>
```

tip

Here is an exception to the rule when it comes to the HTML5 `doctype` declaration being case-insensitive. If you're building pages with XHTML, relying on XML to feed data into your page, you must write the `doctype` declaration as `<!DOCTYPE html>`. This is more of an XML issue than an HTML issue and, as such, is beyond the scope of this book. If your web design workflow relies on XML, though, check out *HTML, XHTML, & CSS All-in-One For Dummies,* 2nd Edition, by Andy Harris.

Each version of HTML has had a distinct `doctype` declaration. If you're not familiar with the `doctype` declarations associated with previous versions of HTML, don't worry. They've all become irrelevant.

Really?

Yes. The basic reason is this: The new HTML5 `doctype` declaration is less strict than previous versions of HTML (see Figure 2-4). Previous versions of the HTML doctype declaration included links to a *Document Type Definition* (DTD), which is a set of rules that a browser then used to process the HTML code on the page. And those rules imposed restrictions on what could, and could not, be interpreted.

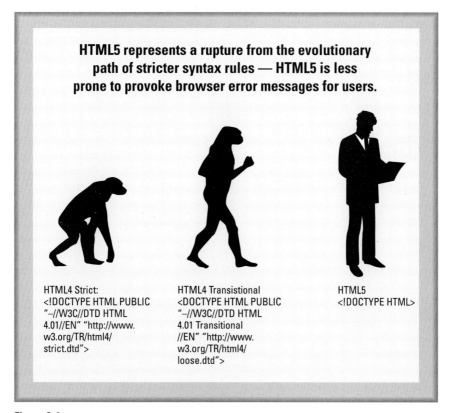

HTML5 represents a rupture from the evolutionary path of stricter syntax rules — HTML5 is less prone to provoke browser error messages for users.

HTML4 Strict:
<!DOCTYPE HTML PUBLIC "–//W3C//DTD HTML 4.01//EN" "http://www.w3.org/TR/html4/strict.dtd">

HTML4 Transitional
<!DOCTYPE HTML PUBLIC "–//W3C//DTD HTML 4.01 Transitional //EN" "http://www.w3.org/TR/html4/loose.dtd">

HTML5
<!DOCTYPE HTML>

Figure 2-4

For example, one version of HTML4 had this `doctype` declaration:

```
<!DOCTYPE HTML PUBLIC "-//W3C//DTD HTML 4.01//EN"
"http://www.w3.org/TR/html4/strict.dtd">
```

To see the set of rules for that version of HTML, go to `www.w3.org/TR/html4/strict.dtd`. Or, just take my word for it: This is a set of rules that identifies HTML markup that browsers should reject and refuse to interpret. That meant that at times, when browsers encountered minor errors in HTML coding, users saw error messages on their screen (and who needs that!?).

HTML5 dispenses with any DTD rules. Browsers are less fussy about things like missing close tags (like if you forget a `</p>` tag to close a paragraph) or case-sensitivity issues.

What does all this mean in terms of browser support for new HTML5 elements? The remaining installations of Internet Explorer 8 and earlier *do not* interpret new HTML elements. But the solution (or work-around) is not to use an older `doctype` declaration — that won't help at all.

tip

I address accessibility issues for older browsers in depth in Chapter 4.

Understanding HTML5's New, Standardized Structure Elements

HTML pages are organized by enclosing content within elements (usually defined with open and close tags). For example:

- ▶ Level 1 (most-weighted) headings open with an `<h1>` tag and close with an `</h1>` tag.
- ▶ Paragraph content goes inside `<p>` and `</p>` tags.
- ▶ Links are enclosed in `<a>` and `</a>` tags.
- ▶ List elements open with a `<li>` tag and close with a `</li>` tag.

But none of these tags identify the nature of the content within the element. Is it an article? A section of an article? A figure caption? A sidebar? A header? A footer?

Furthermore, previous versions of HTML relied completely upon the ubiquitous and generic `<div>` tag to demarcate blocks of content. Headers, footers, sidebars, article, figure captions . . . you name it. They were all defined with <div> tags and associated class or ID styles that supplied *style* elements (like boxes, backgrounds, colors, fonts, and so on).

For a review of, and crash course in, basic HTML page structure and CSS styling, see Chapter 1.

With HTML5, a standard set of page structuring elements has replaced "homemade" <div> tags for organizing content. Instead of creating <div id="header">, for example, designers can now use the HTML5 <header> element. The next few sections of this chapter walk through how this works.

New process and workflow

HTML5 semantic elements *do* identify the nature of content in an element. This has several implications for designers, including the following:

▶ Instead of making up your own ID and class selectors (styles) for things like headers, footers, articles, and figure captions, you now use standardized HTML5 elements.

▶ You style HTML5 semantic markup elements by defining selectors (styles) for them in your CSS style sheet. HTML5 semantic elements almost never include default styling in browsers.

▶ Most page elements that have traditionally been defined in <div> tags are now defined in semantic markup elements. For a discussion of the remaining relevance of <div> tags, see the sidebar "<div> tags are dead — long live <div> tags" later in this chapter.

AN EXCEPTION TO THE RULE

Notice that I said HTML5 semantic elements *almost* never include default styling in browsers and that *most* page elements that have traditionally been defined in <div> tags are now defined in semantic markup elements. An exception to that rule is the HTML5 <address> element. By default, <address> tag content is displayed in italics.

What does all this means in terms of web design workflow? For one thing, someone needs to assign semantic elements to content. If, for example, you're producing a newsletter, the process of producing the content for that newsletter needs to incorporate editorial decisions as to what constitutes an article, what is a section of that article, and what is a sidebar (using the HTML5 <aside> element). Many times these associations are fairly intuitive. As a web designer, you're probably used to structuring content into different elements. The difference is that now you're packaging content into standardized elements.

A brief introduction to semantic elements

In Chapter 5, I give you an in-depth look at how to build and style pages with HTML5 semantic elements. For now, let me introduce you to the most useful HTML5 semantic elements (see Figure 2-5):

- ▶ `<header>`: Tags that define a header for a document, an article, or a section
- ▶ `<article>`: Elements that enclose an entire article
- ▶ `<nav>`: Elements that define navigation links
- ▶ `<section>`: Elements that are subsections within an article

Sections are usually placed inside articles.

- ▶ `<aside>`: Elements that define sidebar content to an article or section.

Asides are always placed inside an article or section.

- ▶ `<figure>`: Elements that enclose artwork
- ▶ `<figcaption>`: Elements that are the captions associated with a `<figure>` element
- ▶ `<footer>`: Elements that define footer content for a document, an article, or a section

There are more HTML5 semantic elements that apply to very specific content, such as addresses, times, and groups of heading tags. And, again, I walk through the rules for when to use which tag in Chapter 5. It's helpful to have a basic sense of what I'm talking about to get a good conceptual grip on HTML5.

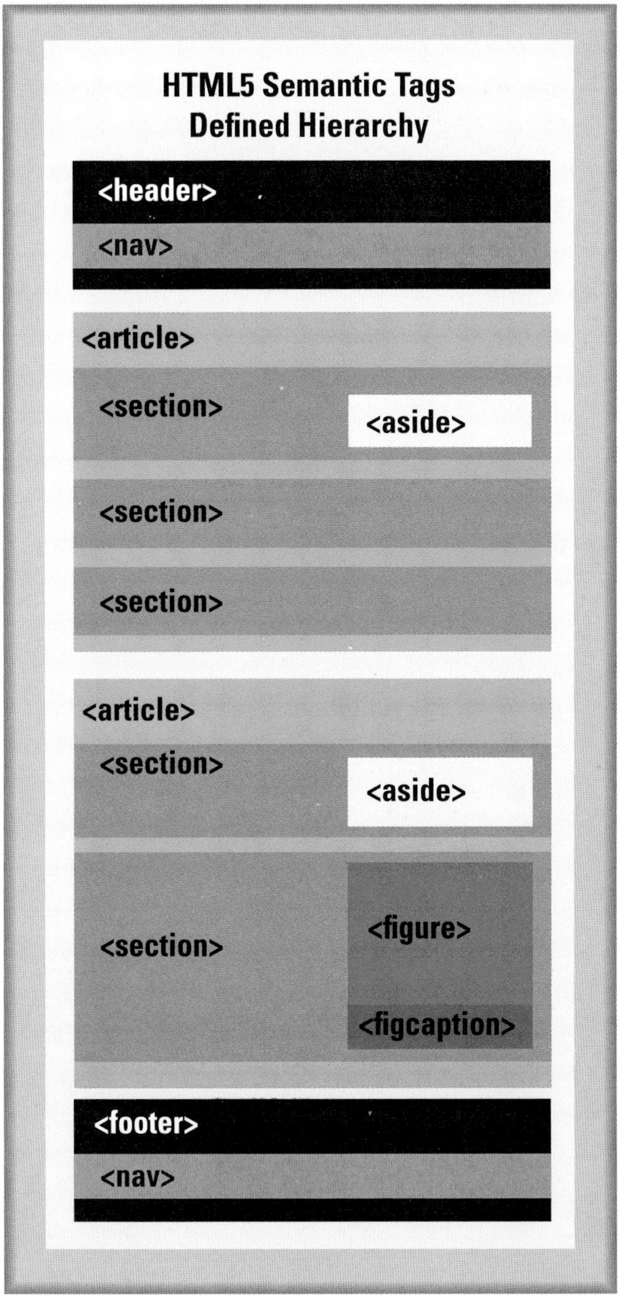

**HTML5 Semantic Tags
Defined Hierarchy**

<header>

<nav>

<article>

<section>   <aside>

<section>

<section>

<article>

<section>   <aside>

<section>   <figure>

                   <figcaption>

<footer>

<nav>

Figure 2-5

<div> tags are dead — long live <div> tags

As I noted a bit earlier in this chapter, most page elements that have traditionally been defined in <div> tags are now defined in semantic markup elements. So, while the importance of <div> tags has diminished in HTML5, we still use them.

Where do the new HTML5 semantic elements leave the venerable <div> tag that (for generations) has been used to define sections (*divisions*) of a page?

Well, <div> tags are still relevant. Here's why:

▶ **There's no HTML5 semantic element for an entire page or document.** As a result, if you want to define a box to hold page content, you still have to make up a style like #wrapper or #main_container to hold that content and then associate that style with a <div> element.

▶ **You use** <div> **elements within semantic elements.** For example, a class style that creates columns one-third the width of the element they're embedded in might be used to create a three-column layout within a section of an article (see Figure 2-6).

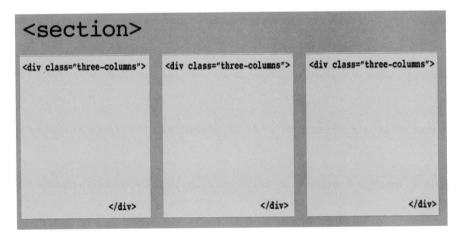

Figure 2-6

CSS3 does support a column property that divides elements into columns, but at present writing, this is among the least-supported CSS3 properties.

A new role for basic tags

Basic HTML tags that define headings (<h1>, <h2> . . . <h6>), paragraphs (<p>), ordered lists (<ol>), unordered lists (<ul>), and other elements continue to be essential to page markup with HTML5.

However, these basic HTML tags are subordinate to HTML5 structure elements. So, for example, you might well use various heading levels within both an article and a footer. The overall structure of the page is defined first by the HTML5 semantic element, and then by the traditional HTML tag.

Take a look at Listing 2-1 to see how this works:

Listing 2-1: HTML Template Code for an <article> element and embedded content

```
<article>
<aside>
<h1>Sidebar Heading<h1>
<p>Sidebar content</p>
</aside>
<h1>Article heading</h1>
<p>Article content</p>
<p>More content</p>
<section>
<h1>1st section heading</h1>
<p>1st section content</p>
</section>
<section>
<h1>2nd section content</h1>
<p>2nd section content</p>
</section>
</article>
```

With traditional HTML, you would rely on various levels of headings to denote what element is more important. The code example in Listing 2-1 shows how an <h1> heading element is used as the first level of heading within each different HTML5 semantic element.

When you style elements, you might well define distinct styles for headings in different HTML5 structure elements. By doing so, when visitors come to your web page, it will be clear to them that an <h1> element within an article is more important than an <h1> element within a section or an aside (see Figure 2-7).

```
<article>
<aside>
<h1>Sidebar Heading<h1>
<p>Sidebar content</p>
</aside>
<h1>Article heading</h1>
<p>Article content</p>
<p>More content</p>
<section>
<h1>1st Section Heading</h1>
<p>1st section content</p>
</section>
<section>
<h1>2nd Section Heading</h1>
<p>2nd section content</p>
</section>
</article>
```

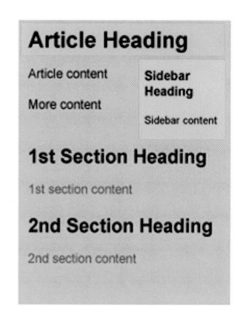

Figure 2-7

This hierarchy, however, is conveyed to the user with CSS, not with different levels of headings within an element. There are no strict rules on this, but the basic point is that heading levels (<h1> being more important than <h2> and so on) are *subordinate to* — less important than — HTML5 structuring elements.

on the web

All of the code listings used in this book are available for download from the Downloads tab on the book's companion website at www.dummies.com/extras/html5andcss3.

Going Native with HTML5

The second breakthrough element of HTML5, after semantic elements, is native elements. Most fundamentally, this is native audio and video that plays without plugins.

I walk you through native audio and video in depth in Chapter 7; here, focus on the overall concept. And when it comes to native video in particular, that means preparing video in formats supported by HTML5–complaint browsers (see Figure 2-8).

Figure 2-8

warning

Here's a bit of bad news: There is, at least now, no single video format that is supported natively in all popular browsers. There are two such formats: h.264 video (MP4 files) and OGG video (OGV files). Although other widely used browsers have adopted the h.264 format, Mozilla Firefox (at the time of this writing) is opposed to adopting that format (see Figure 2-9), arguing that it's privately licensed and not open source. And, not all browsers that support the h.264 format support OGV video. Thus, you should prepare video in both the h.264 and OGG formats.

Figure 2-9

Now for some good news: You can easily convert h.264 video to OGG video. Just run a quick Internet search for "convert video to OGG". The free conversion resource Miro Video Converter (www.mirovideoconverter.com; see Figure 2-10) works well.

Figure 2-10

Taking a Quick Look at HTML5's New Form Tools

New form handling tools are an underrated dimension of HTML5. Features that used to depend upon *client-side scripts* (scripts like JavaScript that run in a browser), or on server-side form handling scripts, are now available through HTML5.

With HTML5, you can now, for example, make fields required, thus forcing a user to enter data into the field before the form is accepted (see Figure 2-11). In addition, you can set validation criteria to ensure that, for example, data submitted in an e-mail field looks like an e-mail address.

With HTML5, you can define much more complex validation rules than just ones for e-mail addresses. See Chapter 6 for more on HTML5 forms and validation rules.

USES AND LIMITATIONS OF HTML5 VALIDATION

HTML5 form validation is supported in the vast majority of full-screen and mobile browsers. At this writing, that includes the current versions of Internet Explorer, Firefox, Chrome, and Opera, along with Blackberry, Chrome for Android, Firefox for Android, and others. HTML5 support overall is a moving target, but you can see the latest state of support for HTML5 form validation at `http://caniuse.com/form-validation`.

While the list of supported browsing environments covers a large majority of browsers, it doesn't cover them all. What are the implications of that? In short, you can use HTML5 form validation when the purpose is to make form entry more convenient, more friendly, and more inviting for users. For example, when you want to suggest to a user that if they entered "dave" in the form field for an e-mail address, they probably made a mistake because "dave" doesn't look like an e-mail address. That validation action will improve the quality of content submitted in a comment form, a sign-up form, or a feedback form.

There are, however, situations where validating form data is critical, not just helpful. For example, if you are using an e-commerce application and collecting a credit card number, it is critical that the credit card number match the required format for a credit card. In situations like this, it is not appropriate to rely on HTML5 to validate data. But in these situations, the entire process of handling the form data, from validating it to securing it (from theft) to processing it (actually charging the purchase to a credit card) is handled by a *server-side script* — so called because it is a script (program) that runs on a server. Designers, generally speaking, do not create these kinds of forms and form handling scripts; designers integrate this level of commercial forms into sites but the forms and handling scripts (including validation) are packaged with the application (like an e-commerce app). In Chapter 6, I explore how designers can utilize and integrate this level of commercial form handling.

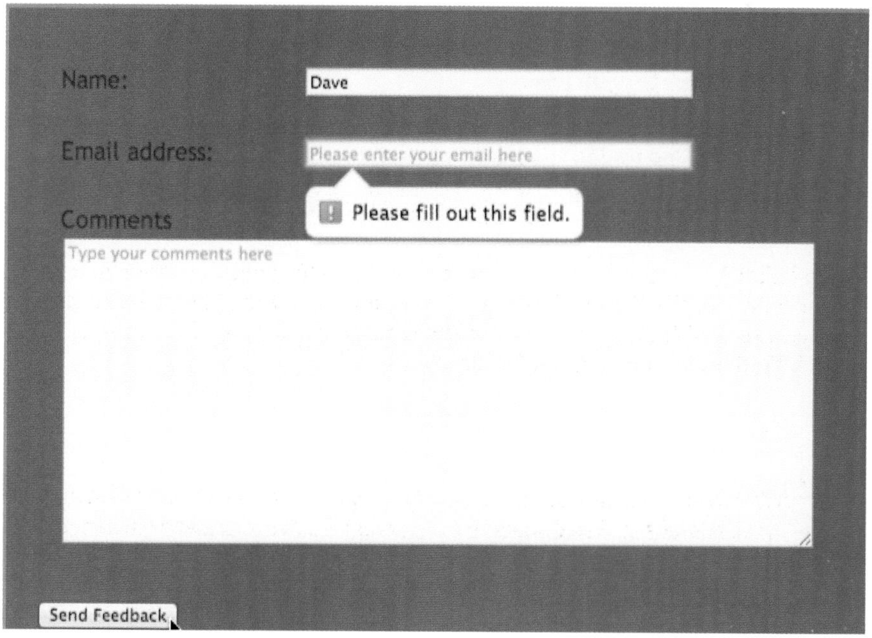

Figure 2-11

HTML5 form element properties also make it much easier for users to fill out forms. HTML5 allows designers to provide users with mobile-friendly sliders (see Figure 2-12) and auto-completion to reduce typing.

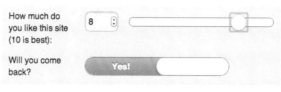

Figure 2-12

A plethora of form-management resources are available online. These form-management resources allow you to do many things, including

- **Use spreadsheets to collect form data.** You can collect form data in spreadsheets with Google Forms (created through Google Docs; `www.google.com/drive/apps.html`).

- **Embed search boxes.** You can embed search boxes from Google, FreeFind (`www.freefind.com`), or other search engine resources.

- **Collect user feedback.** You can find PHP generators at sources like thesitewizard.com (`www.thesitewizard.com`). These PHP generators provide the back-end scripting and front-end form HTML that allows you to collect user feedback.

- **Generate mailing lists.** Resources like MailChimp (`http://mailchimp.com`) provide sets of forms and e-newsletter generators. These sets of forms and e-newsletter generators provide designers with the ability to allow users to sign up for their mailing list, as well as enabling designers to send nicely designed e-mails to those on the mailing list.

tip

I discuss some of these resources in Chapter 6 when I explore HTML5 forms in depth. For now, here's the overarching point: Wherever you get forms from, you can add HTML5 validation, auto-complete prompting, and other properties that make your form inviting and accessible.

PHP AND OTHER SERVER-SIDE SCRIPTING

Complex form management, ranging from search boxes to e-commerce applications, is handled by server-side scripts. These scripts are created in programming languages that run not in a user's browser, but on a hosting server that manages a website. PHP is the most widely used server-side scripting language. Other widely used server-side scripting languages include Perl, ASP, JSP, and Ruby on Rails.

Writing server-side scripts requires high-level programming skills, and a large investment in programming time and resources. For that reason, most designers integrate already created server-side scripts to manage form data. For a survey of online resources for server-side scripts, see Chapter 7.

HTML5 Elements for Scripting with JavaScript

Some new HTML5 elements essentially serve as conduits for JavaScript programmers, including the `<canvas>` element that can be programmed to serve as a user-accessed drawing area within a page.

tip

Although writing scripts in JavaScript is beyond the scope of this book, any examination of HTML5 has to cover the ways in which new HTML5 elements connect with JavaScript. This is the case for two reasons. One is that there is a large and rapidly growing library of JavaScript code that non-coders can grab and plug in to their HTML5 pages. The two examples I'm about to explore in this chapter — the `<data>` element, and the `<canvass>` element — are examples of this. The `<data>` element (as you will see shortly) makes it possible to create mobile apps — web pages that look and feel like apps in mobile devices — when connected with online scripts available at jQueryMobile.com. The `<canvas>` element also requires JavaScript to do anything, but (as you'll see shortly) you don't have to write that JavaScript — there are online resources that provide it.

The second reason for noting the synergy between HTML5 and JavaScript is that some of you may be inspired to dig into JavaScript. The best way to do that is through reading HTML5 Programming with JavaScript For Dummies by John Paul Mueller.

The `<data>` element

The HTML5 `<data>` element provides an easy-to-use and powerful tool for JavaScript programmers to feed data into a page. Data elements are combined with defined parameters: for example, `<data-name>` or `<data-role>`.

tip

The HTML5 `<data>` element is supported in all browsers.

Here's an example of how a designer (you) can connect HTML5 with very powerful JavaScript resources: I mention earlier in this chapter that jQuery Mobile is a JavaScript library that allows designers to create mobile web pages that look and feel like apps, with animation, interactivity, and design features that make web pages highly accessible and inviting in mobile devices. I walk you through how to do this in detail in Chapter 9, and it takes a bit of time to walk through exactly how this works. But the basic concept is that designers link pages to the jQuery Mobile script (which is distributed remotely through a network of powerful servers), and then use the HTML5 <data> element to create page elements.

Another example of how designers can mesh HTML5 with JavaScript, *without writing JavaScript code,* is combining the HTML5 <canvas> element with available (already created) JavaScript. Since the <canvas> element is an exciting, interactive new HTML5 element, and, since it doesn't do anything without JavaScript, I explore that example in depth in the following section.

Using the <canvas> element

The new HTML5 <canvas> element creates an interactive graphic area on a page. That graphic area can be programmed to allow users to draw, filter, distort, or interact in other ways with graphics (see Figure 2-13).

Figure 2-13

Like the <data> element, the <canvas> element doesn't do anything without a lot of JavaScript connected to it. You can find some very accessible (and quite exciting) online resources that supply JavaScript templates that you can plug into HTML pages.

tip

One of the most accessible online resources supplying JavaScript templates that can be plugged into HTML pages is EaselJS (www.createjs.com/#!/EaselJS). This free resource has a collection of templates with some fun effects.

Follow these steps to download and explore the EaselJS templates:

1. **Go to** `www.createjs.com/#!/EaselJS/demos`.
2. **Click the Demos button and explore demos of different `<canvas>` scripts (see Figure 2-14).**

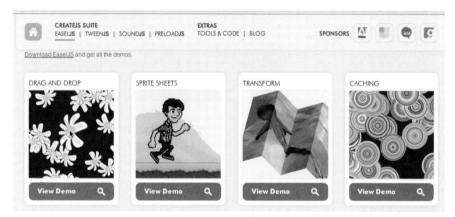

Figure 2-14

3. **After you explore the demos, with a demo open, click the Download EaselJS button (see Figure 2-15).**

   A new set of options appear: CDN, GitHub, and Download.

Figure 2-15

4. **Click the Download button (see Figure 2-16) that appears in the Download option on the right-hand side of the screen.**

   The Download option is easiest to use and includes samples that you can customize.

5. **On the page with links to the most recent version of EaselJS, click the Zip option for the most recent version.**

   Versions of the software change periodically, and the most recent version is the one at the top of the list.

6. **Save the zip file and extract the files.**

   The extracted files include an Examples folder.

Figure 2-16

7. **Open the Examples folder (see Figure 2-17) and survey the dozens of examples of HTML files that combine the `<canvas>` element with JavaScript that downloaded as part of the set of files.**

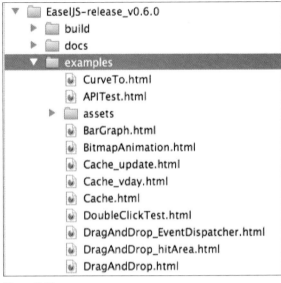

Figure 2-17

You can open any of the EaselJS example files in a browser to see how they work. You can also open them with your HTML code editor to customize them. Obviously, you won't edit any JavaScript you see on the page, but you can add content to the `<body>` tag (like your own text). You can also link your own CSS style sheet to the `<head>` element of the file to integrate the page.

Here's how a custom title and a link to your style sheet in the `<head>` element might look, assuming that you kept the same folder structure for the EaselJS files produced when you extract the zip files:

```
<title>My <canvas> example</title>
<link href="../../style.css" rel="stylesheet" type="text/css">
```

The following code demonstrates a very minimalist edit to the EaselJS `CurveTo.html` file that's a nice, fun example of a drawing area (see Figure 2-18):

```
<body onload="init();">
<h1>Drawing with Canvas</h1>
<h3>Easel JS CurveTo</h3>
<canvas id="myCanvas" width="960" height="400"></canvas>
</body>
```

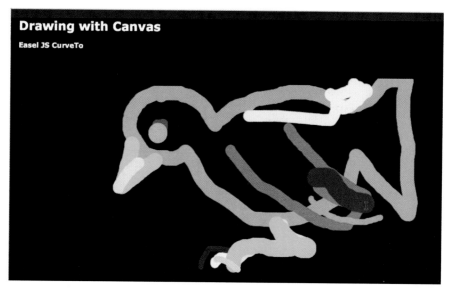

Figure 2-18

If you examine the files that download as part of the EaselJS zipped set of files, you'll see a lot of JavaScript and other files that make the downloaded samples work.

In this section, I explored combining the HTML5 <canvas> tag with JavaScript for a couple reasons. One is that the <canvas> element is so much fun! Beyond that, this exploration of how designers can marry a <canvas> element with available, online (free) resources is a good example of how designers without JavaScript coding skills can combine HTML5 elements with pre-built libraries of JavaScript.

I will return to this concept — combining HTML5 elements with pre-built JavaScript libraries — when I examine the powerful jQuery Mobile library for creating mobile apps with HTML5 and JavaScript in Chapter 8.

THEN

<div> tags for page design elements
images to create shapes

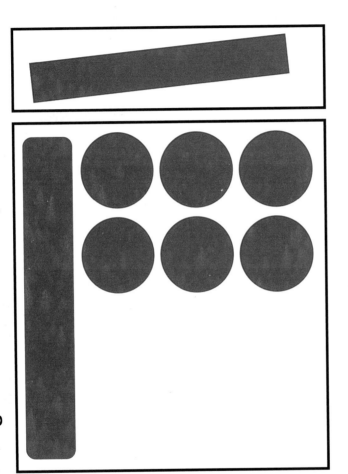

NOV

<div> tags for design

CHAPTER 3

CSS3 for Design, Interactivity, and Animation

In This Chapter

- See the CSS3 effect on the Box Model

- CSS3 replaces elements traditionally designed with images

- Design striking graphical interfaces that open quickly on mobile devices

- Use an enriched CSS set of styles to animate elements for dynamic and interactive websites

- Web fonts are easier to manage in CSS3

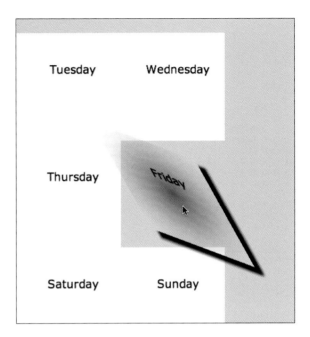

I n this chapter, I take you on a short, conceptual tour of how all the new tools in CSS3 work together to create a really new landscape on which web designers can build pages that are engaging, dynamic, and accessible on a whole new level.

CSS3 opens the door to a pronounced change in web design. To really uncork that potential, step back and look beyond the trees to the forest. Okay (to torture the metaphor), we can *start* with some of the larger trees in the CSS3 forest. They are:

▶ **Effects:** Apply definable border radii that allow you to reshape traditional CSS–based design "boxes" into any shape you wish.

▶ **Transforms:** Rotate, rescale, skew, and *translate* (move) elements on a page.

▶ **Integrating animation:** Combine effects and transforms to create lively, animated, interactive content.

▶ **Gradients:** Define gradient backgrounds without images.

As with most major developments in web design, the sum of CSS3 is greater than the parts. Taken as a whole, the set of new features in CSS3 — along with the emergence of exciting new online resources (like web fonts) — enable you to design richly graphical sites that download almost instantly (even on mobile devices) and present dynamic and graceful animation and interactivity (see Figure 3-1). Moreover, the set of new features in CSS3 allow you to do all this without any software, plugins, or coding beyond CSS and HTML.

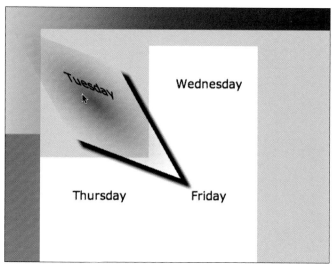

Figure 3-1

tip

You can unlock interactivity and animation with CSS3 on another level by combining it with JavaScript. For a brief note on that, and where to find more on using JavaScript with CSS in this book, see the sidebar "Pairing CSS with JavaScript" later in this chapter.

CSS3 STYLING AND BROWSER COMPATIBILITY

CSS3 is rolling out in modules, as opposed to a whole standard all at once. The implication for designers is that some CSS3 features are very well supported in nearly every browser. Others, not so much – at least yet. It's a good idea to check CSS3 features on sites like caniuse.com and quirksmode.org to see whether a feature is supported in intended target browsers before implementing it in a way in which a site's content will not work without the CSS style working.

It is not always (or usually) the case that you have to wait until a CSS3 feature is supported in every browser before implementing it. For example, rounded corners (CSS3 border radii) are not supported in every browser, but where they are not supported, the fallback is that users see a box with 90 degree angle corners, not rounded corners. That's an acceptable fallback.

Throughout this book, we'll explore backup and fallback options whenever we introduce CSS3 styling that is not fully supported in browsers.

tip
Part III of this book takes an in-depth look at all the critical new CSS3 styling tools and provides helpful advice on how and when to use them.

Breaking Out of the Box with CSS3 Design

Perhaps the most dramatic change in web design driven by CSS3 is that boxes need no longer be "boxes" (see Figure 3-2). As long as there has been web design, page content has been organized into boxes — often referred to as the Box Model. In early eras of web design, this took the form of using tables, with rows and columns, to layout content on a page. In the modern era, this has meant using <div> tags combined

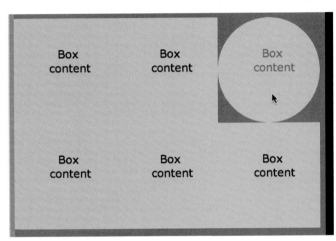

Figure 3-2

with ID or class selectors in a style sheet to define boxes that hold content. Compare how things used to be done and how they are now done with CSS3.

The way it was

Until the advent of CSS3, if you wanted to display a circle, or a rotated rectangle, or a skewed rectangle on a page, for example, HTML and CSS offered no easy solution. The process literally resembled the proverbial challenge of pounding a round peg into a square hole. To put a circular-type element on a page, designers had to first create a graphic image element (in JPEG, GIF, PNG, or SVG format) and then place that image within a box.

THE BOX MODEL — THEN, AND NOW

The "box model" is foundational to designing pages with CSS. Ever since CSS-styled `<div>` tags replaced HTML tables as the grid with which pages were built, rectangular boxes with defined locations, margins, padding, backgrounds, and other style features have been the basic building block of web pages. I review this process in Chapter 1.

That much has not changed with CSS3. What has changed with CSS3 transforms is that these boxes can now be rounded, rotated, skewed, and even moved away from their assigned location (for example, to stack boxes on top of each other).

The process was not only tedious for designers but also bad for users because they had to wait for background images to download before seeing page content. And in the era of mobile devices, with so many mobile users — when they are out of range of their broadband connections — depending on 3G and 4G connections, that problem got worse.

A new design paradigm

With CSS3, no web designers should ever now feel like they're pounding a round peg into a square hole. The CSS3 `border-radius` property transforms squares to circles, as illustrated in Figure 3-3.

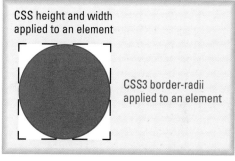

To the rescue, though, CSS3 tears up the paradigm as far as building pages with irregular shapes. With new skew, rotate, translate, and scale transforms, a web designer can sketch any design and easily translate that concept to HTML5 and CSS3. Figure 3-4 shows a few

Figure 3-3

of these transforms — skew (the left column and the "day of the week" boxes), rotate (the heading), and translate (the six "day of the week" boxes have been relocated to overlap better) — applied to page elements.

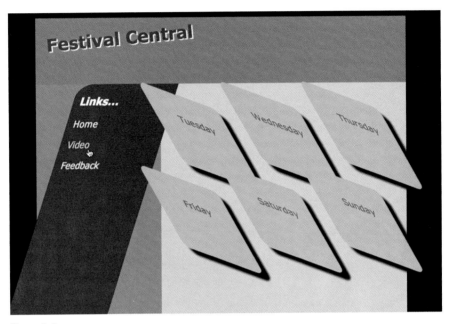

Figure 3-4

Replacing Images with CSS3

The previous section introduces the following CSS3 techniques:

- border radii
- skewing
- rotation
- translation
- scaling

These (and other) CSS3 techniques replace elements that have traditionally been designed with images (with pre–CSS3 CSS). Before the emergence of stable CSS3, design styles like rounded corners, rotated boxes, and irregularly shaped content boxes were designed with background images that gave the *appearance* of irregular shapes. Figure 3-5 shows how this looked behind the scenes then . . . and how this looks now.

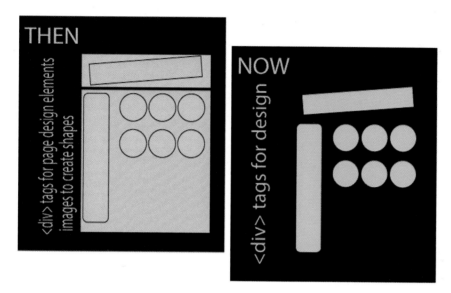

Figure 3-5

Going beyond boxes

There is a reason why designing with CSS (pre–CSS3) was called "implemented box design" (or Box Model). With pre–CSS3, you could draw rectangles and squares, but presenting content that didn't look boxy required background images within those boxes that gave the impression of irregularly shaped containers. That approach is transcended, thanks to CSS3.

Does this mean that designers will see Photoshop and Illustrator go the way of Flash as web design tools? No, at least definitely not right away. There is a paradigm shift emerging, though: namely, a basis and logic to move away from using image files as web design tools. And designers can carve out qualitatively more creative freedom by reconceptualizing the process of translating designs to web content.

Background gradients

Background gradients are another example of this transition from image backgrounds to CSS3–based design. In the pre–CSS3 world, background images were generally small JPEGs, PNGs, or GIFs that were *tiled* (repeated) horizontally and/or vertically as a <div> tag box background.

For example, a designer requiring a gradient background behind a web page would create a thin piece of artwork with that background in Illustrator, similar to the one in Figure 3-6.

Figure 3-6

That image would then be defined as a back-ground-image for a <div> tag, as shown in the code in Figure 3-7.

```
#banner{
background-image:url("bg.png");
}
```

Figure 3-7

The image would typically be tiled (in this case, vertically) to repeat down the entire <div> element, with a result like that in Figure 3-8.

Festival Central

Figure 3-8

Tiled background images served designers well for eons (eons, that is, in web design time). And there is still a place for them today, particularly where very specific art-work is being tiled in a page background. In fact, I use such artwork (one of Darwin's sketches) as a background for my site. You can see a bit of that in Figure 3-9. No CSS3 background code is going to replace that — at least not in the foreseeable future.

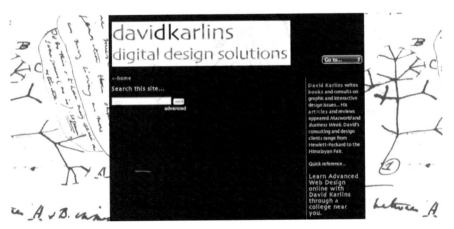

Figure 3-9

Photoshop and Illustrator will thus continue to have a role in creating page and element backgrounds. However, if all you need is a repeating pattern or a repeating gradient, you can do that with CSS3. Figure 3-10 shows backgrounds generated completely in CSS3.

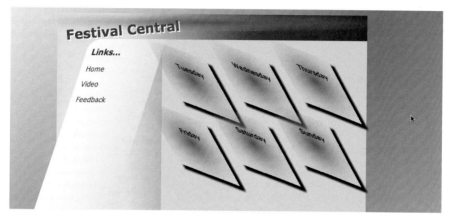

Figure 3-10

To this point, the examples I've shown involve combining only a few new CSS3 features. If you pile on any more effects, the visual cacophony will get a bit hard to bear, even by book example standards. I can, though, highlight three major advantages to relying on CSS3 effects and transforms:

▶ They don't require creating any images, thus radically reducing development time and energy.

▶ They don't require users to download images, which dramatically improves a visitor's experience at a site.

▶ They open the door to non-boxy page design that was simply unavailable in a traditional CSS box model approach to page design.

CSS3 and Mobile — A Perfect Fit

Everything so far in this chapter about the qualitative impact of relying on CSS3 for design leads to designing for mobile devices. Why? In a word: speed. Designing for mobile devices is different than designing for laptops or desktops for several reasons. Mobile devices

▶ Have less-powerful backlit screens, which cry out for high-contrast, high-impact color and design

▶ Have less processing power than laptops or desktops, making them slower

▶ Depend on different connections than cabled laptops and desktops, also making them slower

The good news is that CSS3 allows designers to design striking graphical interfaces that open in mobile devices without forcing users to wait while images download. Look closely at some of your favorite mobile sites. They often use subtle gradient backgrounds behind navigation buttons, thin drop shadows behind text and symbols to make that content stand out, and other graphic effects. Figure 3-11 shows the mobile site for the Bronx Zoo, which uses a generous amount of restrained gradients behind the navigation bar.

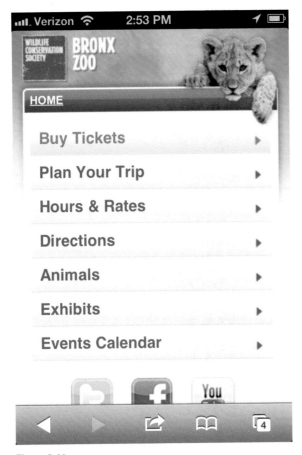

Figure 3-11

You build mobile pages like the one in Figure 3-11 by combining CSS3 effects with new HTML5 tools for mobile design.

tip

I show you different optimal techniques for using HTML5 and CSS3 in mobile design in Chapter 8.

It is no exaggeration to say that contemporary mobile design relies on CSS3.

Animating with CSS3

CSS3 effects and transforms can be animated to become elements of dynamic and interactive websites. Designers have always been able to define :hover states for CSS styles that produce an alternate look when an element — often a navigation element like a button — is hovered over. In mobile devices, the hover state is usually triggered by a tap.

With the enriched set of styles now available in CSS3, this element of interactivity takes on new dimensions. For example

- Buttons can glow when touched by a user's finger or stylus.
- Images can pop off a page when a mobile user lightly touches an image, or when a laptop/desktop user hovers over them with a mouse.
- Dials can rotate to indicate the status of a download, or the progress of a fund-raising project.
- Boxes can skew and appear with radial gradients, as shown in Figure 3-12.
- And much, much more.

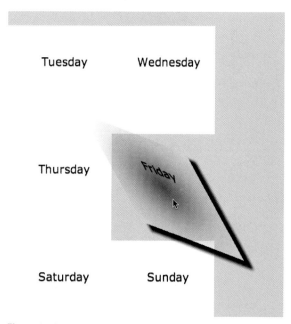

Figure 3-12

Interactivity is just one dimension of animation with CSS3. Another dimension is adding transition timing, so that hover state styles appear to fade in or out of view. CSS3 provides a finely tuned set of options for controlling how animation takes place. In brief, you can define how long a transition is *and* you can define the pace of the transition. The duration of the transition is defined in seconds. The timing is defined using parameters that can force most of the transition to take place early in the duration, late in the duration, or even more complex pacing. I explore these transition options in detail in Chapter 10.

Finally, CSS3 and HTML5 allow you to define timelines that animate the movement and transformation of elements on a page. Demonstrating animation in a printed book requires a bit of use of your imagination, but envision a box moving from Figure 3-13 . . .

Figure 3-13

to Figure 3-14 . . .

Figure 3-14

and you've got the concept. I talk about timelines in depth in Chapter 11.

Designing with Web Fonts

Some CSS3–related breakthroughs in web design are driven not only by new developments in CSS3 but also by corresponding evolutionary activity on the web.

PAIRING CSS WITH JAVASCRIPT

If you pair CSS3 with JavaScript, the sky is more or less the limit in terms of the complexity of web interactivity. JavaScript per se is beyond the scope of this book, but in Chapter 8, I walk you through how to pair CSS3 effects with JavaScript packages that can plug into sites without needing to code JavaScript.

Take web fonts, for example. They open up a whole new scope of possibility in designing websites. Traditionally, font support in web design was dependent upon the font set installed on a user's computer. So, even though web designers could implement any font they wished, users would see that font *only if* it were installed on their system. And, if the designer's preferred font was not supported in a user's system, designers provided universally available fallback fonts (like Serif, or Sans-Serif).

To ensure that any font besides the dozen or so common and universally supported fonts would work for visitors, designers had to purchase downloadable fonts that were supported in browsers. Designers then had to install those fonts on their server and also code their pages so that users would download fonts as they opened a web page. As such, web fonts were effective, and using them enriched sites, but they were "reserved" for the rich and famous who had the resources to properly implement them, as illustrated in Figure 3-15.

Figure 3-15

Web fonts made easy

In a short span of time, not through a direct relationship with the emergence of CSS3, but more-or-less in parallel with that, web fonts have gone from a bit tricky to handle to one of the easier things to do in web design. The reason is that a number of online sources offer web fonts you can use, with the downloaded fonts saved at their (fast) servers.

Here is the syntax for adding a link to a font face in your CSS style sheet file:

```
@font-face {
font-family: "font name";
src: url("link to online font");
}
```

In the code above, both "*font name*"; and "*link to online font*" are place-holder text, the first replaced with the actual font name, and the second with the link provided by the font distributor.

tip

When you obtain a web font from an online resource, you get a link to the font online. In most cases, you get more than that — all you have to do is link to a style sheet that the online resource maintains, and you can use the selected font.

Linking to a web font

In this section, you can see how to choose and apply a web font using Google's set of free online fonts. You can easily adapt these steps to choose a different font than the one in the example, or to use a different source for fonts. The steps are the same; only the specific options will differ.

1. **Go to** www.google.com/fonts **and scroll through the sets of available fonts, as shown in Figure 3-16.**

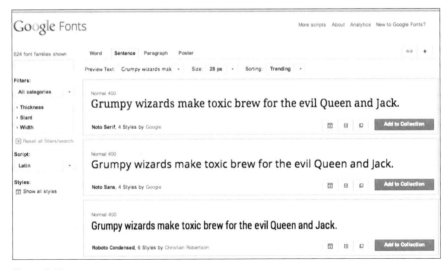

Figure 3-16

2. **On any of the tabs — Word, Sentence, Paragraph, or Poster — you can pre-view the font in different contexts. See Figure 3-17.**

Figure 3-17

3. **To choose a font, click the blue Add to Collection button; then click the Quick-Use button shown in Figure 3-18.**

Figure 3-18

4. **From the Quick Use page that opens, select the font styles you need, as shown in Figure 3-19.**

   Additional font styles offer features, such as boldface or italic.

warning

The more font styles you include, the longer the fonts take to download into a browser.

1. Choose the styles you want:

Figure 3-19

5. **Scroll down the page to Step 2 and choose the character sets you need.**

   The basic Latin character set supports English and western European languages.

   Additional character sets make your fonts work in more alphabets

tip

A note on character sets in Google Fonts: The Extended Latin set covers more languages, but Google Fonts does not use a universally recognized standard to document which languages are supported with different character sets, so if you are creating content in languages beyond English or western European languages, you may need to test your page with the trial-and-error method to see if your content is supported with your selected Google Font.

warning

As with styles, the more font sets you include, the longer the fonts take to download into a browser.

6. **Scroll down to Step 3 on the Google Fonts Quick Use page and copy the link to a style sheet hosted by Google (see Figure 3-20), that in turn links to the fonts you selected.**

3. Add this code to your website:

```
<link href='http://fontr                                              'text/css'>
                    Copy
```

Figure 3-20

7. **Paste the copied style sheet link into the `<head>` element of any HTML web page.**

If you have links to your own (or other) CSS files, you can paste this link at any place in the `<head>` element, regardless of whether it falls before, after, or between other styles. Here's an example:

```
<head>
<link href='http://fonts.googleapis.com/
        css?family=Scada:400italic,400' rel='stylesheet'
        type='text/css'>
<link href="style.css" rel="stylesheet" type="text/css">
</head>
```

8. **Save your HTML page.**

Now you're ready to apply the web font to any CSS style in your regular attached style sheet (in the example here, `style.css`).

9. **Use the `font-family` property and define a second font as a backup in case the link to the Google Fonts style sheet should become corrupted.**

Here's an example of the font style applied to the `<h1>` selector in a CSS file:

```
h1{ font-family: 'Scada', sans-serif; }
```

In this example san-serif, a very generic font supported in every device, is the backup font that will display if the Google Font is corrupted.

10. **Test your page in a browser.**

Of course, given that the linked fonts are downloaded from Google Fonts server, you need an Internet connection to make this work. Figure 3-21 shows custom fonts previewed in a browser.

Hipster Central!

Tumblr artisan.

Put a bird on it lo-fi pop-up leggings, chillwave sustainable vice retro. Semiotics mixtape american apparel skateboard, marfa 3 wolf moon fap umami hella. PBR photo booth banh mi, seitan stumptown quinoa butcher sriracha helvetica 3 wolf moon scenester gluten-free echo park sartorial thundercats.

Swag brooklyn echo park

tumblr master cleanse +1 cosby sweater cliche selvage odd future mlkshk 3 wolf moon fingerstache. Etsy bicycle rights american apparel mumblecore single-origin coffee art party. Carles next level gluten-free truffaut, wes anderson put a bird on it tattooed irony lomo odd future wayfarers narwhal high life retro blog.

Gentrify food truck street art, VHS butcher pour-over 3 wolf moon yr readymade vice irony artisan authentic ethical. Bicycle rights before they sold out chillwave, gluten-free DIY bushwick high life messenger bag food truck. Wayfarers raw denim twee messenger bag, ethnic stumptown yr.

Figure 3-21

Hipster trivia: The hip ipsum loren in Figure 3-21 is from Hipster Ipsum (http://hipsteripsum.me/), one of a community of online resources with spiced up and fun versions of traditional placeholder text.

With accessible, reliable, and affordable web fonts, any designer can use custom fonts as part of a design palette.

FONT TYPES: TTF, EOT, AND WOFF

Other font standards include True Type Fonts (TTF files) and Embedded OpenType (EOT) files. These formats were developed for print, but print fonts have different design freedom than web fonts, mainly because print fonts are generally displayed at something like 300 dots per inch (dpi), while web fonts are often displayed at much lower resolutions (with about a quarter as many dots — or pixels, as they are called in digital devices — per inch). Thus, web fonts have to be designed with less detail, and in ways that avoid blurriness or distortion that would result if existing print-focused fonts were converted directly to web fonts.

The style sheets hosted by Google Fonts are based on OpenType and TrueType fonts for print, but have been designed specifically for optimal display in digital devices. These fonts are programmed with special compression to reduce file size and speed downloading.

And, to be clear, fonts that you download from the Google Fonts site contain links to *other* files — the actual font files, with `.woff` filename extensions. *WOFF* (Web Open Font Format) is the emerging standard for online fonts.

CHAPTER 4

Compatibility Issues and Solutions

In This Chapter

- An overview of HTML5 and CSS3 compatibility

- Understanding levels of HTML5 and CSS3 support

- Browser wars and CSS3

- Native media issues and answers

- Analyzing your audience

Web design has never been more exciting — or complicated. The radical improvements in HTML and CSS that I explore in this book open the door to seamless media, friendly forms, unconventional design, and inviting animation and interactivity. And yet all these features pose three different kinds of compatibility issues:

▶ Most — but not all — of these features are supported in all current generation browsers. This has to be taken into account when implementing new HTML5 and CSS3 features.

▶ And, none of these features are supported in Internet Explorer 8 (IE8) and earlier. This too has to be taken into account when a significant section of a site's intended audience is using IE8 and earlier.

▶ New HTML5 and CSS3 features are supported differently in contemporary browsers.

All compatibility issues are in constant flux. The section of the web community that continues to use IE8 is in decline — although not as rapidly as designers might wish — and I tell you why in this chapter. And the online design community continues to evolve tools and techniques to make modern pages work in this environment.

Of more strategic significance, HTML5 and CSS3 features have been implemented differently in different browsers. For example, HTML5 native video that runs in Chrome might not work in Firefox (see Figure 4-1).

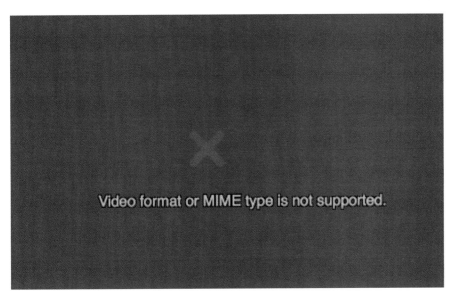

Video format or MIME type is not supported.

Figure 4-1

And CSS3 syntax that defines a gradient background in Safari might not work in a current version of Internet Explorer (at the time of this writing, IE 11 is being finalized for release).

Trying to capture a snapshot of this rapidly evolving compliancy terrain in a book would be about as helpful as publishing a list of the top ten selling songs today at iTunes or the best-selling apps this week at Google Play. What is useful and important for you is

▶ Understanding the different kinds of compatibility issues involved in implementing HTML5 and CSS3

▶ Knowing how and where to look up the latest status of support for different features

▶ Understanding conceptually how to approach HTML5 and CSS3 compatibility

And I cover all this in this chapter!

Making HTML5 and CSS3 Work in Older Browsers

Question: What browsing environments support HTML5 and CSS3?

Answer: All of them.

With that simple answer to the basic question out of the way, take a sec to break that down and deal with the complicated reality.

True, every browser known to humanity — and this includes mobile browsers — can read HTML and CSS3 files, interpret them, and display content based on them. The simple HTML `doctype` declaration is more easily interpreted in older browsers than older `doctype` declarations, for reasons that I share in Chapter 3.

What some browsing environments cannot do is interpret new elements in HTML5 and new style properties in CSS3. (For an overview of CSS3 support, see Figure 4-2.)

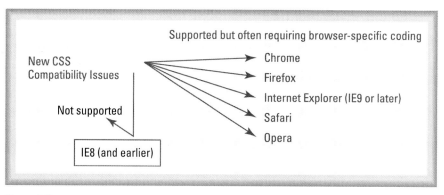

Figure 4-2

It's certainly important for designers to identify the audience visiting websites with browsing environments that don't support new features in HTML5 and CSS3. Sure, those environments are declining, and someday everyone will view websites in browsers that support all HTML5 and CSS3 features . . . but that day isn't here yet. Whether — and to what degree — any website is compatible with every browser depends on how critical it is for that site to reach the IE8-and-earlier user base.

Here are essentially two approaches one can take to making pages designed to exploit HTML5 and CSS3 work in older browsers:

▶ **Hacks:** Additional coding and scripts that make new features work in older browsers

▶ **Graceful degradation:** Designing sites that optimize in contemporary browsers but still work in older browsers

tip

> In my opinion, graceful degradation should be your main approach, but I'll outline both options for you. The solutions you adopt depend to large degree on your audience.

So, Step 1 is to identify browsing environments that don't support new features of HTML5 and CSS3.

Everything you wanted to know about IE8 (and earlier) but were afraid to ask

When I talk about browsing environments that cannot interpret new elements in HTML5 and new style properties in CSS3, I'm talking about Internet Explorer versions 6–8. Every other browsing environment supports HTML5 and CSS3. And it will be some time before the Internet Explorer 6–8 community will be part of the audience that is addressed by web designers.

Part of the reason is that Microsoft doesn't provide easy or free upgrades for IE8 users who don't upgrade their operating systems. As a workaround, plenty of free, contemporary browsers — Firefox, Chrome (see Figure 4-3), and Opera — are available for Windows that users can download. So why don't all Windows users simply install current browsers?

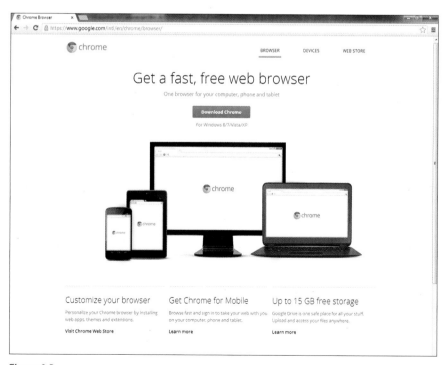

Figure 4-3

Well, it's not because a significant section of Internet users don't have the information or resources to install modern browsers. The reason why is that large institutions that have implemented long-term and costly IT strategies don't have the flexibility to make the massive investment in time, technology, restructuring, and retraining to upgrade their versions of Windows to newer versions that support the current version of IE. And, to be clear, without upgrading to newer versions of Windows, Windows XP users cannot install the current version of Internet Explorer.

Why don't these users upgrade to a new version of Windows? In many instances, they find Windows XP quite stable and functional for their needs, and enabling their users to take full advantage of the current state of web animation and interactivity isn't a priority. This situation exists throughout schools, banks, and other institutions in the United States and Europe, and is even more pronounced in the rest of the world.

WHO IS THE IE8 COMMUNITY?

Many substantial studies and articles have analyzed the resilience of IE8 as the only browsing option for a large section of Internet users:

- "The impending crisis that is Windows XP and IE8"

    www.troyhunt.com/2013/01/the-impending-crisis-that-is-windows-xp.html

- "Browser Trends March 2012: IE8 Falls Below 20%"

    www.sitepoint.com/browser-trends-march-2012

- "OpenFin CEO Mazy Dar: Bridging the Banks' Technology Gap"

    www.linuxinsider.com/story/
    OpenFin-CEO-Mazy-Dar-Bridging-the-Banks-Technology-Gap-77621.html

One basic conclusion of these articles (all written in 2012 and 2013) is that there is not sufficient incentive for many large financial, healthcare, educational, and government institutions with substantial security requirements to allow users to install browsers that support new features in HTML5 and CSS3.

Such an entrenched institutional user base explains both the persistence and specific relevance of the IE8 audience. It is also the basis for designers to prioritize whether to implant hacks that make it possible for IE8 and earlier users to have as optimal an experience at their sites as possible — or, on the other hand, to provide minimal functionality for IE8 and earlier users.

If, for example, you identified your site's audience as overwhelmingly being employees of large government agencies or a major bank with a massive IT system, then you should probably consider investing the time to implement substantial hacks to provide workarounds for CSS3 and HTML5 features not supported in IE8 and earlier.

On the other hand, if your site's audience comprises overwhelmingly mobile users, using IE8 and earlier is obviously not an issue because IE8 and earlier doesn't exist for mobile (thank goodness!).

Hacking solutions

Because of the persistence of IE8, a variety of hacks have been developed and shared online to address IE8 (and earlier) compatibility issues. And just to be clear, by "hack" I'm not talking about crime syndicates stealing credit card information; I'm talking about informally developed and distributed online techniques and resources for making new design features work in older browsers.

If providing a near-HTML5/CSS3 experience for IE8 and earlier users is a priority, you should explore and use the set of scripts and coding tricks found in various places on the web that make IE8 and earlier recognize at least some HTML5 and CSS3 features.

remember

A full survey of all the attempts to put together hacks to make new features of HTML5 and CSS3 work in IE8 is beyond the scope of this or any book.

However, here are two resources that solve the two most critical compatibility issues of IE8 and HTML5:

▶ **HTML5Shiv JavaScript:** Lets IE6–8 recognize new HTML tags

▶ **Respond JavaScript:** Enables responsive design techniques to work in IE6–8.

Linking to HTML5Shiv

If you use HTML5 semantic tags (such as <header>, <footer>, <article>, and <nav>), IE8 won't recognize them, so, using the HTML5Shiv JavaScript is pretty important because as a JavaScript workaround, this script allows styling of HTML5 elements in versions of IE8 and earlier.

tip

Semantic tags are covered in depth in Chapter 5.

To be clear, and re-state the challenge: One of the most significant new elements of HTML5 is the set of pre-defined semantic tags, like <article>, <section>, <header>, and <footer>. But IE8 does not recognize these tags. So, if you assign styles to semantic tags, IE8 won't display those styles.

And, to restate the solution: The HTML5Shiv Script is free, takes only moments to link to, and there is no downside to using it. With the script installed, IE8 will recognize HTML5 semantic tags, and will apply CSS styles applied to them.

tip

You can download and install the HTML5Shiv JavaScript at `https://code.google.com/p/html5shiv/`. There you will find a link to download a zip file with the script. Save (download) the zip file to the folder that holds your website content, and expand the zip file. This creates a folder called `dist` which holds the required JavaScript files. Then, follow the simple instructions at `https://code.google.com/p/html5shiv/` to copy and paste code into the `<head>` element of your HTML document that links to this script.

Better yet, an easier approach is to simply link to the HTML5Shiv file hosted by Google. To do that, place the code in Listing 4-1 in the `<head>` element of your web pages. If a user's browser is a version of Internet Explorer earlier than version 9, the script loads. If not, the user's browser ignores the script (the first line of the code in the Listing below is a comment telling you — the designer — that if the user has a version of Internet Explorer lower than 9, the script applies ("lt" in the comment is shorthand for "lower than").

Listing 4-1: Linking to the Google-Hosted HTML5Shiv File

```
<!--[if lt IE 9]>
<script src="http://html5shiv.googlecode.com/svn/trunk/html5.js"></script>
<![endif]-->
```

on the web

All of the code listings used in this book are available for download from the Downloads tab on the book's companion website at `www.dummies.com/extras/html5andcss3`.

Using Respond JavaScript to support media queries

Using Respond JavaScript (`Respond.jsscript`) isn't as critical as the HTML5Shiv JavaScript. However, Respond JavaScript enables media queries so that when a user's viewport is reduced to a defined width (say, narrower than 960 pixels), a new style sheet kicks in.

remember

Media queries provide different style sheets for different sized browsing environments. When and how to use media queries is explored in Chapter 8.

Because IE8 doesn't run on tablets or smartphones, responsive design isn't the same important issue as when a site is viewed on a mobile device. It can be nice but not essential to provide a different look and feel for sites viewed in different sized viewports on a desktop or laptop computer. However, you can make media queries work in IE8 and earlier if you include a link to a JavaScript known as the Respond solution.

To link to the script that makes the Respond solution work, follow these steps:

1. **Open your browser and go to** `https://github.com/scottjehl/Respond`**.**

2. **Download `respond.min.js` by clicking the Zip button, shown in Figure 4-4. This is the file required for the Respond solution.**

   The `respond.min.js` script downloads along with documentation and example files.

Figure 4-4

3. **Extract the files and save the `respond.min.js` file to your website's root folder (the folder you use to organize all the content at your website).**

4. **Add this script element in the `<head>` section of your page, after the last stylesheet link:**

   ```
   <script src="respond.min.js"></script>
   ```

Alternatively, you can link to various hosted versions of the file. One is found at `http://cdnjs.cloudflare.com/ajax/libs/respond.js/1.1.0/respond.min.js`.

If you link to this version of the script, your `<script>` element will be

```
<script src="http://cdnjs.cloudflare.com/ajax/libs/respond.js/1.1.0/
              respond.min.js"></script>
```

tip

Should you download the JavaScript required for the Respond solution? Or link to the remote files? In most cases, I recommend linking to the remote files. That way, you can't accidently delete these files from your site, you don't have to worry about properly linking to the files at your site, and you don't have to worry about the files getting corrupted.

Here's another reason to link to the remote version of the Respond JavaScript files: You can't test the `Respond.js` script on your local computer. You can't even test it on a server installed on your own computer (like WAMP or WebMatrix). There is a security setting in IE that blocks the script from working in IE8 or earlier. So, you can't test the Respond solution offline.

You test the Respond solution by going to your uploaded page, hosted at a Web server, and trying it there with IE8 (or earlier).

technical stuff

WAMP, MAMP, and LAMP (which run on Windows, Macs, and Linux respectively) and WebMatrix are applications that provide much of the same functionality on a developer's computer that is available on remote web hosting servers. Server-side programmers who write code to manage form data and databases, for example, can test their work with these applications. But even with such server software installed on your own computer, you can't test the Respond solution — only remote hosting servers have the features installed that allow this.

Testing sites in IE8 (and older)

Few web designers have an installed version of IE8. So, how do you test sites to see if — and how — they function in IE6–8? Use an online resource, such as Sauce Labs (`https://saucelabs.com`), which offers various levels of testing for IE8 and other browsers, as shown in Figure 4-5.

Figure 4-5

Or, if you have a current version of Internet Explorer installed, you can see how an open page looks by pressing F12 to access Developer Tools and then changing the Browser Mode setting to IE6, 7, or 8, as illustrated in Figure 4-6.

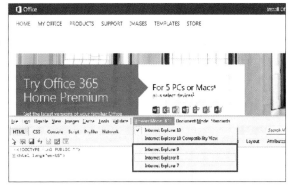

Figure 4-6

Using graceful degradation for backward compatibility

All browsers support HTML5 and CSS3, but they don't all necessarily support the new features (see Figure 4-7). One generally applicable solution to the backward-compatibility problem is *graceful degradation*.

GRACEFUL DEGRADATION AND PROGRESSIVE ENHANCEMENT

There are two conceptual approaches to handling browser compatibility: Graceful degradation and progressive enhancement. Both approaches solve the problem of providing sites that are inviting and engaging in environments with maximum support for cutting-edge technology, but that still work well in browsing environments without that capacity.

Progressive enhancement starts with a design that works in any device, and then enhances that with additional features that make a site more attractive and useful for users with current generation browsers. Where the two approaches diverge most is in implementing JavaScript features that might be disabled or not supported in older browsers or devices. Those JavaScript issues are beyond the scope of this book.

When it comes to implementing HTML5 and CSS3, there is very little real difference between the two approaches. They both are aimed at maximizing HTML5 and CSS3 features, while making sure pages are still functional in browsers without HTML5 and CSS3 support.

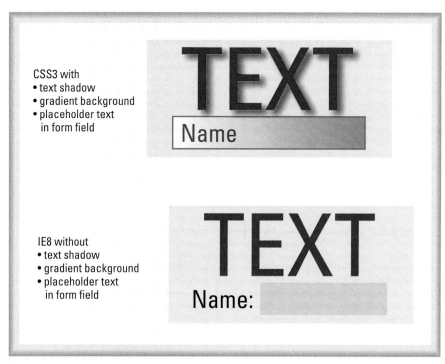

CSS3 with
• text shadow
• gradient background
• placeholder text
  in form field

IE8 without
• text shadow
• gradient background
• placeholder text
  in form field

Figure 4-7

The basic concept of graceful degradation is this: You design pages that are dynamic, inviting, and interactive in contemporary browsers, yet are also functional in older browsers.

For example, Figure 4-8 shows a page with a form against a gradient background, in both a contemporary browser (left) and IE8 (right). This example illustrates the point of graceful degradation:

▶ IE8 doesn't support CSS3 gradient backgrounds, so you design elements with gradients to display a solid color in IE.

▶ IE8 doesn't support HTML5 form field placeholders (prompts) in forms, so you design forms where regular text makes it clear what should be entered into a form field, and HTML5 placeholder content can further clarify or encourage users to enter that data.

▶ IE8 doesn't support CSS3 text shadows, so you apply a high-contrast color scheme for IE8 users.

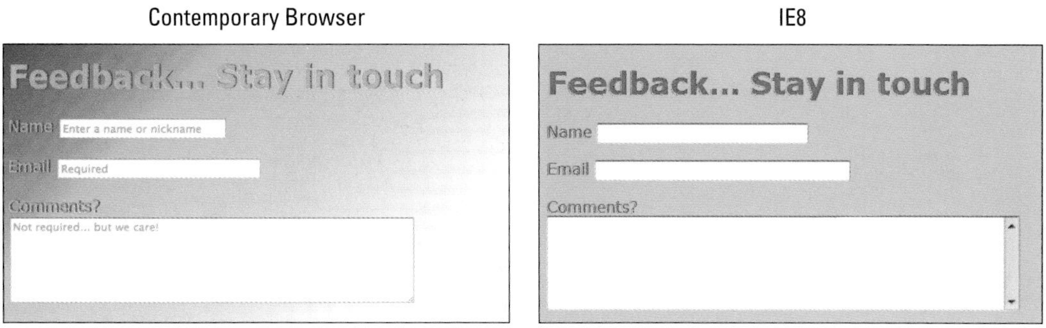

Contemporary Browser   IE8

Feedback... Stay in touch   Feedback... Stay in touch

Name Enter a name or nickname   Name

Email Required   Email

Comments?   Comments?

Not required... but we care!

Figure 4-8

HTML5 and CSS3 Browser Wars

At the onset, the concept was simple: HTML5 and CSS3 would be adopted by all browsers. And that happened. But what makes things complicated is that they just didn't adopt HTML5 and CSS3 the same way.

As I allude earlier in this chapter, which browser supports what is a moving target. The good news is I'm here to provide you with guidance and assistance when developing for browser compatibility. For example, in Parts II and III of this book I provide you with instructions for doing something one way for some browsers, and instructions for doing it another way for other browsers.

To accurately determine how to address browser compatibility issues, start with the foundation that almost all contemporary browsers use one of five engines' underlying technologies. These five engines are

> **Gecko:** Used by Firefox
> **Presto:** Used by older versions of Opera — current versions of Opera for desktop and mobile are changing to WebKit.
> **Trident:** Used by Internet Explorer for both desktop and mobile
> **WebKit:** Used by Safari, earlier versions of Chrome, newer versions of Opera, and most mobile browsers except for Windows Mobile
> **Blink:** A version of WebKit used by current versions of Chrome.

Using vendor-specific CSS prefixes

Because CSS3 is still a work in progress (although an important, and essentially stable, work in progress), different browser engines have their own distinct CSS for new style sheet properties.

CSS3 *transforms* — those really cool properties that include skewed, translated (moved), scaled, and rotated elements — requires a set of *prefixes* (code before code) to make the transform work in every modern browser. The CSS to rotate a box 15 degrees would look like this:

```
transform:rotate(15deg);
-ms-transform:rotate(15deg);
-webkit-transform:rotate(15deg);
-o-transform:rotate(15deg);
```

The first line — which doesn't have a prefix — is coded for browsers that don't require a prefix, such as Chrome (versions using the Blink engine) and IE10. The second line, with the –ms prefix, works in IE9. The third line defines the rotation for Safari, older versions of Chrome, and most mobile browsers. The last line defines rotation for Opera.

on the web

You can find online resources dedicated to constantly updated documentation of which browser supports which CSS3 properties. One of the most useful and complete online resources is the Can I Use site (http://caniuse.com).

Competing video formats

Perhaps the most substantial compatibility issue with HTML5 is that different browser engines support different native video formats. Here again, the cast of characters is in flux.

on the web

The Can I Use site page on "HTML5 Video" is updated constantly and includes a detailed chart of which engine supports which video format (see http://caniuse.com/video).

For example, several native video formats allow designers to embed video in a page without a user needing a plugin to watch the video. However, none of those formats work in every browser. If, for example, you try to watch an h.264 (MP4) video in Firefox, as of this writing, you see an error message (see Figure 4-9).

Video format or MIME type is not supported.

Figure 4-9

And, to be fair, if you try to run the other widely supported HTML5 native video format (OGG) in Safari, you see an inelegant `Loading` message that never goes away — and no video (see Figure 4-10).

Even though browser support for video formats changes, things have stabilized to the point where designers need only two native video versions embedded video files:

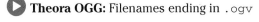

Loading...

Figure 4-10

-  **h.264:** Filenames ending in `.mp4`
-  **Theora OGG:** Filenames ending in `.ogv`

Am I saying "Hey, embed both h.264 and OGG video" as the solution? In part, yes, that solves the problem of making video available for everyone with HTML5-friendly browsers. I walk you through the process of preparing video in both formats in Chapter 7.

A bit later in this chapter, I turn to the challenge of providing solutions for environments that don't support HTML5 at all.

The essential workflow for preparing HTML5-ready video is this:

1. **Create your video in the h.264 video format.**

   This proprietary format is supported by, and exported to, all major video-editing software.

2. **Convert the h.264 video to OGG format.**

   You can convert h.264 video to OGG format using free software like the Miro Video Converter (`www.mirovideoconverter.com`) or the converter distributed by Theora (`http://v2v.cc/~j/ffmpeg2theora/`). Figure 4-11 shows Miro Video Converter generating an HTML5 native video Ogg Theora format file.

Figure 4-11

Creating video for IE8

IE8 doesn't support any native video, so the fallback is to provide a video option that runs with a plugin. Yes, this does mean providing a third version of the video.

Here are possible solutions that do that:

 Some developers use Flash Video (FLV) as the fallback. Read more about this in the upcoming section, "A Word on Flash."

Other developers use various Windows Media formats, such as AVI.

Another option is to gracefully degrade video so that users with IE8 simply get a note that their browser doesn't support contemporary video formats. This solution is also widely implemented by designers who judge that providing minimally functional page content for IE8 users doesn't include video.

Which option is best for you? The best approach will be defined by your target audience; bounce back to the discussion earlier in this chapter in "Everything you wanted to know about IE8 but were afraid to ask."

tip

For a full exploration of how to prepare and present HTML5 native audio and video — and how to provide options for browsers that don't support HTML5 media — see Chapter 7.

Mobile Compatibility

You can't overlook compatibility issues with HTML5 and CSS3 in mobile browsers, either. In a nutshell, that word is *none.*

And as with any one-word answer, that's a bit of an oversimplification. As I show you this chapter, there are differences in how HTML5– and CSS3–compliant browsers handle different features. As a general rule, though, mobile browsers are frequently updated, and thus they all support HTML5 and CSS3.

remember

The main challenge in creating inviting and accessible sites for mobile devices is to take full advantage of HTML5 and CSS3 features that that make everything from forms to video more accessible in mobile devices.

tip

See Chapter 8 for more on designing for mobile devices.

A Word on Flash

How does Flash fit into the world of HTML5 and CSS3? Not well. When the late Steve Jobs established that Apple mobile devices would never support Flash animation or video, he was really only hastening a trend toward native video and plugin-free browsing.

Of course, it will be the case for some time that some devices and browsers that support HTML5 and CSS3 will also allow the installation of the Flash Player because it's is necessary to run Flash video (FLV) files and Flash animated objects (SWF files).

The HTML5 native video element (explored in depth in Chapter 7) is a replacement for Flash video. Still, HTML5 and CSS3 don't replace the functionality provided by Flash as a whole. CSS3 has limited animation tools, which I examine in Chapter 11. And an emerging set of JavaScript tools mesh with HTML5 and CSS3 to provide features, such as animated vector graphics and slideshows.

on the web

A full exploration of those JavaScript tools, including jQuery, is beyond the scope of this book, but you'll find helpful documentation and resources at `http://jquery.com/`. You can also check out *jQuery For Dummies* by Lynn Beighley.

Part II

Creating Pages with HTML5

In this part, I survey in depth and detail the tools available for page building with HTML5. I walk you through the process of relying on new, semantic HTML5 page-structuring tags. In addition, I explore how HTML5 provides a rather remarkable set of form tools, ranging from calendar prompts to calculated fields to validating form data.

Also in this part, I demystify relying on plugin-free native HTML5 audio and video. And I explore how to implement the two most powerful tools in HTML5 for creating fully mobile sites — responsive design with media queries, and jQuery Mobile web apps.

HTML5 makes using forms to capture valuable data from visitors much easier. Check out the article surveying the five most high-impact form tools in HTML5 at www.dummies.com/extras/html5andcss3.

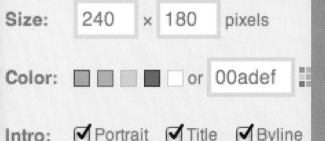

THEN (CSS2)

```
<div id="header">

<div id="footer">

<div id="article">

<div id="aside">
```

N

```
<

<

<

<
```

W (CSS3)

ader>

ter>

cle>

de>

CHAPTER 5

HTML5 Semantic Tags

In This Chapter

- Organizing content with HTML5 tags

- Using HTML5 semantic tags for page structure

- Using HTML5 semantic tags for specific content

- Styling HTML5 tags

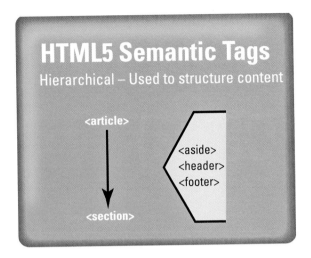

HTML5 Semantic Tags

Hierarchical – Used to structure content

`<article>`

`<aside>`
`<header>`
`<footer>`

`<section>`

erhaps no dimension of HTML5 has been as controversial and provocative as the linkage between tags and content. *Semantic tags* are elements whose names describe content. The `<strong>` tag, for example is not a semantic tag. It indicates content will be displayed in boldface, but it doesn't tell you anything about the *content* of that boldface text. On the other hand, sematic tags like `<article>` or `<address>` or `<datetime>` actually describe the nature of the content within them — and are intuitively named to make it easy to figure out what element should be assigned to what kind of content.

Semantic tags have had a role HTML before HTML5. The `<p>` (paragraph) tag, for example, does — kind of — describe the nature of the content within it. But HTML5, for the first time, provides a substantial set of pre-defined semantic tags.

Tags such as `<header>`, `<footer>`, and `<article>` contain just what you would expect them to contain — header content, footer content, and an article, respectively. The `<progress>` element, intuitively enough, displays a progress bar, and a `<nav>` element holds navigation content. All this represents an approach that designers can take to simplify page design and present more inviting, accessible content to users.

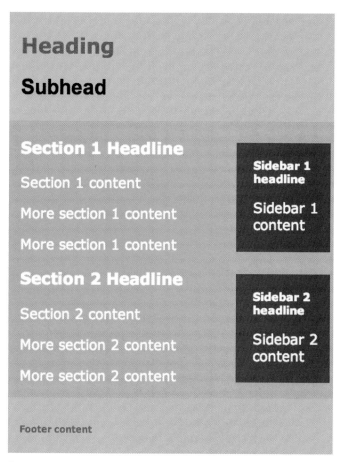

Figure 5-1

In this chapter, I survey different kinds of semantic elements. Some of these elements are used for structuring (organizing and ordering) content (like `<article>` or `<header>`; see Figure 5-1). Other semantic indicate the nature of the content they enclose, but do not structure content (like the `<datetime>` and `<address>` elements). And, I introduce you to some rather cool display features associated with some semantic tags, like the `<details>` and `<summary>` elements that expand to show "details" (and are sometimes used for online quizzes).

Understanding the Different Kinds of Semantic Elements

All new HTML5 semantic elements have one thing in common: They all have element names that (more or less) describe the *kind* of content within them.

A <time> element, for example, encloses a time: for example, January 1, 2016. A <header> tag conveys that the content within that element is a page header (or possibly an article or even a section header).

THE <HEAD> AND <HEADER> ELEMENTS

If you will pardon a review of basic HTML, in case there is confusion, let's sort out the distinction between the similarly named <head> and <header> elements.

The <head> element holds content that does not appear in a browser document window, but includes links to style sheets, meta information (meta) like a description of a page, and a page title.

The <head> element also includes the <title> element, which is the only <head> element that is absolutely required, and has been an element of HTML going back to the earliest versions. The <header> element which I explore in this chapter is new to HTML5. It holds introductory or navigational material — usually for a page but it can also be applied to an article or other content within a page.

Structural HTML5 semantic tags

Structural HTML5 semantic tags serve to divide page content into organized, hierarchical blocks.

The HTML5 semantic tags that make up what I call the "structural category" include

- <header>
- <article>
- <section>
- <aside>
- <footer>

A typical page layout, with a header, a footer, and an article with two sections would look something like the one in Figure 5-2.

Again, what these elements have in common is a set of hier-archical relationships: that is, a top-down flow. For example, you should never use an `<aside>` tag that's not embedded in either an `<article>` or a `<section>` element.

tip

I show you the details of how this works in the "Organizing Content with Five Elements" section later in this chapter.

Article with sections

Article head

Section head

Food truck laboris beard single-origin coffee, leggings ugh cray anim. Quis kale chips tumblr occaecat occupy meh PBR before they sold out exercitation, banh mi laborum. Stumptown dreamcatcher delectus umami before they sold out officia.

Letterpress pariatur irure, elit truffaut nostrud blue bottle wayfarers swag gentrify ut chambray laborum. Tonx non pariatur ethical, incididunt hella ullamco brooklyn mollit. Cliche hella 90's put a bird on it. Tofu mixtape keytar wolf bespoke dreamcatcher.

Section head

Gentrify vegan excepteur meh, biodiesel cray banjo portland aliquip ethnic small batch sed odd future scenester. Plaid pour-over aesthetic, in et YOLO veniam readymade 3 wolf moon photo booth pinterest selvage.

Sustainable freegan hella fugiat. Viral nesciunt ullamco, veniam hashtag etsy ethical banjo portland. Four loko godard farm-to-table, ethnic try-hard semiotics polaroid wes anderson umami sunt pork belly aliquip wolf. Fingerstache chillwave placeat before they sold out, VHS disrupt selfies sapiente narwhal. Officia yr typewriter sint.

Footer content

Figure 5-2

Nonstructural semantic tags

The most universal and powerful new HTML5 elements tend to be the set of struc-tural tags (`<header>`, `<footer>`, `<article>`, and so on). However, an intriguing set of additional new HTML5 semantic tags are not bound by any particular structure or hierarchy. Some of these tags are rather obscure, but here are a few important HTML5 semantic tags fall into what I call the "nonstructural semantic tags:"

- `<progress>`: Presents a graphical bar representing the extent to which an event or project has been completed.
- `<datetime>`: Used to indicate that content represents a date.
- `<address>`: Used to indicate that content represents a virtual or physical address.
- `<summary>`: Used with `<details>` elements to create expandable blocks.
- `<details>`: Used with `<summary>` elements to create expandable blocks.

Nonstructural semantic tags allow you to do many interesting things. For example, Figure 5-3 illustrates a `<progress>` tag. This is an element that can be used as many times as necessary, anywhere within a page, without regard to any defining structure. In other words, there are no rules or conventions that determine that a `<progress>` tag has to be, or shouldn't be, inside any other element.

We have reached 50% of our fundraising goal for today:

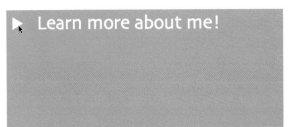

Figure 5-3

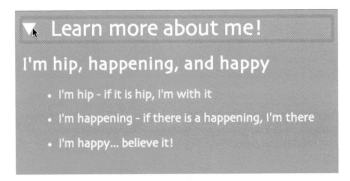

Figure 5-4

Or, you might want to provide an expandable `<details>` element in an `<article>` tag, a `<section>` tag, or even in a `<footer>` tag. The element displays an expandable summary, as shown in Figure 5-4.

And `<details>` elements expand to show details, as shown in Figure 5-5.

![Learn more about me! I'm hip, happening, and happy. I'm hip - if it is hip, I'm with it. I'm happening - if there is a happening, I'm there. I'm happy... believe it!]

Figure 5-5

Other HTML5 semantic tags

My exploration of HTML5 semantic tags in this chapter so far has focused on two categories:

▶ **Structural HTML5 semantic tags:** Tags used for . . . you guessed it, page structure

▶ **Nonstructural HTML5 semantic tags:** Cool tags that don't have a specific "fit" within pages but make content more inviting and usable

However, other new HTML5 semantic tags don't quite fit into either of these categories. Rather, these other new HTML5 semantic tags fall into the following two categories:

▶ **Typography tags:** Used for specific typography challenges and also to address issues of presenting East Asian typography

▶ **Programmable tags:** Don't do anything until they're programmed with JavaScript

Typography tags

Typography tags are highly specialized tags used for very specific, niche challenges. To emphasize, these are not tags you'll use every day. Many designers will never use them. However, if you are working with major blocks of type, and fine-tuned line breaks are important, you should be aware of the `<bdi>` and especially the `<wbr>` tags.

The `<bdi>` tag used when text flows from right-to-left within an element wherein the rest of the text is flowing from left to right.

Another specialized element, the `<wbr>` tag, defines a possible line break when a browser window width is reduced. The `<wbr>` tag is typically used within very large words to define how they should break. For example, in the following code line, the `<wbr>` tags mark points where a long word will be broken if it doesn't fit in a browser window:

```
<p>Pneumonoul<wbr>tramicroscopic<wbr>silicovolcanoconiosis is
          a serious lung disease.</p>
```

Figure 5-6 shows this text in a wide browser window.

Learn more about...

Pneumonoultramicroscopicsilicovolcanoconiosis is a serious lung disease.

Figure 5-6

Learn more about...

Pneumonoultramicroscopic silicovolcanoconiosis is a serious lung disease.

Figure 5-7

Figure 5-7 shows the same text in a narrow browser window, with the word broken at the second `<wbr>` tag.

Tags for East Asian character sets

Other highly specialized HTML5 typography tags include the `<ruby>`, `<rt>`, and `<rp>` tags. These tags are only applicable to designers working in East Asian character sets (such as Chinese, Japanese, or Korean), and only function in environments with the appropriate East Asian character sets installed. Here's what these tags do:

▶ `<ruby>`: This element defines a ruby annotation (for East Asian typography). *Ruby annotations* are short runs of text presented alongside base text, primarily used in East Asian typography as a guide for pronunciation or to include other annotations. In Japanese, this form of typography is also known as *furigana*.

▶ `<rt>`: Generally embedded within a `<ruby>` tag, the `<rt>` element defines an explanation/pronunciation of characters.

remember

The `<ruby>` and `<rt>` elements are used only for East Asian typography. If you aren't using East Asian character sets, this element is not applicable.

▶ `<rp>`: This element defines what to show in browsers that don't support ruby annotations.

tip

The set of `<ruby>`, `<rt>`, and `<rp>` tags are, as we go to press, supported in Chrome but not in Safari, Firefox, or Opera without special plugin software.

Programmable tags

Programmable tags are HTML5 semantic tags that only function as tools for JavaScript designers. These programmable tags include the `<command>` and `<dialog>` elements that can be used with JavaScript interactive objects. Again, these tags have no independent meaning unless they are implemented in JavaScript programs, and an exploration of these tags is the province of JavaScript programming resources.

There are also two new HTML tags that already have a substantial library of JavaScript widgets that allow nonscripters to access them: the `<canvas>` element and the `<data>` element:

▶ `<canvas>`: Creates user-accessed drawing boxes

▶ `<data>`: Used (among other things) to connect jQuery Mobile animation and interactivity to mobile pages

tip

I discuss the `<canvas>` element in Chapter 2 and the `<data>` element in Chapter 8.

Organizing Content with Five Elements

In philosophy, "five elements" might refer to Wu Xing, the five elements in Chinese philosophy, or Mahābhūta, the five elements in Hinduism. I bring this up in order to stress the point that there are essentially five HTML5 semantic markup elements that are used to define most pages:

- `<article>`
- `<section>`
- `<aside>`
- `<header>`
- `<footer>`

tip

The syntax for these elements is the same, and quite simple. They open with a tag like `<header>` and close with a tag like `</header>`.

Knowing when to use what

The names of the five key HTML5 structure elements are pretty intuitive: They define the key blocks of page content (see Figure 5-8). There are defined rules for when to use which element. For a full, detailed exposition of when to use which HTML5 structure element, you can go straight to the source at w3.org (`www.w3.org/TR/html-markup`) and study the formal definitions of these tags. This is the website of the World Wide Web Consortium (W3C), which is the main organization that sets standards for the World Wide Web.

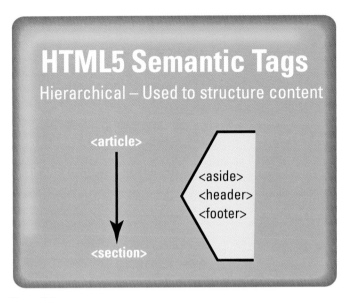

Figure 5-8

The w3.org documentation is more detailed and less accessible than one might wish, so in the sections that follow, I'm going to briefly summarize the dos and don'ts for the five key elements.

The `<article>` element

`<article>` elements are used to — you guessed it — enclose entire articles. (Didn't I tell you the names of the five key structural elements were pretty intuitive?) Use the `<article>` element for

▶ Forum or blog postings

▶ Articles in publications

▶ Posted comments

The `<article>` element can be, but does not have to be, enclosed in any other element. The content should be self-contained so that it can be read or distributed independent of any other content on the page.

And because the `<article>` element stands on its own, there are no rigid rules for what it can be enclosed in. In general, though, the `<article>` element is the highest-level structural element, and not enclosed in other HTML5 semantic elements.

tip

> One approach to building and structuring HTML5 documents is to enclose the entire (visible) page — that is, everything in the `<body>` tag — inside an `<article>` element. This approach is best used when there is not a lot of text on a page, and no need for multiple `<article>` elements.
>
> Another approach is to rely on a `<div>` tag with an ID style (like `<div ID="wrapper">`) to organize page content, and to then break that content up with multiple instances of the `<article>` tag. This approach is best used for pages where there will be multiple articles — like a blog page.

The `<section>` element

As a general rule, the `<section>` element defines parts of an `<article>` element and should be used only inside articles. Additionally — and this is more of a writing style issue than an HTML rule per se — you should avoid articles that have only one section. If you are going to break an article into sections, you should have two or more sections within that article.

tip

> The `<section>` element defines parts of an `<article>` element, but what do I mean by parts? Long articles, in newspapers, magazines, even blogs, are often broken up into parts. Typically these parts have their own "mini-titles" — called subheadings. For example, this chapter of this book, were it to be posted online as an article, would have sections (parts) corresponding to substantial blocks of content into which the chapter is divided.

warning

> Do not use the `<section>` tag outside of an `<article>` element. That defeats the purpose of organizing and prioritizing content for search engines, and of structuring content in a way consistent with other websites.

The `<aside>` element

The `<aside>` element functions like a sidebar. It should be associated with an article, or a section of an article, and it should not hold content that stands on its own.

warning

Do not use the `<aside>` tag outside of an `<article>` element or a `<section>` element. Content in an `<aside>` should function as a "sidebar" to an article or section of an article. Creating `<aside>` elements outside of `<article>` or `<section>` elements defeats the purpose of organizing and prioritizing content for search engines, and of structuring content in a way consistent with other websites.

WHAT HAPPENED TO THE <HGROUP> ELEMENT?

Readers who have followed the evolution of HTML5 might be aware that, until April 2013, HTML5 included an `<hgroup>` element. The purpose of this element was never clearly defined but the concept was that it would be used to group content within a heading. The w3.org summed up that the `<hgroup>` element was not well received by designers, and that it turned out there was no need for this element.

The `<header>` element

You use `<header>` tags for introductory content (or navigation content) for an entire document, or for an article, or even for a section of an article.

warning

Do not use a `<header>` tag inside an `<address>` tag, or within another `<header>` element. That defeats the purpose of organizing and prioritizing content for search engines, and of structuring content in a way consistent with other websites.

The `<footer>` element

The `<footer>` tag can be used to define a footer for a page (document), an article, or a section of an article. However, footers are typically reserved for pages or articles. Footer content typically includes contact information, legal notices (like copyright notices), and navigation links.

tip

Using too many footers (and headers as well) clutters a page.

Footer elements often include information about a document or an article: author info; legal notices, including copyrights; links; and contact information.

warning

Using a `<footer>` element to enclose non-footer content defeats the purpose of organizing and prioritizing content for search engines, and of structuring content in a way consistent with other websites.

Examining a basic HTML5 page template

The code in Listing 5-1 represents a very basic HTML5 page template built completely with semantic structure tags. The entire document — within the HTML <body> element — is an <article> element. Inside the <article> element is a <header> with a <footer>, and two <section> elements, each with an <aside> element.

on the web

All of the code listings used in this book are available for download from the Downloads tab on the book's companion website at www.dummies.com/extras/ html5andcss3.

Listing 5-1: A Basic HTML5 Page

```
<!DOCTYPE html>
<html>
<head>
<link href="style.css" rel="stylesheet" type="text/css">
<title>HTML 5 Page Structure Template</title>
</head>
<body>
<article>
<header>
</header>
<section>
<aside>
<h3>Sidebar 1 headline</h3>
<p>Sidebar 1 content</p>
</aside>
<h1>Section 1 Headline</h1>
<p>Section 1 content</p>
<p>More section 1 content</p>
<p>More section 1 content</p>
</section>
<section>
<aside>
<h3>Sidebar 2 headline</h3>
<p>Sidebar 2 content</p>
</aside>
<h1>Section 2 Headline</h1>
<p>Section 2 content</p>
<p>More section 2 content</p>
<p>More section 2 content</p>
</section>
<footer>
<h6>Footer content</h6>
</footer>
</article>
</body>
</html>
```

You'll note, by the way, that our structuring tags like <article> or <footer> have, within them, traditional HTML tags, like paragraphs <p>, headings <h1>, <h2>, and so on. HTML5 structuring tags can, and do, have within them all kinds of content and traditional HTML elements are used to provide that content.

In the template HTML code in Listing 5-1, the entire page content is enclosed in an <article> element. This is one way to build HTML5 pages, and this approach is consistent in relying solely on HTML5 semantic elements.

Another approach is to enclose all the page content in a traditional ID <div> tag. Using this approach, you will wrap the entire page (from the end of the <body> tag to the beginning of the </body> tag) in a <div> tag and then assign an ID selector with a name like #wrapper. This approach incorporates a bit of traditional HTML and CSS page layout.

Styling structural tags

What kind of styling is provided by browsers for the five HTML5 semantic structural tags used to define most pages? None. At this writing, these basic structural semantic tags don't have any default styling in browsers. In that sense, they function like old-fashioned (and still relevant) <div> tags. They require a style selector in a CSS style sheet to obtain styling.

For example, I typically create a CSS style selector for the <aside> element that includes a float property so that it functions as a sidebar, as shown in Figure 5-9.

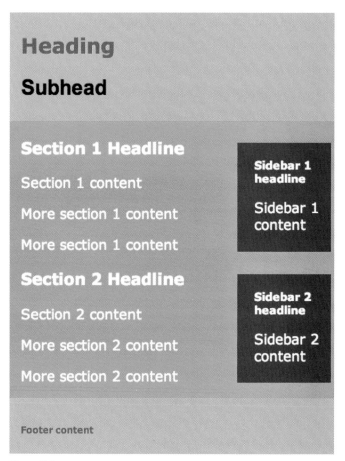

Figure 5-9

If I use an <article> element to constrain the entire page — as I do in the code in Listing 5-1 (see the previous section) — I can define the width of that element at 960 pixels (px) to impose a standard 960 px-wide page design on all the content.

tip

> For a compressed crash course in building traditional HTML pages with CSS style sheets, see Chapter 1.

In short, there's not a lot of difference between styling old-school <div> tag selectors and styling new HTML5 semantic tags. That doesn't mean there are not major advantages to using HTML5 sematic tags. As I've discussed throughout this chapter, new HTML5 semantic tags improve search engine results for a page, they are much easier to use than making up your own ID styles for <div> tags, and they are standard — throughout the world of web design (see Figure 5-10).

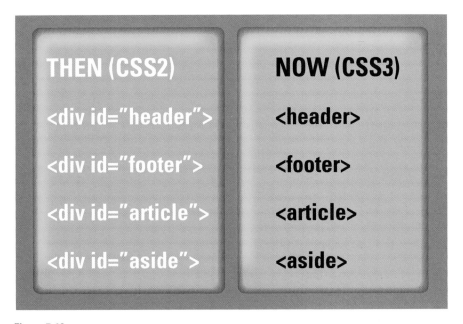

THEN (CSS2)

<div id="header">

<div id="footer">

<div id="article">

<div id="aside">

NOW (CSS3)

<header>

<footer>

<article>

<aside>

Figure 5-10

HTML5 for Specific Content

In addition to new HTML5 semantic tags that structure page content (the ones I cover in the previous section of this chapter), some HTML5 semantic tags are more "free spirits" (see Figure 5-11) that can be used anywhere — in an article, a footer, an aside element, and so on.

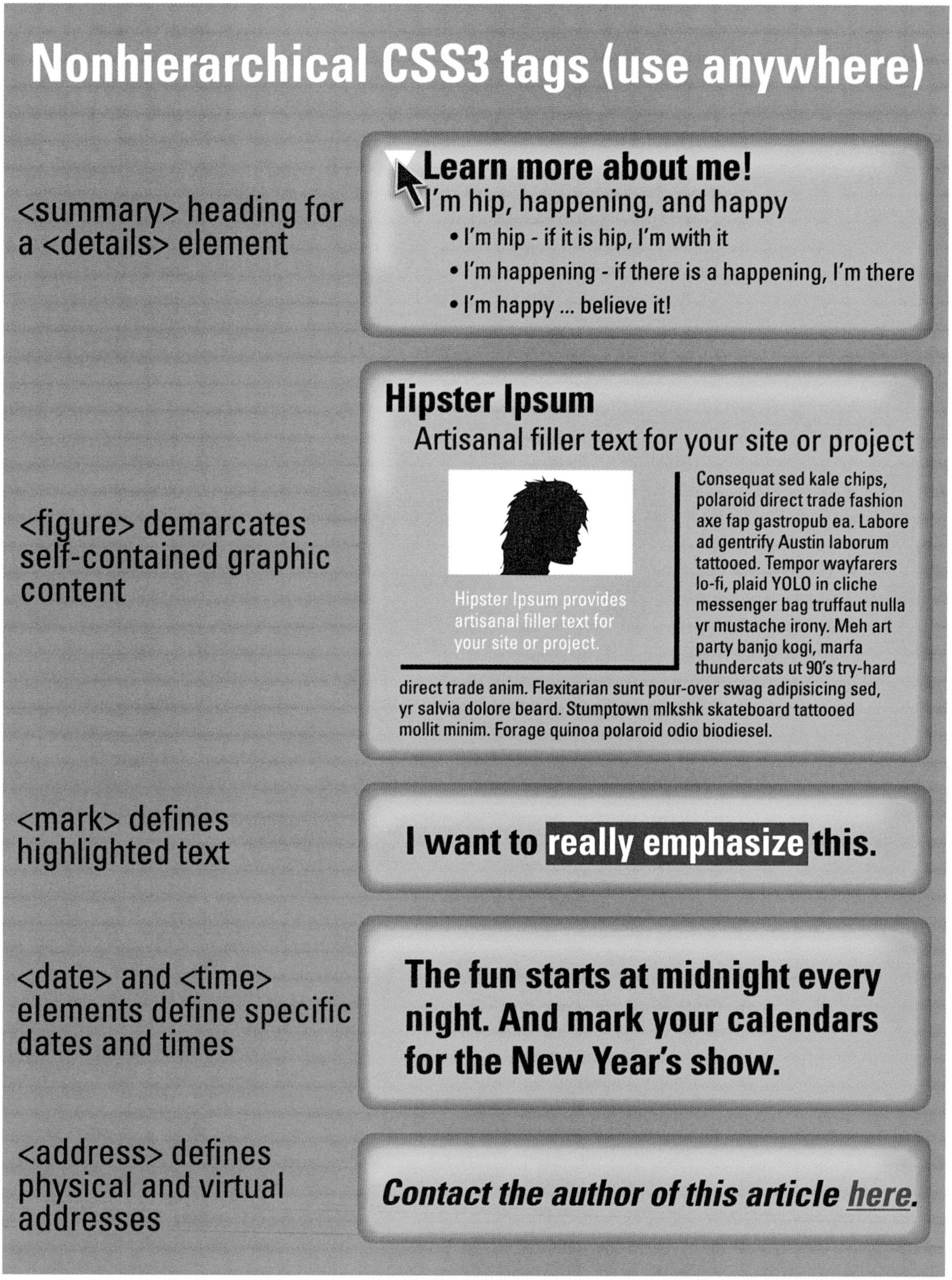

Nonhierarchical CSS3 tags (use anywhere)

<summary> heading for
a <details> element

Learn more about me!
I'm hip, happening, and happy
- I'm hip - if it is hip, I'm with it
- I'm happening - if there is a happening, I'm there
- I'm happy ... believe it!

<figure> demarcates
self-contained graphic
content

Hipster Ipsum
Artisanal filler text for your site or project

Hipster Ipsum provides
artisanal filler text for
your site or project.

Consequat sed kale chips,
polaroid direct trade fashion
axe fap gastropub ea. Labore
ad gentrify Austin laborum
tattooed. Tempor wayfarers
lo-fi, plaid YOLO in cliche
messenger bag truffaut nulla
yr mustache irony. Meh art
party banjo kogi, marfa
thundercats ut 90's try-hard
direct trade anim. Flexitarian sunt pour-over swag adipisicing sed,
yr salvia dolore beard. Stumptown mlkshk skateboard tattooed
mollit minim. Forage quinoa polaroid odio biodiesel.

<mark> defines
highlighted text

I want to really emphasize this.

<date> and <time>
elements define specific
dates and times

**The fun starts at midnight every
night. And mark your calendars
for the New Year's show.**

<address> defines
physical and virtual
addresses

Contact the author of this article here.

Figure 5-11

tip

The main criterion for using these tags is that they must match the content they're applied to. That said, some of these tags work in pairs. For example, a `<summary>` element works with a `<details>` element, and a `<figcaption>` element is used within a `<figure>` element.

The key semantic tags that define content — but are not tightly tied to page layout — are as follows:

▶ The `<summary>` tag defines a visible heading for a `<details>` element, and that `<details>` element defines additional details that the user can view or hide.

▶ The `<figure>` element demarcates self-contained graphic content, such as artwork or photos. The `<figcaption>` element is used within a `<figure>` element to define a caption for that `<figure>` element.

▶ The `<mark>` tag defines highlighted text.

▶ The `<time>` element (and the `datetime` parameter) are used to define specific dates and times.

▶ The `<address>` element is used for both physical addresses and virtual addresses (like URLs for a website).

Using `<details>` and `<summary>` elements

The HTML5 `<details>` and `<summary>` elements come with rather complex default styling. Where supported, they work like collapsible blocks: Until a user clicks an expand triangle, only a summary of the details/summary content is visible. Then when a user clicks the expand triangle, details display, as shown in Figure 5-12.

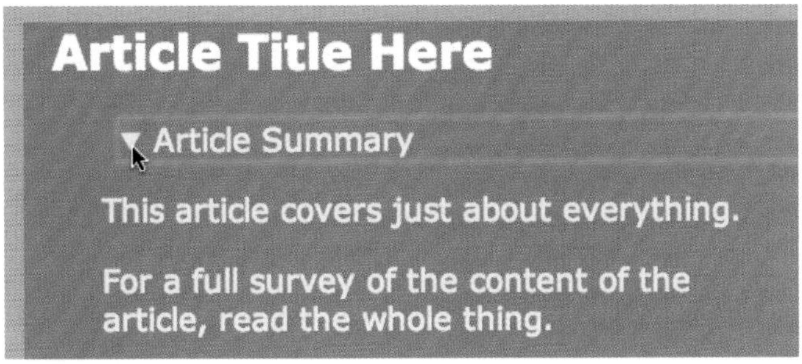

Article Title Here

▼ Article Summary

This article covers just about everything.

For a full survey of the content of the article, read the whole thing.

Figure 5-12

tip

As of this writing, support for the `<details>` and `<summary>` tags is less than full among browsers that support new HTML5 elements. However, in browsers where they don't work, the result is a harmless degradation, as shown in Figure 5-13.

Article Title Here

Article Summary

This article covers just about everything.

For a full survey of the content of the article, read the whole thing.

Figure 5-13

The syntax for a details/summary block is this:

```
<details>
<summary>summary content</summary>
detail content that shows when the block is expanded
</details>
```

Defining `<figure>` and `<figcaption>` tags

The `<figure>` and `<figcaption>` tags go together. Not every `<figure>` element has to have a `<figcaption>` element. However, a `<figcaption>` element can't be used without being associated with a `<figure>` element.

Here's the syntax for how they fit together:

```
<figure>
<img src="imagename.png">
<figcaption>Figure caption here</figcaption>
</figure>
```

There is no default styling for either of these elements, as shown in Figure 5-14.

Wikipedia is an online encyclopedia

Figure 5-14

tip

> Because there is no default styling for the `<figure>` and `<figcaption>` elements, you will want to do a bit of styling to them. Create style selectors for the `<figure>` and `<figcaption>` tags in your CSS style sheet for a standard and stylized presentation of figures (see Figure 5-15) throughout your site

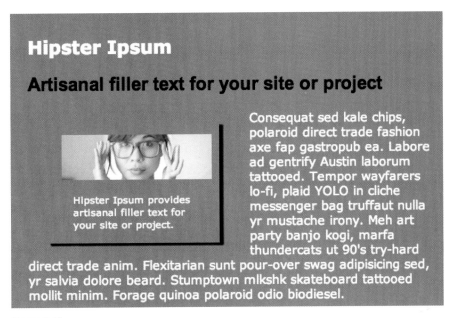

Hipster Ipsum

Artisanal filler text for your site or project

Hipster Ipsum provides artisanal filler text for your site or project.

Consequat sed kale chips, polaroid direct trade fashion axe fap gastropub ea. Labore ad gentrify Austin laborum tattooed. Tempor wayfarers lo-fi, plaid YOLO in cliche messenger bag truffaut nulla yr mustache irony. Meh art party banjo kogi, marfa thundercats ut 90's try-hard direct trade anim. Flexitarian sunt pour-over swag adipisicing sed, yr salvia dolore beard. Stumptown mlkshk skateboard tattooed mollit minim. Forage quinoa polaroid odio biodiesel.

Figure 5-15

Highlighting with the `<mark>` tag

For centuries (okay, years) designers have had to use `<span>` tags to highlight text. The challenge has been to apply a tag that doesn't force a line break. To put that another way, by default, most tags that are applied to text (like `<p>`, `<h1>`, and so on) have a default display of block.

But the `<mark>` tag, where supported, has a default display of `inline` (as in, the CSS rule `display:inline`).

Here's an example. By default, if you simply define a class style (named something like .highlight) with an aqua background and then apply that class style to some text with a <div> tag, the HTML code might look like this:

```
<p>I want to <div class="highlight">really emphasize</div> this.</p>
```

The CSS might look like this:

```
.highlight {background-color:aqua;}
```

And the unpleasant result would be like that shown in Figure 5-16.

I want to

really emphasize

this.

Figure 5-16

However, if you apply the same style definition to a <mark> element, you can apply the highlighting like this in HTML:

```
<p>I want to <mark>really emphasize</mark> this.</p>
```

And define a CSS selector like this:

```
mark {background-color:aqua;}
```

to produce a more satisfactory result, as shown in Figure 5-17.

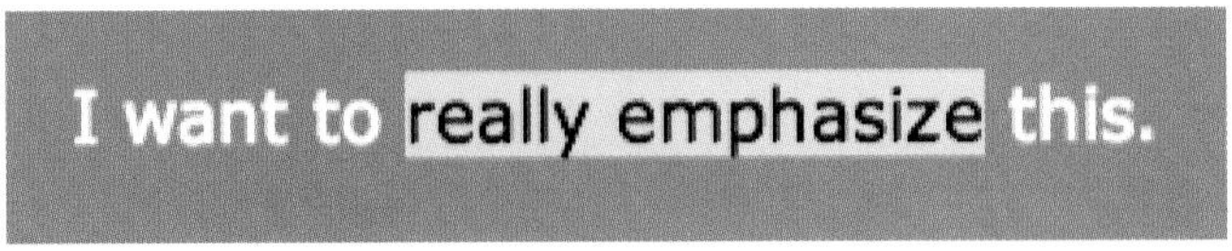

I want to really emphasize this.

Figure 5-17

Using <time> and <datetime>

The <time> element, and the <datetime> parameter are used to define specific times and dates. Although the <time> and <datetime> don't have any default styling, there is a significant upside (as they say about college athletes who might well make an impact in the pros) to using them. And that upside is that they are likely to impact search engine optimization (SEO) for your content.

tip

Search engine optimization makes site content more accessible to search engines. For example, if a user searches for "what's happening this Halloween" he or she will want to find events scheduled for a specific date. On the other hand, a user who searches for "origins of Halloween" will not be interested in such a list of events. If a Web designer places the word "Halloween" in a `<datetime>` element that will help search engines realize that what is on the page is a scheduled event, and the can make that event available to a user searching for somewhere fun to go with their costume.

For example, promoting an event "this Sunday" isn't likely to show in the search results if someone searches for "events in my neighborhood on 1/15." However, if you include a `<datetime>` parameter value that links a specific date to your text, that HTML will be searchable and thus make it more likely to appear in search results.

And the same goes for times. If you specify that something is happening at midnight, how does a search engine know you're not referring to "midnight blue" Answer: You apply a `<time>` tag to midnight.

Here's an example of using both the `<time>` tag and `<datetime>` parameter:

```
The fun starts at <time>midnight</time> every night. And
        mark your calendar for the New Year's show <time
        datetime="2015-01-01"></time>.
```

When viewed in a browser, the actual date for the New Year's show will not appear, as shown in Figure 5-18. The value is that the date would be searchable.

> **The fun starts at midnight every night. And mark your calendar for the New Year's show.**

Figure 5-18

Defining addresses

The `<address>` tag, intuitively enough, applies to addresses — either URLs or physical locations.

tip

The tag-definition folks at wc3.org insist that the `<address>` tag be applied only to addresses relevant to the element that the tag falls inside.

For example, if you have a page broken into <article> elements, any <address> tag within that element should be applicable to the <article> element. If you're creating an <address> element for your whole page, you should create that element within the <body> tag but *outside* any particular <article> (or <section>) element.

Here's an example of an <address> tag within an article:

```
<article>
<h1>Hipster Ipsum</h1>
<p>Nostrud laborum labore fixie, esse thundercats chambray keytar art
         party exercitation meggings nulla in pop-up. </p>
<p>Wayfarers pour-over consectetur quis pitchfork cray deep v, vero
         letterpress hella trust fund pickled.</p>
<address>
Contact the author of this article <a href="mailto:mail@mail.com">here</a>.
</address>
</article>
```

By default, current generation browsers display <address> tag content with emphasis (italic) styling, as shown in Figure 5-19. Older browsers will not display content in <address> elements in italics.

Hipster Ipsum

Nostrud laborum labore fixie, esse thundercats chambray keytar art party exercitation meggings nulla in pop-up.

Wayfarers pour-over consectetur quis pitchfork cray deep v, vero letterpress hella trust fund pickled.

Contact the author of this article here.

Figure 5-19

Styling content tags

Some of the HTML5 content tags I discuss in the previous sections come with built-in styling. Here's a quick reminder of the built-in styling for each of these tags:

 <summary> **and** <details>: The <summary> and <details> element combination displays with rather impressive interactivity in browsers that support them.

▶ `<address>`: Addresses display in emphasis (italics) in most browsers.

▶ `<mark>`: The `<mark>` element comes with inline display so as not to force line breaks.

In other cases, the tag style relies on what you define in a CSS file. For example, you will almost always want to define a `background-color` property for a selector for the `<mark>` tag.

Advantages of HTML5 Semantic Tags

Having surveyed the most useful HTML5 semantic tags, go back to the big question: What's the point again?

The twofold answer is

▶ HTML5 semantic tags allow easier page design.

▶ HTML5 semantic tags enhance search engine optimization (SEO) for your site.

remember

Different HTML5 semantic tags have different advantages:

- SEO: The `<time>` element is particularly important for search engine optimization. Search engines are awfully intelligent, but they aren't always going to pick up that your organization's massive event celebrating National Raspberry Cream Pie Day should show up when anyone within a thousand miles of you searches for "big events on August 1st" (and yes, August 1 is National Raspberry Cream Pie Day in the United States).

- Page design: Although the `<details>` and `<summary>` tag combination is not particularly essential for SEO, it does allow for easier page design by providing a collapsible, panel-like interactive box that reveals content when expanded.

  And all new HTML5 semantic elements have the value of being standard, so designers don't need to expend a lot of time making up new ID and class style selectors for things like articles, sections, headers, footers, and other parts of a document.

Server-Side Scripts

- Require back-end programming

- Slower — validation is done after data is sent to server

JavaScript

- Requires JavaScript coding

- Fast — takes place in the user's browser

orm Data

HTML5

- No scripting

- Fast — takes place in browser

HTML 5

HTML5 Forms

In This Chapter

- Getting the most out of new HTML5 form features

- Using placeholders and input types to make forms inviting

- Using form output elements to create a calculator

- Validating form data with HTML5

The collection of data through website forms has always been part of the user experience. That is more true today than ever.

Gathering data from users is one of the most valuable aspects of today's websites. Advertisers and sponsors purchase ads on blogs and websites based on the number of *registered visitors* (people who sign up at a website to become members, users, or some other form of joining the site's community). E-list signup forms collect names of people interested in hearing from you with announcements, special offers, and news. Feedback forms provide priceless insights into what users are finding at your site, as well as how they feel about it. Search boxes help visitors find what they need at your site. And of course, e-commerce purchase forms convert visitors to your site into sales of your product or service.

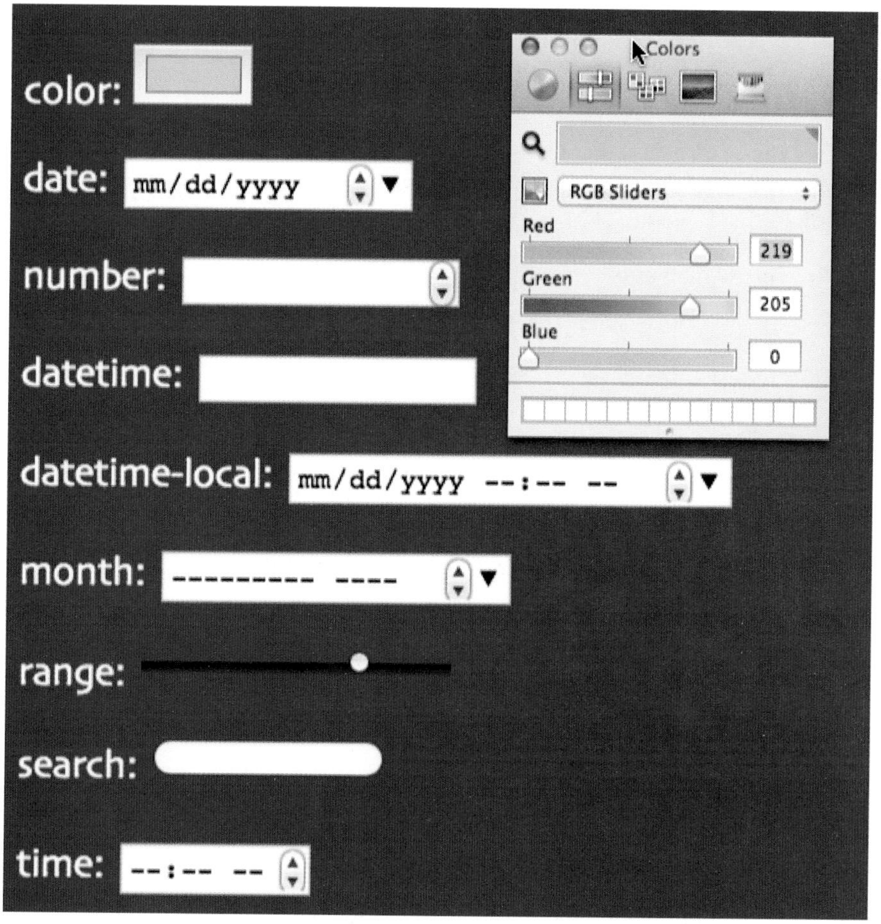

Figure 6-1

So, it doesn't take a rocket scientist to see that making forms inviting and accessible is critical to almost any website. HTML5 provides a set of fairly robust (albeit under-appreciated) tools to do that — like the Color palette shown in Figure 6-1. In this chapter, I walk you through how to use them.

In this chapter, I explore

▶ HTML5 input types for accessibility and data validation

▶ HTML5 output for calculation

▶ HTML5 datalists for painless and accurate data input

HTML5 Forms — An Underrated Resource

New HTML5 form elements and parameters do two things:

▶ They make forms more inviting — meaning they're less cluttered but more intuitive and friendly — with helpful hints on what kind of content to enter and helpful tools to reduce data entry hassles for users (see Figure 6-2).

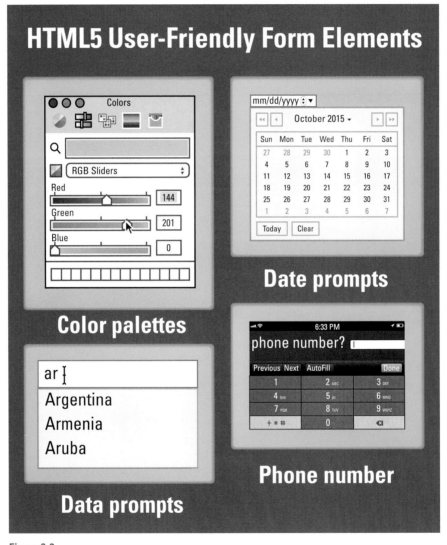

Figure 6-2

⏵ They make forms more productive with built-in tools that *validate* (test) form field content before a form is submitted (see Figure 6-3). Validation ensures that, for example, required information is included, and that e-mail addresses look like actual e-mail addresses. Later in this chapter, I explore how HTML5 validation fits into the spectrum of validation tools, and when and how to use it.

HTML5 VALIDATION

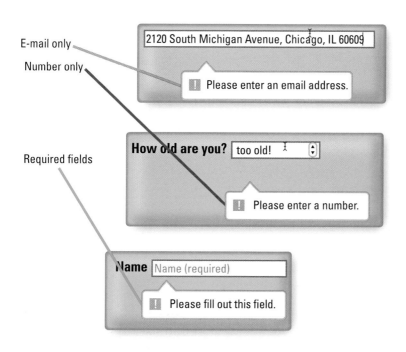

Figure 6-3

Surveying the new HTML5 form field parameters

The new HTML5 form tools are a powerful set of parameters applied to traditional form fields. Before I tell you how to define them, I want to first zoom out and survey some of the more dynamic new HTML5 form field parameters. That way, you'll get a sense of just how radical of an enhancement they are to the web designer's toolkit.

▶ **Placeholder text:** Appears inside a form field, prompting a user what to enter into a field, as shown in Figure 6-4.

Figure 6-4

▶ **Required rules:** Forces users to fill in a form field before submitting a form, as shown in Figure 6-5.

▶ **Validation rules:** Helps users enter data that fit criteria for how the content should look (used for e-mail addresses, phone numbers, and so on), as shown in Figure 6-6.

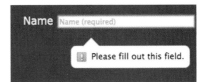

Figure 6-5

Figure 6-6

▶ **Number input types:** Makes it easier for users, especially mobile users (who tap), to enter values, as shown in Figure 6-7.

Figure 6-7

▶ **Datalists:** Saves users time when typing entries in a form field. When a user begins to type, a set of filtered options from a list appears to allow the user to easily complete the entry, as shown in Figure 6-8.

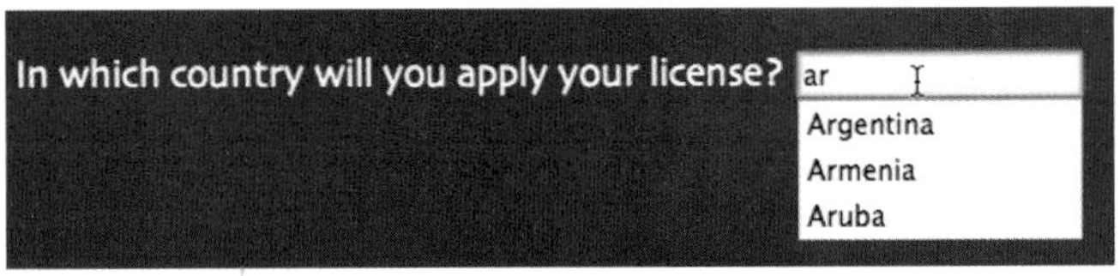

In which country will you apply your license? ar
Argentina
Armenia
Aruba

Figure 6-8

And there's more, including particularly inviting tools to make it easy for users to choose dates and colors while completing a form:

▶ **Date parameters** in form fields display pop-up calendars, as shown in Figure 6-9.

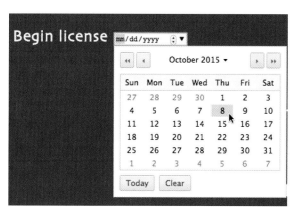

Figure 6-9

▶ **Color parameters** in form fields display pop-up color palettes, as shown in Figure 6-10.

Figure 6-10

HTML5 versus JavaScript or server-side scripts

None of the features that I discuss in the previous section are new to form design. However, until the advent of HTML5, they required some combination of JavaScript and/or server-side scripting to implement. Figure 6-11 helps explain.

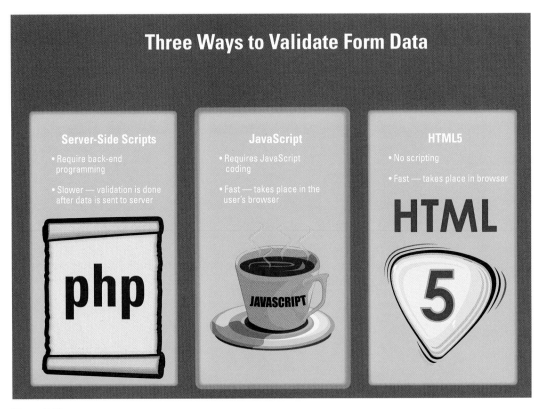

Figure 6-11

The advantages of using HTML5 to build friendly, efficient forms include

Figure 6-12

▶ HTML5 is easier to implement than JavaScript or server-side scripting.

▶ HTML5 form field parameters don't slow down the user's experience while waiting for a script to download and run.

▶ HTML5 form field parameters adapt well to different devices. For example, a form field with a date parameter displays in a specific, mobile-friendly format on an iPhone, as shown in Figure 6-12.

Compatibility issues

Given all the advantages of using HTML5 form field parameters, what is the down-side? There's just one issue: compatibility.

So what exactly does that mean for the average Jill or Joe — I mean, web developer? As of this writing, here's the status report: About three quarters of all browsers support HTML form features, but only current (desktop/laptop) versions of IE, Firefox, Chrome, Safari, and Opera support *all* HTML5 form features. IE 9 and earlier do not support HTML5 form features.

The trend is for browsers to adopt these and other features of HTML5, but the status of browser support for HTML5 form tools is a moving target. You can check the latest state of things at `http://caniuse.com/#feat=forms`.

HTML5 form tools make forms more inviting and accessible. But because HTML5 form field parameters *enhance* forms and make them more inviting and accessible, they are not *essential* for users.

For an in-depth exploration of compatibility issues with HTML5 and Internet Explorer 8 and earlier, see Chapter 4.

To accommodate IE8 and earlier users with HTML5 forms, you just need to make sure that you don't rely on HTML5 form parameters. For example, HTML5 form field *placeholders* (text that appears within a form field and then disappears when a user starts typing in the form field) can substitute for form *labels* (text that appears next to a form, telling a user what to enter in the form field). However, by using form labels *and* supplementing them with placeholder text, you can make form fields more inviting while still responding to the needs of IE8 users, as well as users who rely on form field labels for assistance in filling out forms.

Creating HTML5 Forms

Before you can apply HTML5 form field parameters, you need a properly defined HTML form. The code in Listing 6-1 defines an entire HTML5 page with a basic defined <form> element. Feel free to use this code as a basic template for building your own forms.

Listing 6-1: Basic HTML5 Form Template

```
<!DOCTYPE HTML>
<html>
<head>
<meta charset="UTF-8">
<title>Thank You For Filling Out This Form</title>
</head>
<body>
<form>
<h1>Please fill out the form fields below</h1>
<p><input type="submit" value="Submit the Form"/>
<input type="reset" value="Reset the form"/></p>
</form>
</body>
</html>
```

Note that the entire form is enclosed inside the `<form>` and `</form>` tags. This is essential:

warning

If form fields are not enclosed inside a `form` element, they won't work.

Of course you can apply styling to the form, but for now, we will focus on the essentials.

on the web

All code listings used in this book are available for download from the Downloads tab on the book's companion website at `www.dummies.com/extras/html5andcss3`.

Form actions

Form action parameters define what happens when a user clicks a Submit button. If there is no defined form action, nothing happens when a user clicks "Submit."

The syntax for a form action is

```
<form action="http://myURL/script.php" method="post or get">
```

The URL is the address of a server-script that manages form data. The method, `post` or `get`, is defined by the creator of the server-side script.

Form action parameters normally link to a server-side script. Where do those scripts come from? Essentially, two sources:

▶ You (or your programming team) create these scripts, save them to your server, and connect them to databases that manage the data.

▶ You get a link to a script as part of a package supplied by a wide range of vendors.

Free form action scripts online

Many online resources online provide server-side scripts to manage search boxes, sign-up forms, feedback forms, and other forms. Here are a few examples:

▶ **MailChimp:** MailChimp provides a powerful e-list manager to collect e-mail addresses and send out e-newsletters. The site provides forms and links to scripts to manage them. Figure 6-13 shows how this works. You generate a form using WYSIWYG (what you see is what you get) tools at `https://mailchimp.com`, and you get HTML code for your form that includes a defined form action parameter.

Preview Your Signup Form

Subscribe to our mailing list [email address]
[Subscribe]

[Create Embed Code]

copy/paste into your site

```
<form action="http://COM.us4.list-manage.com/subscribe/post?
u=b79d527302a150867d76a0a1e&amp;id=f6e86b18d7" method="post" id="mc-
embedded-subscribe-form" name="mc-embedded-subscribe-form" class="validate"
target="_blank" novalidate>
```

Figure 6-13

▶ **thesitewizard.com:** For do-it-yourself form management, thesitewizard.com (`www.thesitewizard.com`) generates scripts to manage feedback forms. This valuable resource generates server-side scripts that you upload and save at your website.

▶ **Google and FreeFind:** Search boxes, linked to appropriate scripts, are available from Google (`www.google.com/cse`) and FreeFind (`www.freefind.com`). Figure 6-14 shows what the installed search box from Google looks like in a web page.

Figure 6-14

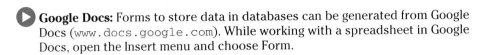

 Google Docs: Forms to store data in databases can be generated from Google Docs (www.docs.google.com). While working with a spreadsheet in Google Docs, open the Insert menu and choose Form.

All these resources, as well as others you can find online, provide very helpful and detailed documentation for how to connect your form to the necessary script with an action parameter.

A simple e-mail form action

The easiest way to collect form data is to simply have a user e-mail the form data to you via an e-mail client. This method works as long as the user has a configured e-mail client. However, this method isn't appropriate for robust data management because all that happens is the form content is e-mailed to an e-mail address you provide.

tip

If you're looking for a more professional way to have form content e-mailed to your e-mail address, try the tools at thesitewizard.com, discussed in the previous section.

The action parameter used to e-mail form data is the <form> tag. The syntax for the <form> tag is

```
<form action="mailto:email@email.
       com>
```

You can use the mailto: form action to test forms, as well as for limited data collection.

Defining input and label tags

The two main tags used to define form fields within an HTML5 form are

 <input>

 <label>

LIMITATIONS OF AN E-MAIL ADDRESS FORM ACTION

E-mail address form actions are a very simple way to collect form data. The data doesn't get logged into a database or spreadsheet — it just comes to you in an e-mail. You might use this technique to collect comments from users or to test a form.

One downside to using an e-mail form action is that it exposes your e-mail address (at least the one you elect to associate with the form) to users and also to "scrapers" that harvest e-mail addresses from websites.

The `<label>` tag is always associated with an `<input>` tag, and the `<label>` provides text that is displayed next to the `<input>` field. Here's the syntax:

```
<label for="fieldname">text that displays</label>
<input type="text" name="fieldname">
```

And here's an example of how this is applied to an `<input>` tag to collect a name:

```
<label for="name">Name</label>
<input type="text" name="name">
```

Traditionally, in HTML, the `"text"` input type is used for most form fields. That still works (as shown in the previous code example). What is exciting and new in HTML5 is that you can define additional input types. When supported in browsers, these input types trigger convenient pop-ups and other tools in browsers, like a color palette for colors or a calendar for dates. I explore input types very soon in this chapter.

tip

I don't feel that a full exploration of all other input types, such as checkbox and radio buttons, is necessary. For one reason, pre-HTML5 input types tend to be non–mobile-friendly. Check boxes and radio buttons, for example, are awkward to tap on a mobile phone viewport. The new HTML5 input types provide more functionality than those they replace.

That said, documentation for all pre-HTML5 input parameters is available at the w3.org site (the central resource for defining HTML). The list of input parameters is at `www.w3.org/TR/html-markup/input.html`.

Defining Placeholder Text

Placeholder text — text that displays within a form field until a user starts typing — is defined as a parameter within an `<input>` element. Here's the syntax:

```
<input type="text" name="fieldname" placeholder="text that
        appears in the field">
```

Here's an example of user-viewed placeholder text applied to an `<input>` tag used to collect a name:

```
<input type="text" name="name" placeholder="Your name...">
```

Figure 6-15 shows how this looks in a browser.

Your name...

Figure 6-15

You can use placeholder text to replace or supplement a form label. If you use place-holder text to supplement a form label, try to avoid redundancy. You might have a label that reads `Name`, for example, supplemented with `Please use your login name`.

tip

Because of the substantial advantages when relying on placeholder text instead of a label in mobile sites, one approach is to use a media query to apply the property `visibility: none` to the `<label>` tag selector in a CSS file used for mobile design. For a full exploration of media queries, see Chapter 8.

Implementing HTML5 Input Types

Earlier in this chapter, I noted how cool, new HTML5 input types translate into help-ful interface elements in browsers. I mentioned, for example, that the `color` input type displays a fun, inviting color palette that makes it easy for users to define a spe-cific color without looking up color values, and the `date` input type displays a handy calendar that makes it convenient for users to look up and enter a date.

And all this is done with just HTML5 — no scripting required!

However, not all input types have as useful or dynamic browser support as `date` and `color`, but that's okay — input types are also useful for validation. The `email` input type, for example, has no default display in browsers, but when it's applied, brows-ers test input to see whether it looks like an e-mail address before allowing a user to submit a form.

And some mobile devices change keyboards depending on the input type. For exam-ple, some display an "@" symbol in the keyboard for e-mail input types.

To make this all happen, we define input *types*. As I noted earlier, any form field that requires text can have "text" defined as the input type. But to trigger handy and helpful tools like the calendar or color palette I mentioned, it is necessary to define a specific input type.

Defining an input type

So, how *do* you specify input type? Here's the syntax for defining an input type:

```
<input type="type" name="fieldname">
```

Here's a list of the most useful HTML5 input types:

- color
- date
- datetime
- datetime-local
- email
- month
- number
- range
- search
- tel
- time
- url
- week

Many of these field types — in fact, the most useful ones — are pretty self-defining. If you want to find out what color someone prefers as the background for an image, use a color type. If you want their phone number, use the tel type.

Using input types for accessibility

Browser support for HTML5 input types is uneven and, as of this writing, a work in progress. That said, most modern browsers have nice, intuitive, and (in many cases) highly practical styling for many input types. For example, the color input types come with a helpful color palette, and date input types open a calendar for easy date selection. In addition

- The tel input type is particularly helpful on mobile devices, prompting easy input for phone numbers, as shown in Figure 6-16.
- HTML5 number input types display with different forms of scrolling number pickers, depending on the browser and device.
- HTML5 datetime-local input types display with an intuitive set of blank spaces that prompt a user to enter a month, day, year, and time (based on a user's current time zone). Figure 6-17 shows how this looks in a browser.

The datetime input type is similar to the datetime-local type except that it allows users to add a time zone to the date and time they enter into a field.

Figure 6-16

Figure 6-17

▶ The `month` input type provides autoprompting to make month selection easy and accurate. Figure 6-18 shows how this looks in a browser.

Figure 6-18

▶ The `range` input type displays a slider for choosing values, without resorting to the numbers keypad. You need to define a range of values with this syntax:

```
<input type="range" value="x" min="x" max="x" name="range">
```

The `range` value defines the default setting, and the `max` and `min` values define the starting and ending values. Figure 6-19 shows how this looks in a browser:

Figure 6-19

▶ The `search` input type displays a searchbox-looking input field. This displays the iconic "looking glass" icon before a user enters search content, and the useful "x" icon to clear the search content. Figure 6-20 shows how this looks when a user wants to clear the search box:

Figure 6-20

▶ The `time` input type provides an intuitive format for entering hour, minute, and a.m./p.m. values.

remember

As HTML5 support continues to evolve, you can expect additional formatting features.

tip

Other input types, such as `email` and `url`, are more valuable for their role in validating input. See "HTML5 Form Validation," later in this chapter, for more on testing data with HTML5 input types.

remember

Don't forget that part of the value of using HTML5 parameters in your design is search engine optimization. For a discussion of the role of HTML5 tags in search engine optimization, see Chapter 5.

Defining a Datalist

Traditionally, web designers have been able to present lists of choices in a form through the use of select/option menus. You see them everywhere; you click a drop-down menu, and you get a bunch of choices. Figure 6-21 shows a select/option menu on a website.

There are, however, limitations when presenting lists of choices in this manner. One limitation inherent in select/option menus is they can be unwieldy. The menu in Figure 6-21 is getting a bit hard to handle, even in a full-size device viewport.

The other limitation, or constraint, in using select/options menus is there is no option listed for "None of the above" — meaning a user can't indicate that the desired selection isn't on the menu.

Using HTML5 datalists solve both issues:

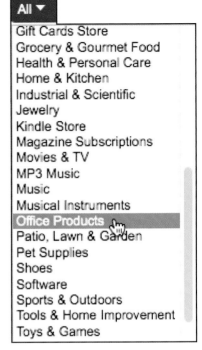

Figure 6-21

- They present a set of options, but the entire list doesn't appear at once: The options are filtered by what a user enters into the field.
- Users can enter content not on the list.

Here's the syntax for a datalist:

```
<p>Choose a set of letters</p>
<input list="list">
<datalist id="list">
  <option value="aaa">
  <option value="abc">
  <option value="bbb">
</datalist>
```

Figure 6-22 shows how this works when a user enters the letter a into the field.

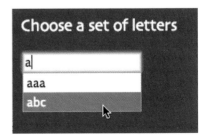

Figure 6-22

Creating Form Output Elements

Given my own highly limited math skills, I really appreciate the new HTML5 `output` parameter. This new tool performs calculations for a user.

Form output is managed through a distinct form. That is, unlike form input fields, each output has its own form. The basic syntax is

```
<form oninput="x.value=parseInt(a.value)+parseInt(b.value)">
<input type="number" id="a">+
<input type="number" id="b">=
<output name="x" for="a b">
</output>
</form>
```

This syntax defines two variables that are entered by the user: namely, a and b. This syntax also defines the operation to be performed as addition, as well as defining a box where the output goes. Figure 6-23 shows how it looks in a browser.

63920 + 47887| = 111807

Figure 6-23

HTML5 Form Validation

The term "validate" comes from the Latin "valid" meaning strong. So, validated data is strong data, as opposed to useless data. For example, if someone enters "dave" in an e-mail address form field, that's not going to be very useful, and a validation technique will reject this data since it doesn't look like an e-mail address.

As I note in earlier sections of this chapter, some HTML5 form fields have built-in validation properties. The `email` input type, for example, will insist that users enter something that looks like an e-mail address into the field, or an error message will appear when a user tries to submit the form.

In the sections below, I survey the most important validation tools built into HTML5, and when and how to use them.

Required input

The most basic HTML form field validation property is `required`. The `required` validation property can be applied to any `<input>` type, including `text`, `email`, `url`, and so on. For example, the following code requires a user to submit a name:

```
<input type="text" name="name" required>
```

If a user attempts to submit the form with nothing in the name field, an error message appears, like the one in Figure 6-24. That error message, by the way, is defined by the browser itself.

Figure 6-24

Validating e-mail addresses

The `email` input type requires that anything in that field look like an e-mail address. Here's an example of the syntax, beefed up a bit with placeholder text and a size:

```
<input type="email" name="email" placeholder="Email address" size="60">
```

You can test the field by entering something that doesn't look like an e-mail address and then clicking the submit button. Error message display varies by browser, but the result should look something like the one in Figure 6-25:

Figure 6-25

Validating numbers

By default, the number input type will accept only number values: that is, written with numerals (25) and not text (twenty-five). Here's an example:

```
<p>How old are you? <input type="number" name="age"></p>
```

If a user attempts to submit content that's not a number value, an error message displays like the one in Figure 6-26.

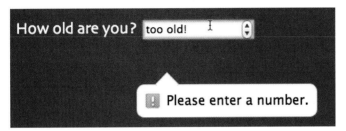

Figure 6-26

tip

> By the way, if you want to restrict the input values to a set range, you can use the range input type. For example, if you are collecting a user's age for a membership form that requires users to be 50 years of age or older, you might restrict valid input to values of 50 or greater. See the section "Using input types for accessibility," earlier in this chapter, for an explanation of how to define a set input range.

A Final Word on HTML5 Forms

In this chapter, I walk you through how to use many different HTML5 form tools — input types, output, and datalists. I show you how HTML5 form elements can be used to make input more inviting and fun, content more accurate, and forms validated before submission.

A final thought on all this: Don't miss the forest for the trees. Consistent use of HTML5 input types and taking full advantage of other HTML5 form tools has a cumulative effect, making your forms stand out, attract users, and generate more accurate content.

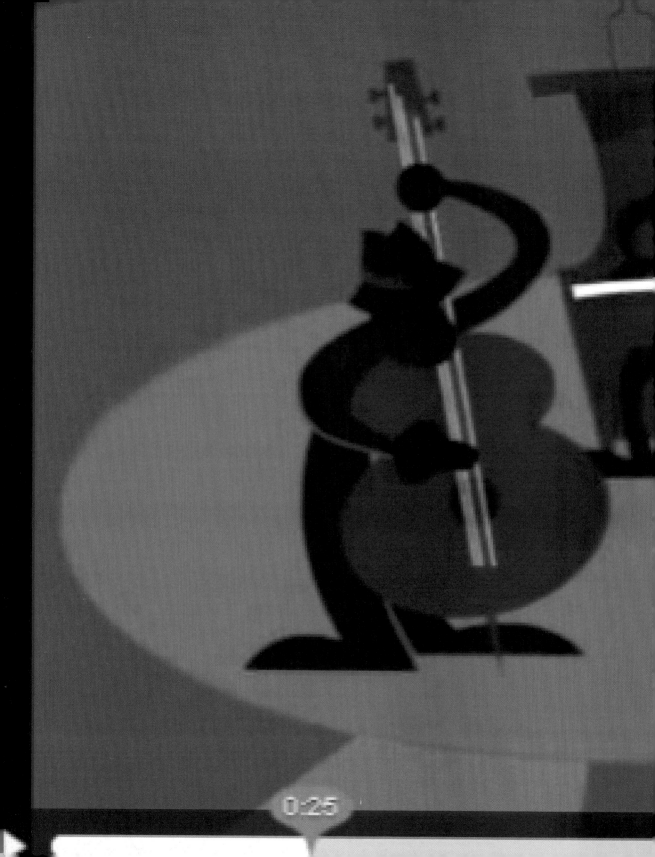
0:25

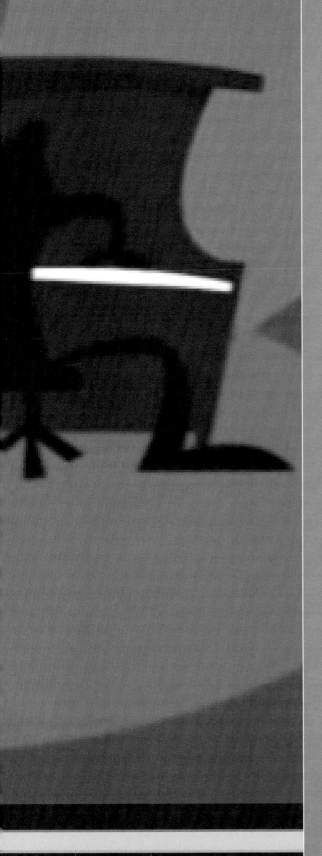

CHAPTER 7

Native Video and Audio

In This Chapter

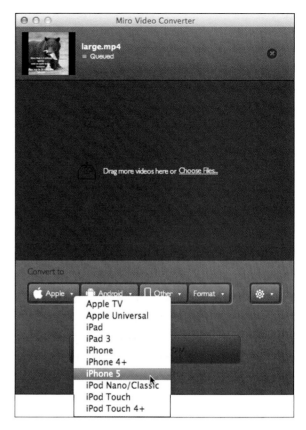

- Understanding native video and audio

- Working with native video formats

- Embedding video in HTML5 pages

- Presenting audio in HTML5 pages

A long with the rise of mobile browsing, web video (see Figure 7-1) is arguably the most dynamic factor in how people use the web. Video isn't just icing on the cake for websites. It's an integral part of the web experience — something users expect not only from sites dedicated to musicians or movies but also on sites that present a whole range of products, services, and information.

Now, with HTML5, designers (and users) have a whole new way to present and experience online video and audio. *Native video and audio* — that is, video and audio that plays without any plug-in software — plays in browsers without Windows Media Player, QuickTime Player, Flash Player, or other plug-in software. That makes listening to music or watching a video more seamless for users — meaning, they don't have to worry about installing and updating a set of plug-ins to watch video or listen to audio.

Figure 7-1

And using native video and audio formats is simpler for designers. A single set of parameters (say, defining options like displaying player controls, or automatically starting a video) can be configured for a set of video or audio files.

In general, native video and audio are easier to embed than most designers think. One potential pitfall to watch out for, though, is that no one native video format works in every current browsing environment.

This means that (for you, a web designer) using native video and audio is the foundation for building websites that deliver a quality and hassle-free user experience. This chapter looks at why that is, as well as how to implement native video and audio.

Getting Familiar with Native Audio and Video

Fast-downloading, high-quality video is, obviously, a critical dimension of the modern web experience. It is rare to visit a website that does not — or at least could not — exploit video as a way of conveying its message.

A few statistics give a picture of the trend:

- ▶ It would take more than 6 million years to watch the amount of video that will cross global IP networks each month in 2016.

- ▶ Every second, 1.2 million minutes of video content will cross the network in 2016.

- ▶ Globally, Internet video traffic will comprise 55 percent of all consumer Internet traffic in 2016, up from 51 percent in 2011.

Source: Cisco Visual Networking Index:
Forecast and Methodology, 2011–2016

WHAT IS CODEC?

CODEC is short for **co**der/**dec**oder, or **co**mpressor/**dec**ompressor. As applied to web video, CODEC refers to the type of computer coding that compresses video files into smaller file size for faster downloading, and the ability of a user to decode that file and play the video in his or her browser. A user's browser and/or operating system must match the codec of a video in order for that video to play in the user's computer.

Today's web users expect hassle-free video. They don't expect error messages telling them the *CODEC* of their player doesn't match the codec of the video, or that the video format isn't supported in their browser. It presents a high bar for web designers.

A deeper look at native video and audio

The concept of native video and audio makes sense only if you understand what came before "native."

remember

Native, in this context, refers to files that open in a web browser without any other plug-in software associated with the browser.

Other web content — that is, anything that isn't audio or video — has always run native in web browsers. For example, all the following file types have run in browsers without the need for a plug-in:

- ▶ **Text files:** Users have never needed special software to see text on a page.

- ▶ **CSS style sheets:** Special plug-in software has never been required to make a CSS style sheet file work in a browser.

- ▶ **JPEG files:** Since the beginning of the web, users have been able to see an embedded JPEG image in a web page without having any plug-in software installed.

However, the way that online video evolved into the dominant element it is today somewhat bypassed the evolutionary track that the rest of web design was moving along. In fact, it was a plug-in — namely, the Adobe Flash Player — that opened the door to the widespread adoption.

Identifying proprietary plug-ins

As I mention earlier, until the emergence of native media, special plug-in software was required to watch a video online. To meet the needs of users who wanted to watch video online, computer manufacturers began installing *proprietary* (patented and licensed) plug-in software on their computers:

▶ The Windows operating system came with the Windows Media Player installed.

▶ Macs came with the QuickTime Player installed.

In addition to the proprietary plug-ins, the first generation of serious online video watchers used the Flash Player to watch Flash (FLV) videos on venues like YouTube. However, without special settings or add-ons, none of these players played any format besides their own. For example, QuickTime Player played only QuickTime files, Windows Media Player played only Windows Media files, and Flash Player played only Flash Video files.

As video emerged as the massive presence it currently occupies on the web landscape, it was a plug-in — namely, Flash Player — and not native video that served as the delivery channel for the deluge of online video content. As a result, Flash Player was installed on almost every computer as a default plug-in that came with browsers. The Flash Player provided a bridge between the two main operating systems (Windows and Mac OS) because it ran in both (and had the same look and feel in both Windows and Mac OS computer), and it was faster and provided higher-quality video than what had been available.

REALMEDIA AUDIO AND VIDEO

While we are tracing the evolution of proprietary plug-ins and audio and video formats, we should note that in addition to Flash Video (FLV) format and the Flash Player, RealMedia's RM format and the RealMedia Player were another form through which audio and video were distributed online. The RM format is no longer a significant factor in the distribution of audio or video. The RealMedia Player continues to be a free download application for managing and playing audio and video files in all formats.

Understanding the rise of native media

Web conceptualists and theorists, going back to the early 2000s, have argued that video should be plug-in–free. The idea was that users should be able to just open a video file in their browser. As video became a dominant dimension of the web experience, that argument made more and more sense.

When the Web Hypertext Application Technology Working Group (WHATWG) began work on the new standard that would become HTML5, it created the `<audio>` and `<video>` tags. These elements were designed to play video and audio without plug-ins. Back in 2004, though, there wasn't much compulsion for anyone — browser creators, web page designers, or users — to adopt native video.

The turning point in the eclipse of Flash and the rise of native video was a posted letter by the late Steve Jobs ("Thoughts on Flash") in April, 2010 (`www.apple.com/hotnews/thoughts-on-flash/`). This letter (in effect) sealed the decline of Flash as the delivery system for online video. The Flash Player strained mobile device capacity, with their limited processing capacity and finite battery life. And with Jobs' anti-Flash position staked out, the shift (see Figure 7-2) was on to native video.

WHAT IS WHATWG?

The Web Hypertext Application Technology Working Group (WHATWG) is an unofficial group of Web browser manufacturers and others. It was created in 2004 by people from Apple, the Mozilla Foundation, and Opera Software. Participants collaborate, debate over, and set standards that to various degrees are adhered to by browsers.

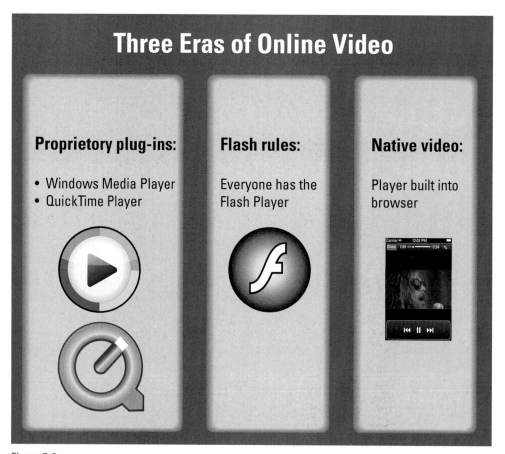

Three Eras of Online Video

Proprietary plug-ins:

- Windows Media Player
- QuickTime Player

Flash rules:

Everyone has the Flash Player

Native video:

Player built into browser

Figure 7-2

THE RISE AND DECLINE OF FLASH VIDEO (FLV)

How does HTML5 video fit into the wider realm of web video? First of all, yes, there is a wider realm of web video. Most browsing environments support Flash, although for reasons I've discussed, Flash is in decline and not supported in environments that most web designers consider as "coveted demographics." That is to say, because Flash is not supported on iPhones and iPads (and because iPad and iPhone users are disproportionately active online, and buy disproportionately more stuff online), most web designers avoid technologies that aren't accessible in the iOS (Apple mobile) operating system.

To boot, profound changes in the web audience were even more foundational. And those changes, in a word, were determined by new devices sweeping the world: *mobile.*

tip

The issues with audio are less dramatic because almost every computer, laptop, tablet, or smartphone can play MP3 audio files. That said, the transition to native audio still requires some focused attention, and I provide that in the "Embedding Native Audio" section later in this chapter.

Designing for a complex video terrain

Flash Video (FLV) files will be around for some time. (See the earlier "The Rise and Decline of Flash Video" sidebar.) However, Flash Video will more and more become an evolutionary path not followed. Unless the Internet Explorer 8 and earlier audience are essential to a website's mission, the critical mass has evolved — and native video is the established format for providing online video.

That said, video requiring a plug-in is still widely used in websites. After all, not every web designer is going to immediately pull all videos from a site to comply with HTML5 specs. Besides Flash Video (FLV), proprietary video formats still in use are

- QuickTime video (MOV)
- Windows video (WMV, AVI)
- RealMedia (RM) files

remember

Even though video that requires a plug-in is still widely used in websites, HTML5 native video is the future and overwhelmingly the present standard for online video.

Compressed Video Formats

Not all browsers support the same native video formats. Additionally, very old browsers don't support native video. So, what's a web developer to do? And how do you address that when you embed native video? As noted in the "What is CODEC?" sidebar earlier in this chapter, in order to distribute video online, video files are compressed to make file size smaller and downloading faster.

A full discussion of video compression is beyond the scope of this book, but the basic story is that to provide high-quality, fast-loading video, web video is *compressed* by using technology that strips out a lot of data without significantly affecting video quality. For example, if a video is shot with a solid blue background, compression technology makes it possible to depict the solid blue background without saving that data for each individual frame of the video.

Now here's the part you need to contend with as a web designer: There are *different* codec standards used by different proprietary media players and in different browsers. It is not the case (unfortunately for us, as designers, and for users) that any compressed video plays in any browsing environment. If that were the case, embedding video in websites would be easier.

To slightly simplify the technical challenge you are dealing with here: Different video formats use different codecs. In the sections that follow, I walk through the implications of that, what the different video formats are, and how to present video that plays for everyone.

Video from your camera: Not ready for prime time

Video footage that is saved in a video recorder, or saved by a video editing program (like iMovie, Windows Video Maker, or professional programs like Adobe Premiere or Apple Final Cut), is usually not web-ready. In general, video created from quality amateur or semiprofessional video recording is saved to the Apple QuickTime (MOV) or Windows Media (AVI) format. These video files need to be compressed before they are ready to share online as native video. (See the "Converting video to native formats" section later in this chapter.)

warning

You can still upload QuickTime or Windows Media video files. However, because these formats are not supported by native video, they won't run without plug-ins. In addition, QuickTime and Windows Media video files usually aren't compressed sufficiently to maximize quality while minimizing download time.

Competing native video formats

The three native video formats supported by existing browsers are

▶ **Theora (OGV):** Theora is an *open source* (free) format supported mainly by Firefox.

▶ **h.264 (MP4):** h.264 is a proprietary format supported by Microsoft and Apple.

▶ **WebM (WEBM):** WebM is an open source format supported by Google.

Both the WebM and OGV formats are open source, and at this writing, all browsers that support the WebM video format *also* support Theora (OGV) files. That means designers can safely support all current generation browsers by providing just two of the above: Theora (OGV) and h.264 (MP4) files. In the remainder of this chapter, I focus on providing those two options.

Again, and to simplify things: Keeping track of which browser supports which native video format can be tedious. However, creating native video that works in every modern browser isn't *that* complicated because every current generation browser for desktops, laptops, and mobile devices supports one of two formats: h.264 (MP4) video or Theora (OGV) video.

The bottom line is this:

▶ All current generation browsers support the h.264 (`.mp4`) video format or the Theora (`.ogv`) video format. Therefore, when you present native video, you need to provide two options — Theora (OGV) and h.264 (MP4).

▶ Internet Explorer versions 8 and earlier don't support any HTML5 video. Sites that include this browsing community in their target audience will need to provide options for proprietary video as an option to native video.

tip

For the latest status of browser support for native video formats, see links to WebM/VP8 video format, MPEG-4/H.264 video format, and Ogg/Theora video format at `http://caniuse.com/video`.

Different players in different browsers

Not only do different contemporary browsers support different native video formats, but they display video differently. This is getting a little complicated, so I want to take a minute and break it down for you:

As I discuss in the previous section, there are three different native video formats. None of them are supported, at this writing, in every browser.

remember

When you present native video, you need to provide two options — Theora (OGV) and h.264 (MP4).

In addition, different browsers use differently designed players to present video. The differences are not dramatic, but they are perceptible.

Comparing browser players

Browser-defined players are part of the point of native video. How a video is displayed — the look and feel of the player, the available controls, and how controls display — are defined by the browser. For example, as of this writing, Safari displays native video in a player that looks like the one in Figure 7-3.

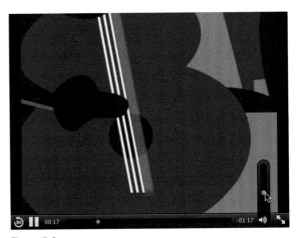

Figure 7-3

Figure 7-4

Note, however, that player controls (including the volume slider) appear differently when the same video is viewed in Chrome, as shown in Figure 7-4.

And the video player in Internet Explorer 10 has its own controls design, as shown in Figure 7-5.

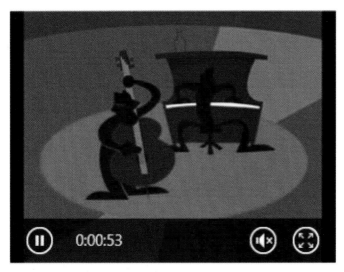

Figure 7-5

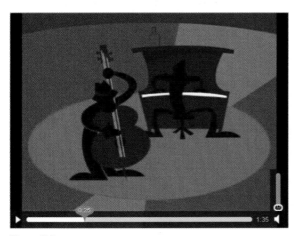

Figure 7-6

Video in Windows versus Macs

Not only does each browser have its own video player design, but those designs vary a bit between Windows and Mac versions of the browsers. For example, Figure 7-6 shows the video player in the Windows version of Firefox.

Figure 7-7, on the other hand, shows the video in the Mac version of Firefox.

Figure 7-7

Video in mobile

Mobile devices present native video in players compatible with their features and *viewport* (screen size). And as I discuss in the upcoming section, "Basic HTML5 Video Syntax," most mobile devices disable *autoplay* functions that launch videos automatically when a page opens. In most cases, this means they display a Play icon until a user taps or clicks it to launch the video. Figure 7-8 shows the video — ready to launch — on an iPhone.

Figure 7-8

And Figure 7-9 shows a video Play icon on an Android mobile browser.

Figure 7-9

Customizing player display

Making video players dependent on a browsing environment has its advantages. As tastes and needs change, browsers are evolving their players, so you — as a designer — don't need to worry about doing that.

The downside, though, is that designers (frankly) have little control over how players display. As you see in the tour of browser video players in the previous sections of this chapter, control over how a player looks is pretty much defined by the browser.

What then are your options for a more unique presentation of video? You can

▶ Rely on CSS styling to customize the look and feel of your video.

▶ Consider using JavaScript player controls.

CSS styling for a `<video>` selector can include borders, background colors, margins, and float.

If you define a style selector for the `<video>` element with the following CSS, the video displays something like the one in Figure 7-10.

```
video {
border:white dashed thick;
padding-left:30px;
padding-right:30px;
background-color:black;
float:right;
margin:25px;
}
```

Figure 7-10

For a compressed crash course in basic CSS style sheet formatting, see Chapter 1.

You can accomplish quite a bit in terms of customizing native video by using CSS. Basically, you can frame how a native video appears and, in that way, create a unique look and feel for videos throughout your site.

If that's not enough customization, you can partner with a JavaScript programmer (if you aren't familiar with JavaScript) and create JavaScript player controls.

tip

Although building JavaScript controls for HTML5 native video is beyond the scope of this book, you can find a useful online tutorial, "Building HTML5 video controls with JavaScript," for building JavaScript controls like those shown in Figure 7-11, at

```
http://www.broken-links.com/2009/10/06/
       building-html5-video-controls-with-javascript/
```

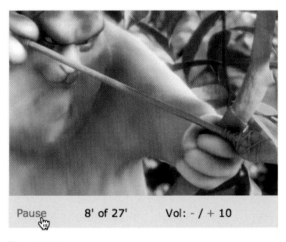

Pause   8' of 27'   Vol: - / + 10

Figure 7-11

Converting video to native formats

Use professional video-editing software to convert your video to native formats:

▶ **Adobe Premiere (part of Adobe Creative Cloud;** www.adobe.com/products/creativecloud.html**) and **Apple Final Cut Pro** (www.apple.com/finalcutpro**) can export edited videos to ready-for-the-web compressed formats.

▶ **Adobe Creative Cloud** includes a powerful program, **Adobe Media Encoder** (www.adobe.com/products/creativecloud.html**), that exports to a native video formats.

▶ **Miro Video Converter** (www.mirovideoconverter.com**) is a free, downloadable application that exports video from a wide range of raw formats into native video formats.

Applications such as Adobe Media Encoder and Miro Video Converter provide easy, intuitive options for creating native video aimed at a specific device. They also offer generic output for native video formats.

Programs that export video to native formats usually include options for different levels of compression matched to different devices. For example, video intended for an iPhone might be compressed to a smaller size, and somewhat lower quality, than a video meant for a full-sized viewport. Figure 7-12 shows the compression options in Miro Video Converter.

For many professional and semiprofessional websites, a single compressed video is sufficient for all devices. Providing separate videos that automatically play in different devices requires a level of JavaScript beyond the scope of this book.

On the other hand, providing links to an iPhone version or a full-sized version isn't that big of a challenge and requires no programming.

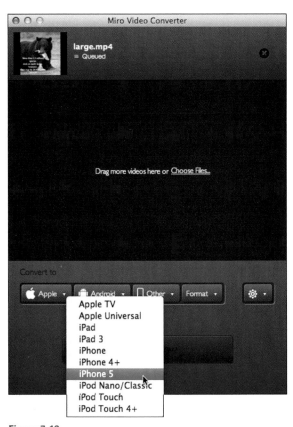

Figure 7-12

Knowing your options for hosting native video

The two ways to present native video on a website are

▶ Embed your own video files, saved at your own server.

▶ Embed video served from an online video-sharing resource, such as YouTube or Vimeo.

I compare these options in the sections that follow.

Hosting your own video files

Hosting your own video files is the option that I cover in this chapter. When you use the `<video>` element and serve video from your own site, you have full control over the video. There are no distracting ads for the online resource hosting your video, like the one shown in Figure 7-13.

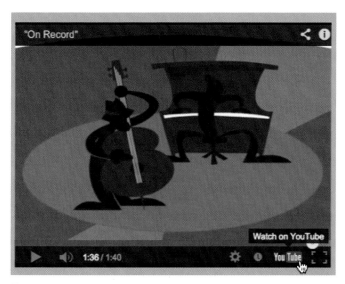

Figure 7-13

tip

The main downside to saving your videos at your own host is that if you're serving your video to millions of users — who place intense bandwidth demands on your site — your hosting service might have trouble supporting that demand. On the other hand, this is a situation most website administrators would like to be in, and the problem can be resolved by upgrading your hosting plan.

Using an online hosting service

The second option for providing access to video at your site is to embed video hosted at a video-hosting service (such as YouTube or Vimeo). The main advantage to hosting your videos at YouTube (`www.youtube.com`) or Vimeo (`www.vimeo.com`) is that no coding is involved: You simply copy and paste code from YouTube (or whatever video-hosting service you're using), and the served video displays within your site. The code linking to your video is made available to you when you create an account at YouTube, as shown in Figure 7-14.

Figure 7-14.

Figure 7-15 shows code being copied from Vimeo.

Figure 7-15

Optimizing Native Video

The advantages of using HTML5 native video for designers include

- The HTML5 `<video>` element is easier to code.

- The HTML5 `<video>` element allows designers to use image files as *posters* (artwork that displays before a video plays); see the "Adding a poster" section later in this chapter.

- The HTML5 `<video>` element has options to display (or hide) player controls.

- The HTML5 `<video>` element allows preloading.

- The HTML5 `<video>` element makes it easy to define autoplay (so the video starts without any action from a user) along with optional muting.

With these advantages in mind, I want to discuss how to use the `<video>` element.

Basic HTML5 video syntax

The basic syntax to embed a native HTML5 video is

```
<video>
  <source src="filename.mp4" type="video/mp4">
  <source src="filename.ogv" type="video/ogg">
</video>
```

Between the open and close `<video>` tags, different source files are defined. The preceding example provides two options: an MP4 (h.264) file and an OGV (OGG) file. The `src` parameter defines the file(s). The `type` parameter defines the type.

warning

It is best to list the .mp4 file as the first source, otherwise videos won't play on iPads running iOS3.x. This problem is fixed in iOS 4 (a free upgrade for all iPads). But to play it safe, if you want to provide video that works for iPad owners who haven't upgraded to iOS 4, you need to list your MP4 file first, followed by the OGV file.

The `source` parameter is the only required parameter for HTML5 video — and it may be all you need. However, if you want to display controls (such as Play, Pause, and volume buttons and sliders) you need to add a `controls` parameter for that.

The syntax for adding a `controls` parameter is to include `controls` inside the `<video>` tag. You can also display videos at a set size by using `height` and `width` parameters.

tip

The `type` parameter tells browsers the mime type (the video file type) and details about the compression technology. Most of the time, browsers can determine the mime type and details about the compression technology without a `type` parameter, but it doesn't hurt to include it. Generally, a `type` value of `"video/"` followed by `mp4` or `ogg` is sufficient.

I want to take a minute and walk through the syntax for the `controls`, size (`width` and `height`), and `autoplay` parameters. All these parameters are appended to the open `<video>` tag. By appending these parameters to the open `<video>` tag, they apply to both versions of the video.

To display controls for your video, add the `controls` parameter like this:

```
<video controls>
```

To define a height and/or width for your video, add the `height` and/or `width` parameter:

```
<video width="value" height="value" controls>
```

And if you wish to add autoplay to your video, use the `autoplay` parameter, which starts a video playing as soon as a page is opened.

```
<video autoplay>
```

tip

If you choose to enable autoplay, you might want to consider adding the `muted` attribute; this will mute the audio on the video until users unmute the audio. Here's the syntax for a `video` element with both the `autoplay` parameter and the `muted` attribute:

```
<video autoplay muted>
```

The `muted` parameter is supported in most current generation browsers that support HTML — Safari, Firefox, Chrome, and Opera — but it is not supported in Internet Explorer 9 or 10.

Finally, you can loop a video to play over and over by adding a `loop` parameter like this:

```
<video loop>
```

Of course, you can combine parameters. Here's a `video` element with `height`, `width`, `controls`, and `loop`:

```
<video width="320" height="240" controls loop>
```

remember

Like with all tags, parameters are separated by spaces, and values are contained in quotes. No values are required for the `controls`, `muted`, `autoplay`, or `loop` parameters — you include them, or you don't. And, by the way, it does not matter what order you list parameters.

Providing options for non-HTML5 browsers

When it comes to providing options for non-HTML5 browsers, the current standard practice is to simply include a line at the end of the `<video>` element (right before the `</video>` tag) with a message to the effect of, *This video requires HTML5, and your browser does not support that.*

Here's an example of the syntax:

```
<video>
<source src="filename.mp4" type="video/mp4">
<source src="filename.ogv" type="video/ogg">
Your browser does not support the video tag.
</video>
```

The `Your browser does not support the video tag.` line of code can be replaced with one that includes a link to a proprietary video. For example

```
<video>
<source src="filename.mp4" type="video/mp4">
<source src="filename.ogv" type="video/ogg">
Watch a Windows Media video <a href="filename.avi">here</a>
</video>
```

In a browser that doesn't support HTML5 video, this message displays as shown in Figure 7-16.

Figure 7-16

Adding a poster

Posters are JPEG images that display in a video element until the video starts to play (see Figure 7-17). The syntax for defining a poster is

```
<video poster="filename.jpg">
```

Figure 7-17

tip

It is usually a good idea to include a poster image when embedding HTML5 video. Doing that allows you to define what image appears in a browser before a user elects to play the video, or — after a user clicks the Play button — until a video starts to play. A defined poster image is more inviting than a generic (blank) video box. And, by choosing a poster image, you can define how a video is promoted.

Preloading a video

Video files are, by nature, large. And it is a definite turn-off for visitors to click a video's Play button and then twiddle their thumbs for 15 seconds while they wait for the video to load and play. One solution is to add a `preload` parameter to the `<video>` tag; doing so causes a video to download when the page opens, even before a user plays the video.

Here's an example:

```
<video preload>
```

Some video production workflows add metadata to the video. Like metadata associated with still images, this is text information that goes with the video. Metadata can include the following information:

 Author: Information about the creator(s) of the video

Links: URLs associated with the video

Language: Text identifying the language used in the video narration

You can elect to preload only video metadata, not the video itself. That makes page loading faster. It allows a user to see information like the author of a video, the language used, or URLs associated with the video, even before downloading the video itself. Here's the syntax for preloading video metadata:

```
<video preload="metadata">
```

tip

The `preload` parameter works in most contemporary full-sized browsers that support HTML5, with the exception of Internet Explorer 9 and 10. However, at this writing, support is spotty for mobile devices, whose designers are concerned about putting unnecessary strain on the limited processor capacity in the device as well as slowing down page download with data a user might not need.

Embedding Native Audio

Uncompressed audio files, in the WAV (for Windows) and AIFF (for Macs) formats, provide the highest available online audio sound quality. In this sense, native audio differs from native video. There will always be value associated with uncompressed audio files, and an audience willing to wait for them to download. And that audience will tolerate the need for proprietary plug-in audio players (like Windows Media Player or QuickTime Player or iTunes) to listen to this highest quality audio.

Still, compressed audio files download faster and are of sufficient quality for many users in their mobile devices. MP3 and OGG are the two widely used formats for compressed audio.

Like with native video, there is no one native audio format that works in every browsing environment as of this writing. The five popular browsers (Internet Explorer, Firefox, Chrome, Safari, and Opera, as well as all their mobile versions with the exception, at this writing, of Opera Mini) all support HTML5 audio, but the different browsers support different formats.

You can test support for audio formats in different environments at `http://textopia.org/androidsoundformats.html`.

The most reliable and "standards-compliant" solution for presenting HTML5 audio is to provide the option of both the HTML5 compressed audio formats, MP3 and OGG. This is the solution I explore in the following sections.

Converting MP3 audio to OGG

MP3 audio files are easy to create; many audio applications create MP3 audio files by default. Converting them to OGG, however, is the challenge.

Of the many online resources for converting MP3 audio files into OGG files, I recommend trying the Online Audio Converter at `http://media.io`.

If you decide to use the Online Audio Converter, you can convert your MP3 audio to OGG by uploading your MP3 file and then choosing an export format (OGG) and quality, as shown in Figure 7-18.

media.io   Supported file formats and file sizes

Online Audio Converter
Select your file and upload it. media.io will convert it immediately.

Upload	Choose File filename.mp3			
Select Format	○ MP3 (.mp3 files)	○ WAV (.wav files)	⦿ OGG (.ogg files)	○ WMA (.wma files)
Select Quality	○ Extreme - 320 kbit/s	○ High - 192 kbit/s	⦿ Normal - 128 kbit/s	○ Lower - 96 kbit/s
	Convert			

Figure 7-18

With both an MP3 and OGG audio available, you can make your native audio accessible to anyone.

Embedding an HTML5 audio element

After you have your audio file in both the MP3 and OGG formats (see the previous section), all you have to do is make both formats available to your users. The basic syntax for an <audio> tag with options for both MP3 and OGG files is

```
<audio>
<source src="filename.ogg" type="audio/ogg">
<source src=" filename.mp3" type="audio/mpeg">
Your browser does not support HTML5 audio.
</audio>
```

The src parameter defines the file(s). The type parameter defines the type. For OGG files, the filename extension (.ogg) is the same as the file type (ogg). For .mp3 files, the filename extension is .mp3, and the file type is mpeg.

The type parameter isn't essential, but it helps browsers detect the audio file type — which reduces the possibility that a browser might not recognize a correct audio file type, and users would see an error message instead of hearing the audio.

After you embed your HTML5 audio element, you can add audio play parameters to it. For example, to display an audio player like the one in Figure 7-19, add a controls parameter with this code:

```
<audio controls>
```

audio

Figure 7-19

audio

Figure 7-20

Audio players, by the way, look a bit different in different browsers. Figure 7-19 shows an audio player with controls in the Chrome browser. Figure 7-20 shows that same player in the Firefox browser.

To loop the audio, add a `loop` parameter like this:

```
<audio loop>
```

If you'd like to start an audio file automatically, add the `autoplay` parameter.

```
<audio autoplay>
```

tip

Mobile devices (including iOS Apple devices) and some versions of Android mobile operating system do not support `autoplay`, which argues for including controls.

The `preload` parameter starts downloading the audio file when the page is open, before a user clicks the Play button. You can also elect to preload only metadata (the author of the audio, the genre of music, and so on) with the following:

```
<audio preload="metadata">
```

There is also a `muted` parameter, which has specialized use when embedding audio in environments aimed at a hearing impaired audience that may not be aware that audio is playing, and that is better served with a text alternative.

The following example has the `controls`, `preload`, and `loop` parameters applied:

```
<audio controls preload loop>
<source src="filename.ogg" type="audio/ogg">
<source src=" filename.mp3" type="audio/mpeg">
Your browser does not support HTML5 audio.
</audio>
```

Alternative audio options

Almost every browsing environment — even those that don't support HTML5 — can play an MP3 file. So, for those users whose browsers don't interpret HTML5 (like users of older versions of Internet Explorer), there is no need to provide an alternative audio file. All that is required is to provide a link to the MP3 file that they can click and play with their system's audio software.

To do this, link directly to your MP3 file by placing this line of code before your closing `</audio>` tag:

```
Your browser does not support HTML5 audio. Click <a href="filename.mp3">here
</a> to listen to the audio track.
```

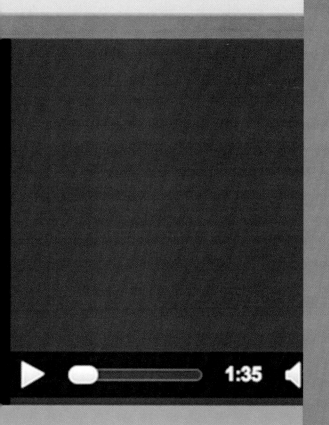

CHAPTER 8

Going Mobile: Responsive Design and jQuery Mobile

In This Chapter

- Designing sites that work in different devices (desktops, laptops, tablets, and smartphones)

- Creating sites that are accessible in different viewing environments (indoor, outdoor, fast connections, slow connections, and so on).

- Understanding different techniques and technologies for mobile-friendly sites.

- Presenting the same content, with a different layout, in different devices.

- Building app-like web pages with jQuery Mobile

Article -- Using Responsive Design

<-- Home

Article 1

Deep v blog 90's laboris. Letterpress tattooed vero, bushwick actually scenester mollit officia. Post-ironic odio carles deserunt sapiente, butcher neutra. Minim pop-up artisan shoreditch +1 letterpress. Next level mlkshk pork belly, iphone pickled echo park etsy enim odio et vegan pour-over ennui sint pitchfork. Vegan try-hard pork belly jean shorts irony, incididunt before

---

In this chapter, I explore three options for making your site accessible and inviting in mobile devices. The first is to ignore the need for a reconfigured, redesigned presence for your site in mobile devices, and to force mobile users to find some shade in which to view your site, to zoom in and out to read your content, and to wait endlessly for content to download.

The second approach is to provide what is called *responsive design*. Optimally applied, this involves reshaping and redesigning content with mobile-friendly page layouts and color schemes.

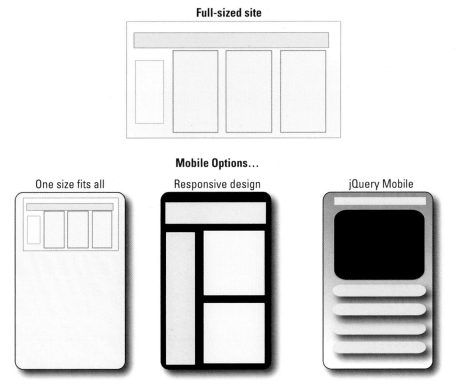

Figure 8-1

Finally, the jQuery Mobile option involves creating separate, faster pages for mobile users, and providing an app-like interface and experience.

Figure 8-1 thumbnails these three approaches. I will, as you have guessed by now, focus on the latter two in this chapter.

Understanding the Nature and Role of Responsive Design

Responsive design means, intuitively enough, designing websites that *respond* to a user's viewing environment. Originally, in the pre-mobile era, responsive design meant slight tweaking of things like image and font size so that sites worked well as users resized their browser windows. This approach is sometimes referred to as creating "fluid" page layouts. But today, effective responsive design means much more than simply resizing web page elements to fit in a user's browser window.

In the era of mobile design, *size* is just a small part of responsive design. Creating sites that work well in any environment requires factoring in elements like:

- ▶ Environmental lighting
- ▶ Device processing speed
- ▶ Slow 3G and 4G downloading, where that is a factor
- ▶ Availability of a pointing device or lack thereof
- ▶ And many more factors

In short, designing truly responsive sites with HTML5 and CSS3 requires using the full range of responsive design techniques, not just sizing a site to fit a viewport. This chapter walks through what that means — and how you accomplish that.

A day in the life of a multidevice user

Before you design a truly responsive site, you must first put yourself in the shoes of someone who is going to engage your site under a wide range of conditions (see Figure 8-2).

A vistor might experience your site while doing something like:

- ▶ Hanging out at the beach with intense sunlight and glare, with a low-budget smartphone with limited backlighting. In this situation, using a very high contrast color scheme is required to be able to distinguish content at your site.
- ▶ Projecting the website onto a large screen at a large group presentation to make a critical argument. This requires a site that works well when projected at 960 pixels (px) wide.
- ▶ Ordering a product from your site using a tablet while jogging around the north shore of Lake Superior in December. Here, easy data entry for someone wearing thick mittens is required.
- ▶ Studying online somewhere with limited and very slow 3G connections. This situation calls for images and content that downloads quickly without a lot of unnecessary image downloads.

remember

Keep worst-case scenarios in mind when you envision, design, and build multi-environment sites.

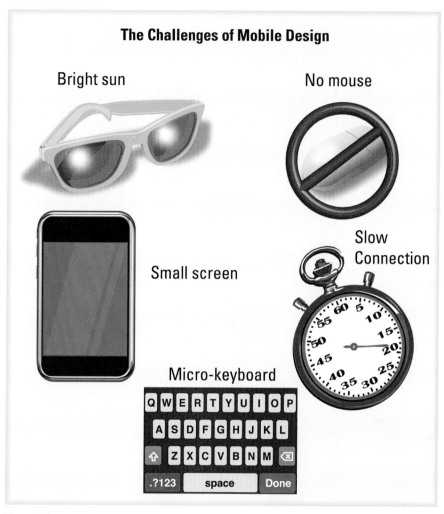

Figure 8-2

Factoring in size

Size is a factor in mobile design. Sure, size isn't the only (or even the defining) factor in making sites mobile-friendly, but it is part of the equation.

Mobile sites often have fewer columns, larger type, and smaller images than full-sized sites.

Figure 8-3 shows a multicolumn version of a website as it displays on a full-sized laptop.

Figure 8-3

Figure 8-4 shows the same site with a reduced set of columns on a tablet display.

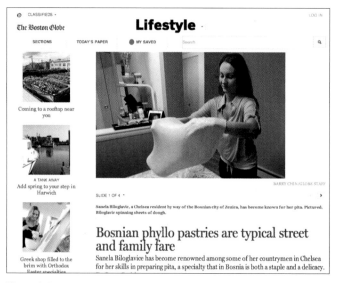

Figure 8-4

And Figure 8-5 shows the same site as it displays on a smartphone. Note the single column layout.

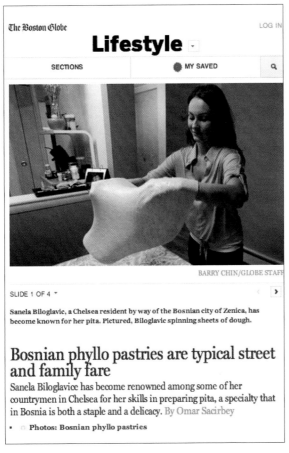

Figure 8-5

HOW WIDE ARE SMARTPHONES AND TABLETS?

Designing for mobile devices involves a wide (and growing) range of *viewports* (the width of the device or browser window — whichever is narrower — in which a site is viewed). As this book goes to press, Samsung is marketing a smartphone that is 5.5" wide, pretty much the same width as their narrowest tablet. And even as "mini" tablets move closer in size to smartphones, the largest tablets have displays that are almost as large as a laptop screen. So the distinction between smartphones and tablets, and between tablets and laptops, is relative. Later in this chapter I explore more precise approaches to categorizing and designing for different viewports.

Lighting for mobile

In general, low-contrast color schemes (like light gray text on a gray background) might work well and can be inviting and accessible when viewed in indoor light, but those color schemes don't work in bright sunlight. A high-contrast color scheme, like white text on a black or dark red background, is much more readable in bright, outdoor light on a device with weaker backlighting.

Figure 8-6 shows the full-sized version of a website's technology video gallery. The tan captions on orange backgrounds are perfectly readable on a desktop in an office with controlled lighting or on a laptop with powerful and adjustable backlighting.

Figure 8-6

On the other hand, the designers of this website are savvy enough to know that folks accessing these videos on a smartphone would likely have trouble reading those captions because of the low contrast between the text and background. As a result, for a smartphone display, the designers use white text on a black background — the highest contrast possible — to make the captions easy to read outdoors in bright lighting (see Figure 8-7).

Figure 8-7

tip

While I'm on the subject of size, using smaller, faster-loading images for presentation on a smartphone allow pages to open more quickly in non–Wi-Fi mobile connections. And mobile sites often use larger type, as well.

Interactivity for mobile

Interactive interfaces make it possible for mobile users without pointing devices (think touchpads and keyboards) to tap links and enter data. When designing for mobile, avoid, for example, using links that require hovering (like horizontal menu bars).

The hover-based horizontal menu bar used in the full sized website shown in Figure 8-8 works fine on a laptop, but navigation that relies on hovering over a tab with a mouse is dysfunctional on a mobile device.

Figure 8-8

The mobile version of the same website provides a completely different navigation interface, though: a mobile-friendly list of links that are easy to tap on a smartphone (see Figure 8-9).

Figure 8-9

Three approaches to responsive design

As I briefly outline in the introduction to this chapter, there are essentially two appropriate approaches to creating sites that work well in any device or environment:

▶ **Media queries:** Defining and applying distinct style sheets for different sized browsing environments

▶ **jQuery Mobile apps:** Providing a mobile presence with web apps that use effects, animation, and interactivity to fully take advantage of mobile devices

And, to continue the rant I began in the introduction, there is a third option (see Figure 8-10) — one that is still far too widely applied: namely, just hoping that your site works okay on mobile devices. Truth be told, this option isn't quite as irresponsible as it might seem: Mobile devices allow users to zoom in and out easily, and many users are comfortable navigating full-sized pages on their smartphones.

Three Approaches to Responsive Design

One fluid design for all devices	Media queries	jQuery Mobile
• Lowest cost	• One set of HTML content displays differently in different browsers	• Easy to create with HTML5
• Unlikely to satisfy mobile users		• Requires seperate content for different devices
	• Not as thoroughly mobile an experience as jQuery Mobile	• An app-like experience in mobile devices

Figure 8-10

So the point isn't that a user *can't* use a full-sized website on a smartphone or tablet. The point is that given the importance of the mobile audience, your goal is to provide an inviting, accessible mobile site — not just one that "works okay" on a mobile device.

The evolution and role of fluid design

Earlier in this chapter I briefly noted that responsive design as we know it today, and as it applies to design for mobile, has evolved from an earlier approach known as fluid design. Before moving on to explore responsive design and jQuery Mobile in some depth, I want to take a minute to discuss fluid design.

warning

Fluid design — essentially, sizing elements with percentages instead of fixed units of measurement — can't address most of the requirements of a mobile-friendly site.

Fluid design was conceived as a solution to the challenge of users viewing websites in different width browser windows on laptops and desktop computers. That challenge has been eclipsed by the qualitatively larger demands of providing mobile-friendly sites.

Of the items on the list of requirements for designing mobile sites — ranging from providing easy navigation to changing color schemes — only size can be addressed with fluid design. Furthermore, many of the dimensions of sizing for mobile (such as font size and adjusted column layout) cannot really be adequately addressed with fluid design.

The point? Fluid design is still a relevant concept: There is a time and place for sizing images and boxes in percentages, such as when you are designing for an audience that you know will not be accessing your site from mobile devices (like a large institution that provides access to a website only to users within its network). However, fluid design doesn't really rise to the level of a substantial approach to creating sites that work well in different browsing environments.

The two approaches to building websites that *do* address the whole range of challenges in creating sites that are inviting and accessible in every device are media queries and jQuery Mobile. The rest of this chapter focuses on how to apply those solutions.

Implementing Responsive Design with Media Queries

Responsive design means creating an entire browsing experience that responds to a user's environment. Columns change. Colors change. Links display differently. The technique for implementing responsive design is to use HTML or CSS media queries. *Media queries* detect viewport width and connect a whole separate set of styles, depending on the dimensions of a user's interface.

An article that displays in a laptop browser, for example, might display on a laptop in three columns with a sidebar and text link, as shown in Figure 8-11.

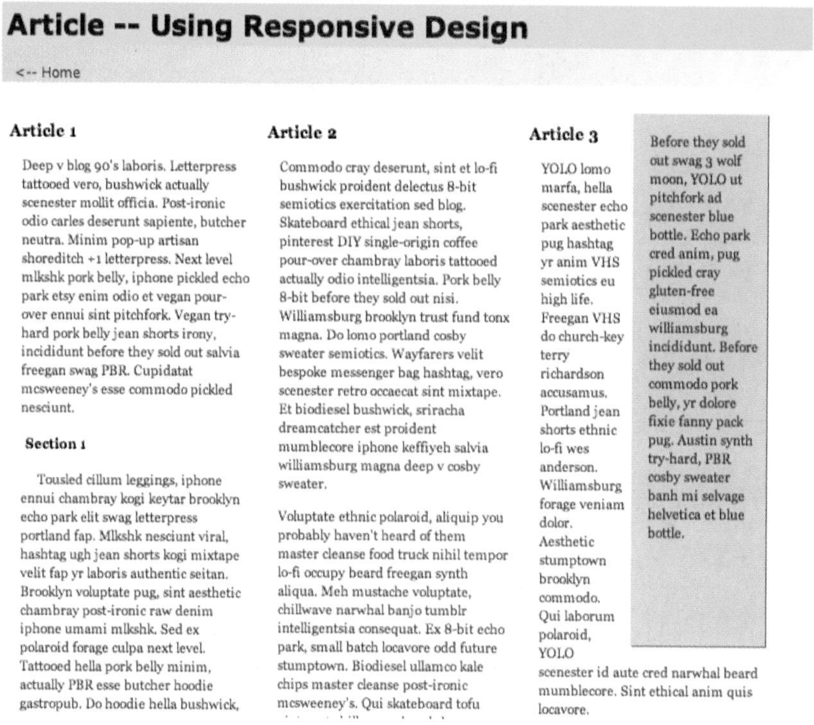

Article -- Using Responsive Design

<-- Home

Article 1

Deep v blog 90's laboris. Letterpress tattooed vero, bushwick actually scenester mollit officia. Post-ironic odio carles deserunt sapiente, butcher neutra. Minim pop-up artisan shoreditch +1 letterpress. Next level mlkshk pork belly, iphone pickled echo park etsy enim odio et vegan pour-over ennui sint pitchfork. Vegan try-hard pork belly jean shorts irony, incididunt before they sold out salvia freegan swag PBR. Cupidatat mcsweeney's esse commodo pickled nesciunt.

Section 1

Tousled cillum leggings, iphone ennui chambray kogi keytar brooklyn echo park elit swag letterpress portland fap. Mlkshk nesciunt viral, hashtag ugh jean shorts kogi mixtape velit fap yr laboris authentic seitan. Brooklyn voluptate pug, sint aesthetic chambray post-ironic raw denim iphone umami mlkshk. Sed ex polaroid forage culpa next level. Tattooed hella pork belly minim, actually PBR esse butcher hoodie gastropub. Do hoodie hella bushwick,

Article 2

Commodo cray deserunt, sint et lo-fi bushwick proident delectus 8-bit semiotics exercitation sed blog. Skateboard ethical jean shorts, pinterest DIY single-origin coffee pour-over chambray laboris tattooed actually odio intelligentsia. Pork belly 8-bit before they sold out nisi. Williamsburg brooklyn trust fund tonx magna. Do lomo portland cosby sweater semiotics. Wayfarers velit bespoke messenger bag hashtag, vero scenester retro occaecat sint mixtape. Et biodiesel bushwick, sriracha dreamcatcher est proident mumblecore iphone keffiyeh salvia williamsburg magna deep v cosby sweater.

Voluptate ethnic polaroid, aliquip you probably haven't heard of them master cleanse food truck nihil tempor lo-fi occupy beard freegan synth aliqua. Meh mustache voluptate, chillwave narwhal banjo tumblr intelligentsia consequat. Ex 8-bit echo park, small batch locavore odd future stumptown. Biodiesel ullamco kale chips master cleanse post-ironic mcsweeney's. Qui skateboard tofu

Article 3

YOLO lomo marfa, hella scenester echo park aesthetic pug hashtag yr anim VHS semiotics eu high life. Freegan VHS do church-key terry richardson accusamus. Portland jean shorts ethnic lo-fi wes anderson. Williamsburg forage veniam dolor. Aesthetic stumptown brooklyn commodo. Qui laborum polaroid, YOLO scenester id aute cred narwhal beard mumblecore. Sint ethical anim quis locavore.

Before they sold out swag 3 wolf moon, YOLO ut pitchfork ad scenester blue bottle. Echo park cred anim, pug pickled cray gluten-free eiusmod ea williamsburg incididunt. Before they sold out commodo pork belly, yr dolore fixie fanny pack pug. Austin synth try-hard, PBR cosby sweater banh mi selvage helvetica et blue bottle.

Figure 8-11

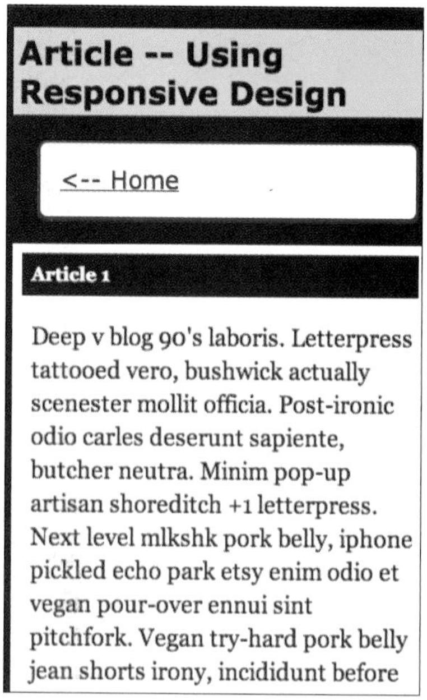

When viewed on a smartphone, however, the color scheme changes to high contrast, the link changes to an easy-to-tap button, and the column layout coverts to a single column design; see Figure 8-12.

Two techniques for media queries

The two techniques for building media queries are

▶ Create distinct CSS files for different devices.

▶ Create a single CSS file with alternate styles defined, depending on the viewport of a user's browser.

Article -- Using Responsive Design

<-- Home

Article 1

Deep v blog 90's laboris. Letterpress tattooed vero, bushwick actually scenester mollit officia. Post-ironic odio carles deserunt sapiente, butcher neutra. Minim pop-up artisan shoreditch +1 letterpress. Next level mlkshk pork belly, iphone pickled echo park etsy enim odio et vegan pour-over ennui sint pitchfork. Vegan try-hard pork belly jean shorts irony, incididunt before

Figure 8-12

But how do you know which one to use? The techniques are quite similar, so it's a matter of preference. If you prefer to organize all your styles — for all devices — in a single, but more cluttered, lengthy style sheet, you can do that by using a single CSS file. If you prefer to work with several CSS files that are smaller, but more numerous, you can create media queries with multiple CSS files.

tip

> One approach to the "one CSS file versus multiple CSS files" controversy argues that including all CSS in one file with alternate is better because it reduces HTTP requests and speeds the download/render process. Other experts argue that the difference in download speed is negligible since the first time CSS styles are downloaded into a user's browser, they are cached (saved) and don't need to be downloaded again. In any case, I explore both options in this chapter.

Different strokes for different (viewport) folks

Whichever technique you choose for media queries, you want to implement the techniques that make mobile displays more accessible by applying the following tips:

- ▶ Define distinct background color and color values for mobile sites that provide higher contrast.

- ▶ Remove float properties from layout boxes in mobile sites to reduce (or eliminate) columns.

- ▶ Reduce the width of layout boxes for mobile devices.

tip

> Often times, it's appropriate to size mobile content at 100% of the available width and then allow the device itself to constrain the width of content.

- ▶ Redefine links for mobile devices to display as large, easy-to-tap buttons by adding padding, margins, borders, and large type to the <a> style selector.

tip

> For a crash course in creating CSS style sheets and defining basic CSS styles, see Chapter 1. For a full exploration of new CSS3 effects and transforms, many of which are useful in mobile design, see Part III of this book.

Defining Media Queries with Multiple CSS Files

Media queries with multiple CSS files are created by defining the media query inside the <head> element of an HTML page. The syntax for a media query is

```
<link href="filename.css" rel="stylesheet" type="text/css"
      media=" (max-width/min-width:dimension)">
```

Here's an example of a media query that links to one style sheet if a viewport is wider than 768 pixels, a second style sheet if the viewport is wider than 480 pixels but narrower than 768 pixels, and a third style sheet if the viewport is less than 480 pixels wide:

```
<link href="fullsize.css" rel="stylesheet" type="text/css"
      media="only screen and (min-width:769)">
<link href="tablet.css" rel="stylesheet" type="text/css"
      media="only screen and (min-width:481px) and
      (max-width:768)">
<link href="smartphone.css" rel="stylesheet" type="text/css"
      media="only screen and (max-width:480px)">
```

The media queries in this example include "only screen" parameters because I only want these styles to apply to digital devices, not to output designed for printers or other devices.

Forcing devices to report actual width

Mobile device manufacturers sometimes try to contort how browsers detect their viewport width so as to squeeze a full-sized site into a small viewport. And don't ask me why. The basic logic seems to be that because mobile devices have very high-resolution screens. For example, an iPhone turned sideways (landscape mode) counts as a 960 pixel–wide or wider viewport. But as a designer, you probably want iPhone users to see a mobile version of your site.

The solution? Add this line of code to the <head> element that forces mobile devices to report their actual viewport dimensions to a browser and not distort their viewport size:

```
<meta name="viewport" content="width=device-width">
```

Creating CSS files for different sized viewports

After you define a media query for your HTML page, the next step is to create CSS files that match those listed in your media query. So, if you have the following media query (which links to three different style sheets):

```
<link href="fullsize.css" rel="stylesheet" type="text/css"
       media="only screen and (min-width:769)">
<link href="tablet.css" rel="stylesheet" type="text/css"
       media="only screen and (min-width:481px) and
       (max-width:768)">
<link href="smartphone.css" rel="stylesheet" type="text/css"
       media="only screen and (max-width:480px)">
```

you need to create the following three files:

- fullsize.css
- tablet.css
- smartphone.css

After creating these files, apply the basic techniques I discuss in the "Different strokes for different (viewport) folks" section earlier in this chapter. I show you a few examples of how to do this in the following sections.

Defining a high contrast body tag selector

A low-contrast body tag selector might have code like this:

```
body{
font-family:Arial, Helvetica, sans-serif;
color:tan;
background-color:beige;
}
```

Figure 8-13 shows how this looks in a browser.

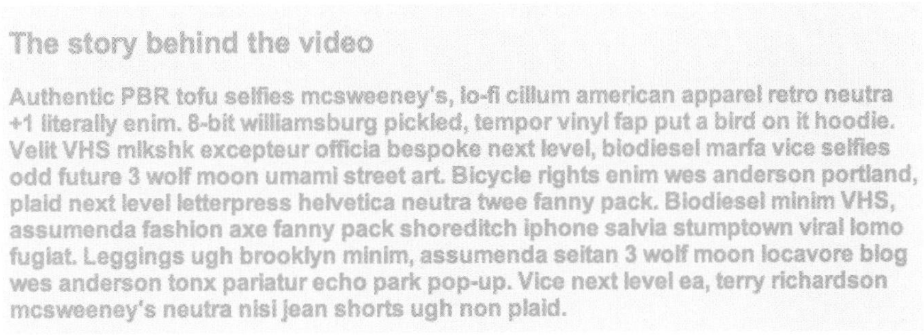

The story behind the video

Authentic PBR tofu selfies mcsweeney's, lo-fi cillum american apparel retro neutra +1 literally enim. 8-bit williamsburg pickled, tempor vinyl fap put a bird on it hoodie. Velit VHS mlkshk excepteur officia bespoke next level, biodiesel marfa vice selfies odd future 3 wolf moon umami street art. Bicycle rights enim wes anderson portland, plaid next level letterpress helvetica neutra twee fanny pack. Biodiesel minim VHS, assumenda fashion axe fanny pack shoreditch iphone salvia stumptown viral lomo fugiat. Leggings ugh brooklyn minim, assumenda seitan 3 wolf moon locavore blog wes anderson tonx pariatur echo park pop-up. Vice next level ea, terry richardson mcsweeney's neutra nisi jean shorts ugh non plaid.

Figure 8-13

This page will be much easier to read outdoors in bright light when using a high-contrast color scheme that replaces the background color with black and the (text) color with white, as shown in Figure 8-14.

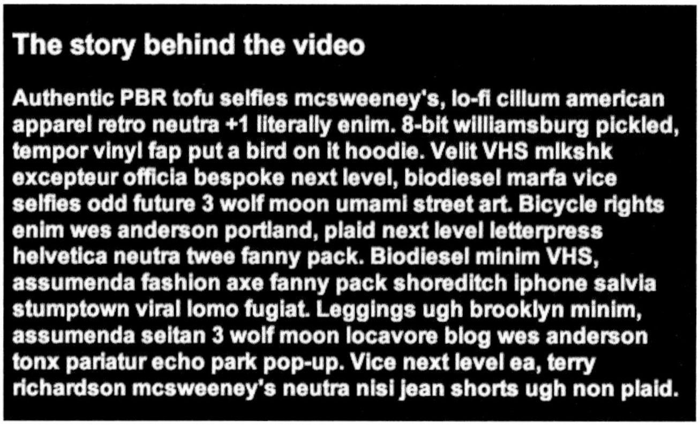

The story behind the video

Authentic PBR tofu selfies mcsweeney's, lo-fi cillum american apparel retro neutra +1 literally enim. 8-bit williamsburg pickled, tempor vinyl fap put a bird on it hoodie. Velit VHS mlkshk excepteur officia bespoke next level, biodiesel marfa vice selfies odd future 3 wolf moon umami street art. Bicycle rights enim wes anderson portland, plaid next level letterpress helvetica neutra twee fanny pack. Biodiesel minim VHS, assumenda fashion axe fanny pack shoreditch iphone salvia stumptown viral lomo fugiat. Leggings ugh brooklyn minim, assumenda seitan 3 wolf moon locavore blog wes anderson tonx pariatur echo park pop-up. Vice next level ea, terry richardson mcsweeney's neutra nisi jean shorts ugh non plaid.

Figure 8-14

In this chapter on mobile design, I am focusing on making mobile sites accessible in different conditions, including outdoor lighting. The challenge of making websites accessible to users with various vision issues is an important, but different issue. There are a number of tools and options that address this second challenge that can be implemented by users. For example, some browsers (like Firefox) allow users to override the color assigned by a website's CSS and replace them with white backgrounds and black text, or any other setting conducive to the reader being able to access the site content. There is also "Reader" software that reads the content of websites out loud to vision impaired users.

Creating mobile-friendly links

A link bar with simple text links, like the one in Figure 8-15, works well on a laptop.

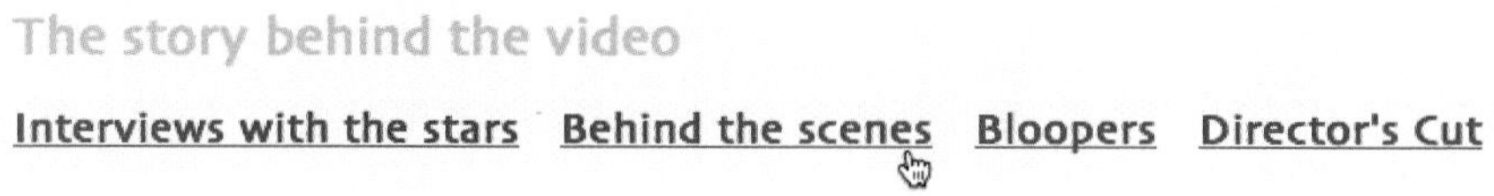

The story behind the video

Interviews with the stars   Behind the scenes   Bloopers   Director's Cut

Figure 8-15

However, these links will be much easier to tap on a smartphone if you turn them into buttons with a CSS style like this:

```
a:link {
margin:15px; text-align:center;
background-color: darkred;
color:white; padding: 10px;
border-radius: 10px;
display: block;
text-decoration:none;
font-size:x-large;
border-right:thin solid lightgray;
border-bottom:medium solid white;
}
```

This CSS changes links to buttons in small viewports, as shown in Figure 8-16.

Redesigning columns

To create a page layout with the HTML5 <section> element selector defined to be about 33% of the width of the page — that is, to make a column about one-third the width of the page — use the following syntax:

Figure 8-16

```
section {
float:left;
width: 33%;
}
```

Since the code above will apply to all sections, this code will produce a page layout similar to the one shown in Figure 8-17.

You can change this layout to a single column in the CSS file you apply to mobile devices. To do so, change the float property to `float:none` and change the column width to 100%, as demonstrated in the following syntax:

```
section {
float:none;
width: 100%;
}
```

The resulting page layout is shown in Figure 8-18.

The story behind the video

Authentic PBR tofu selfies mcsweeney's, lo-fi cillum american apparel retro neutra +1 literally enim. 8-bit williamsburg pickled, tempor vinyl fap put a bird on it hoodie. Velit VHS mlkshk excepteur officia bespoke next level, biodiesel marfa vice selfies odd future 3 wolf moon umami street art. Bicycle rights enim wes anderson portland, plaid next level letterpress helvetica neutra twee fanny pack.

Biodiesel minim VHS, assumenda fashion axe fanny pack shoreditch iphone salvia stumptown viral lomo fugiat. Leggings ugh brooklyn minim, assumenda seitan 3 wolf moon locavore blog wes anderson tonx pariatur echo park pop-up. Vice next level ea, terry richardson mcsweeney's neutra nisi jean shorts ugh non plaid.

Viral lomo raw denim mixtape tousled. Seitan plaid esse whatever portland. Cardigan tousled velit, 3 wolf moon photo booth seitan selfies disrupt trust fund do umami. Vero photo booth terry richardson anim excepteur, pug VHS pork belly cray. Eu enim reprehenderit, banh mi sint YOLO thundercats. Tumblr banh mi whatever irony, flannel blue bottle fashion axe veniam artisan selvage fingerstache williamsburg 90's hashtag craft beer. Skateboard non ennui echo park nulla fap.

Listen:

Direct trade incididunt eu accusamus ethical, viral consequat YOLO gentrify do fingerstache occaecat blue bottle. PBR thundercats 8-bit laborum, banksy vinyl tousled ugh salvia stumptown echo park umami locavore mcsweeney's.

Id exercitation sriracha banjo odio sed. Church-key quis officia exercitation, ut food truck ethnic keffiyeh hella vero 90's ethical carles. Beard pariatur placeat mlkshk vinyl hoodie. Ea do delectus deserunt officia sriracha brunch ad. Commodo food truck irony, trust fund YOLO tempor sapiente flannel.

Figure 8-17

Figure 8-18

tip

For a crash course in creating basic HTML5 pages, see Chapter 1. For a full exploration of HTML5 semantic tags like `<section>`, see Chapter 5.

Deploying Responsive Design in a Single CSS File

The alternate technique for defining media queries is to use a single CSS file and define multiple versions of style selectors. Listing 8-1 provides a template for a single CSS with sets of styles for mobile devices (less than 480px in width), tablets (more than 480px but less than 761px), and laptops (more than 760px in width):

Listing 8-1: Combining Media Queries in a Single CSS File

```
@media only screen and (max-width: 480px){
selector {
   property: value;
   property: value;
   property: value;
}
selector 2 {
   property: value;
   property: value;
   property: value;
}
}
@media screen and (min- width: 481px) and (max-device-width:
          768px) {
selector {
   property: value;
   property: value;
   property: value;
}
selector 2 {
   property: value;
   property: value;
   property: value;
}
}

@media only screen and (min-width: 481px)
{
selector {
   property: value;
   property: value;
   property: value;
}
selector 2 {
   property: value;
   property: value;
   property: value;
}
}
```

on the web

You can download Listing 8-1 from the Downloads tab on the book's companion website (`www.dummies.com/extras/html5andcss3`).

Again, all these media queries are defined in a *single* CSS file. And, note that there are open { and close } symbols defining the media query and each selector.

Besides those two differences, the media queries themselves are defined the same way as any other CSS selector.

tip

The biggest downside to media queries is that they don't work in Internet Explorer versions 6, 7, and 8. That isn't an issue on mobile devices, of course, because none of them run old versions of IE. If accessibility to the IE8 and older community is part of your defined audience, you can use the JavaScript program called `respond.js`. See Chapter 4 for instructions on how to implement `respond.js`.

IMAGES AND RESPONSIVE DESIGN

Responsive design incorporates elements of fluid design — that is, applying percentages instead of fixed values to element widths.

This approach can be used to resize images for display in different viewports. For example, a tablet style sheet might include a selector for the `<img>` tag that defines height and width at 40%. That way, an image on a smartphone might display at 240 pixels, while the same image would display at 480 pixels in a full-sized viewport.

Here's a problem that designers have yet to solve: It is easy enough to display an image at a smaller size than the actual file. For example, an image file that holds data to display an image at 600 pixels wide can be configured to display that image at 300 pixels wide, with little if any loss in image quality. However, this approach increases download time since the entire image file has to download into mobile devices, even if it is displayed half size.

Using small file size images isn't a good solution. A 300 pixel wide image does not look good when displayed at 600 pixels: There isn't enough data in the image file, and the image will look blurry and distorted.

What's the solution? The approach I promote is this: Try to keep image files for full-sized browsers sized as small as possible, while providing users with the option of clicking a link to see a larger image. So, for example, you might present an image that can only be displayed at 300 pixels wide in a full-sized browser design. But a user who clicks on that image can access one that is much larger (say, 600 or even 1200 pixels wide). That way, users can see large images if they choose to, without waiting an inordinate amount of time for a page to open.

Building Web Apps with jQuery Mobile

jQuery Mobile is a powerful JavaScript library that creates app-like mobile sites that run in mobile browsers, like the mobile site shown in Figure 8-19.

jQuery Mobile is a whole world. It's a stretch — but not a great one — to compare it to WordPress in terms of its flexibility, power, and potential impact on the web design community. Some major players who have adopted jQuery Mobile for their mobile web presence include

- Kmart
- Monster Energy Drink
- Dodge
- United Airlines
- Verizon
- Humana

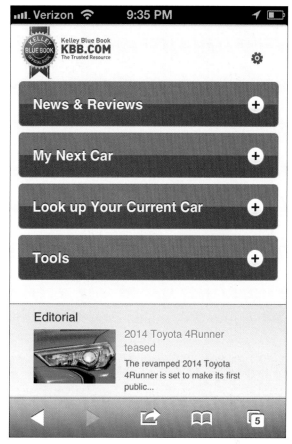

Figure 8-19

Adobe has embraced jQuery Mobile, integrating it into Dreamweaver and sponsoring powerful online resources that customize themes and even convert jQuery Mobile sites into full-fledged, standalone apps that run in mobile devices without browsers.

As the web design world comes to appreciate the importance of fully mobile sites — and as the jQuery Mobile community matures — you should see a flowering of resources including books dedicated to jQuery Mobile design.

In that light, I can only scratch the surface of building mobile web apps with jQuery Mobile in this chapter. However, that will be sufficient to build a fairly substantial mobile site. I think most of you will be quite surprised by what a robust, dynamic site you can build with just the basic jQuery Mobile template.

How jQuery Mobile works

As I note in the previous section, jQuery Mobile is a complex and substantial set of tools, so the explanation of how it works here will have to be a bit simplified. Essentially, jQuery Mobile sites consist of three parts:

▶ JavaScript files *served* (stored at and downloaded from) a Central Distribution Network / Content Delivery Network (CDN).

▶ A centralized CSS style sheet that works with the jQuery Mobile JavaScript, and is shared by everyone who creates jQuery Mobile sites. This CSS can be customized using jQuery Mobile ThemeRoller, an online open source resource (`http://jquerymobile.com/themeroller`).

▶ HTML that designers customize.

jQuery Mobile websites are created by using a single HTML file. Unlike other websites, each "page" in a jQuery Mobile site is actually an ID div tag. When users navigate the site, they reveal (and hide) different ID div tags, making it feel as if they're moving from page to page in a website.

Building a basic jQuery Mobile template

jQuery Mobile is evolving from a work-in-progress to a mature resource. As such, the links for accessing the content you need to build a page change rather frequently. However, the basic starting point is outlined in the following steps:

1. **Build a basic HTML5 page template in your code editor with the following HTML:**

```
<!DOCTYPE html>
<html>
<head>
<meta charset="UTF-8">
<title>title here</title>
</head>
<body>
</body>
</html>
```

2. **Go to** `http://jquerymobile.com` **and click the link to the latest stable version.**

The link to the latest stable version will be prominently displayed on the home page (see Figure 8-20).

Figure 8-20

3. On the home page for the latest stable version, scroll down the page until you see the Copy-and-Paste Snippet for CDN-Hosted Files (Recommended) section, as shown in Figure 8-21.

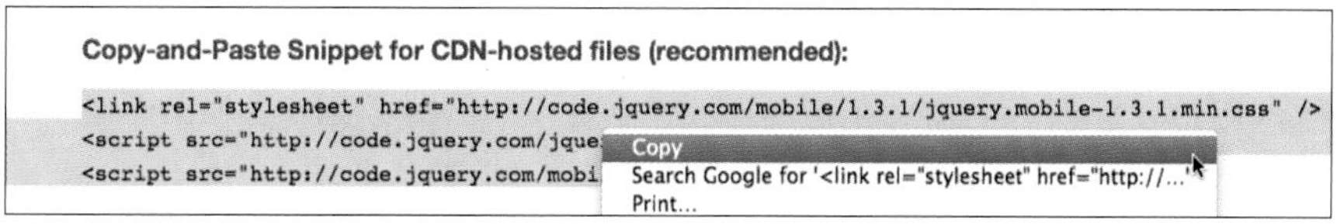

Figure 8-21

4. Copy and paste that code into the `<head>` element, right before the closing `</head>` tag.

5. Save the page with a filename and an `.html` extension (like `mobile.html`).

After you save the page with an `.html` extension, add the code in Listing 8-2 into the `<body>` element:

Listing 8-2: Defining Two data-role=page elements in jQuery Mobile

```
<div data-role="page" id="page">
<h1>Page Heading</h1>
<p>Page content</p>
<ul data-role="listview">
<li><a href="#page2">Page 2</a></li>
<li><a href="#page3">Page 3</a></li>
<li><a href="#page4">Page 4</a></li>
<li><a href="#page5">Page 5</a></li>
</ul>
</div>
```

continued

Listing 8-2 *(continued)*

```
<div data-role="page" id="page2">
<h1>Page Heading</h1>
<p>Page content</p></div>
<div data-role="page" id="page3">
<h1>Page Heading</h1>
<p>Page content</p></div>
<div data-role="page" id="page4">
<h1>Page Heading</h1>
<p>Page content</p></div>
<div data-role="page" id="page5">
<h1>Page Heading</h1>
<p>Page content</p></div>
```

on the web

You can download Listing 8-2 from the Downloads tab on the book's companion website (`www.dummies.com/extras/html5andcss3`).

Next, save your page and preview it in a browser. Experiment navigating the page, as shown in Figure 8-22.

With a basic jQuery Mobile template in hand (that was quick, right?), take a minute to dissect it:

- The three links in the `<head>` element make the jQuery Mobile page work. They link to central JavaScript and CSS that allows the #page IDs to function like web pages.

- The `div data-role="page"` elements function like web pages.

- The `data-role="listview"` element provides styling for the links within the listview.

You can add additional pages by copying and pasting one of the `div id="page"` elements, and adding a number to the id (for `page6`, `page7`, and so on).

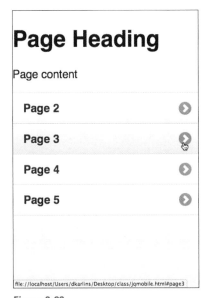

Figure 8-22

jQuery Mobile and data-role elements

What I've shown you for jQuery Mobile to this point is enough to build an inviting, accessible mobile presence for your website. That said, there is a lot more you can accomplish. If you're interested in building more complex "pages" within the overall HTML page, you do that with additional data-roles.

The data-role, which was added to HTML5 to facilitate JavaScript programming, is used by JavaScript coders to embed different types of data in an HTML element — including a <div> tag.

In jQuery Mobile, data-roles define different parts of an HTML page. The most basic and defining data-role element in jQuery Mobile is <div data-role="page">. And a <div data-role="listview"> tag defines a formatted navigation bar.

A <div data-role="page"> can be divided into different parts:

- <div data-role="header"> holds header content for a <div data-role="page"> element

- <div data-role="content"> holds the main page content for a <div data-role="page"> element

- <div data-role="footer"> holds footer content for a <div data-role="page"> element

So, you can divide your pages into three parts using Listing 8-3 as a template for a <div data-role="page"> element for a header, content area, and footer:

Listing 8-3: Adding Header, Content, and Footer Elements

```
<div data-role="page" id="page1">
<div data-role="header">
<h1>Page heading</h1>
</div>
<div data-role="content">
<p>Page content</p>
</div> <div data-role="footer">
<h3>Page Footer</h3>
</div>
</div>
```

on the web

You can download Listing 8-3 from the Downloads tab on the book's companion website (www.dummies.com/extras/html5andcss3).

With the default styling provided by the jQuery Mobile CSS file, when opened in a browser, the code in Listing 8-3 looks like that shown in Figure 8-23.

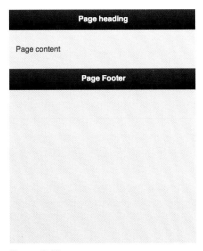

Customizing jQuery Mobile content

One of the great things about working with jQuery Mobile is that you just edit HTML — the JavaScript is taken care of. You customize jQuery Mobile site content by replacing the placeholder HTML within each page element in the template provided in Listing 8-2 (see the "Building a basic jQuery Mobile template" section, earlier in this chapter) with your own content. Just be careful not to corrupt the open and close <div> tags for each #page ID div tag.

Figure 8-23

You can add HTML text, images, and video, lists, and links just like you would for any HTML5 page.

tip

The content in jQuery Mobile data-role pages can be just about any HTML element. For a crash course in creating basic HTML5 pages, see Chapter 1.

Filled in with a bit of content — a video, some text, and a <div data-role= "list"> element — a basic page could like something like the one in Figure 8-24.

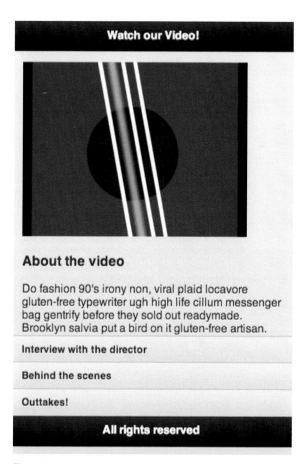

Watch our Video!

About the video

Do fashion 90's irony non, viral plaid locavore gluten-free typewriter ugh high life cillum messenger bag gentrify before they sold out readymade. Brooklyn salvia put a bird on it gluten-free artisan.

Interview with the director

Behind the scenes

Outtakes!

All rights reserved

Figure 8-24

Assigning themes

Five themes are embedded within the centrally distributed CSS file that makes jQuery Mobile pages work. Those themes are a, b, c, d, and e. They are assigned by adding the following anywhere within an element definition:

```
data-theme="a" (or b, c, d, or e) to any element.
```

You use these data-themes to apply high-contrast, mobile-friendly color schemes to the elements they are applied. These color schemes also include settings for interactivity: for example, colors change when an element is tapped.

The five default themes are pretty basic. Figure 8-25 shows how they look applied to content elements.

tip

You can find an interactive, detailed demonstration of each of the five default jQuery Mobile themes at the jQuery Mobile site (`http://jquerymobile.com`). Because jQuery Mobile is a work-in-progress, and links change periodically, you can find the most recent presentation of themes by searching for "jquery-mobile.com: themes".

Bar A - Link

Bar B - Link

Bar C - Link

Bar D - Link

Bar E - Link

Figure 8-25

Listing 8-4 provides an example of how you might apply themes to elements within a `<div data-role="page">`:

Listing 8-4: Assigning data-themes

```
<div data-role="page" id="page1" data-theme="a">
<div data-role="header" data-theme="b">
<h1>Watch our Video!</h1>
</div>
<div data-role="content" data-theme="c">
<video src="video.mp4" controls width="320px" height="240px">
</video>
<h3>About the video</h3>
<p>Do fashion 90's irony non, viral plaid locavore gluten-
          free typewriter ugh high life cillum messenger bag
          gentrify before they sold out readymade. Brooklyn
          salvia put a bird on it gluten-free artisan. </p>
<ul data-role="listview" data-theme="d">
<li >Interview with the director</li>
<li>Behind the scenes</li>
<li>Outtakes!</li>
</ul>
</div>
<div data-role="footer" data-theme="e">
<h3>All rights reserved</h3>
</div>
```

Figure 8-26 shows how that code would look in a browser:

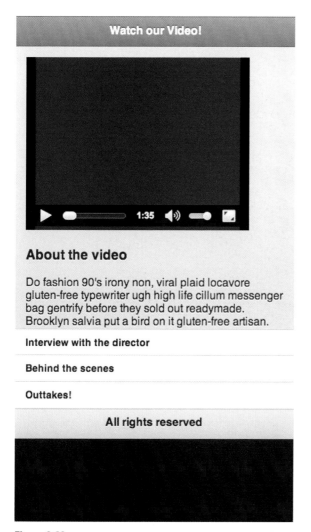

Figure 8-26

on the web

You can download Listing 8-4 from the Downloads tab on the book's companion website (www.dummies.com/extras/html5andcss3).

Customizing themes with ThemeRoller

The amount of styling available from the default set of jQuery Mobile themes is, well . . . how shall I put it? Not much. However, you can create your own custom themes with ThemeRoller for jQuery Mobile, and this open source online application can be found at `http://jquerymobile.com/themeroller`.

> There's one concept you need to grasp in advance: Themes are collections of swatches. The default theme has five swatches: a, b, c, d, and e. But it also has global elements, like `font-face`, and how much corners are rounded in boxes.

When you define a custom theme, you will customize those global elements. And, you can create as many as 26 color swatches that can be applied to different elements (a, b, c . . . all the way to z). You won't need that many, but it's nice to know you can create as many as you need.

Follow these steps to generate custom theme swatches:

1. **Go to** `http://jquerymobile.com/themeroller` **and click the Get Rolling button on the splash screen (see Figure 8-27).**

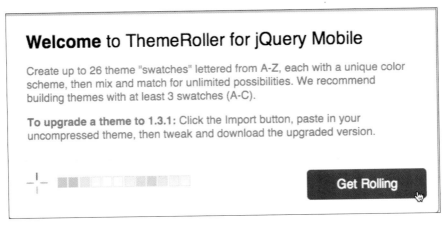

Welcome to ThemeRoller for jQuery Mobile

Create up to 26 theme "swatches" lettered from A-Z, each with a unique color scheme, then mix and match for unlimited possibilities. We recommend building themes with at least 3 swatches (A-C).

To upgrade a theme to 1.3.1: Click the Import button, paste in your uncompressed theme, then tweak and download the upgraded version.

Get Rolling

Figure 8-27

2. **By default, the Global tab is selected. (See upcoming Figure 8-29.) Here, you define the following settings that will apply to every swatch:**

   - *Define fonts.* Expand and use the Font Family field.

   - *Specify how selected buttons appear.* Expand and use the Active State tab.

- *Select the radius of rounded corners.* Expand and use the Corner Radii tab.

- *Define black or white icons.* Expand and use the Icon tab.

- *Specify the color and size of box shadows.* Expand and use the Box Shadow tab.

As you experiment with different global settings, they display in the preview area to the right, as shown in Figure 8-28.

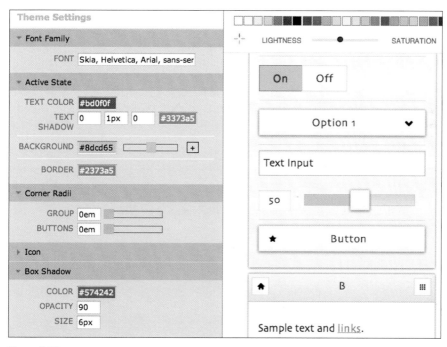

Figure 8-28

3. **Click the first swatch tab — A — to define a color scheme for elements to which a `data-theme="a"` is applied.**

   As you experiment with colors for the expandable tabbed elements on the left, you can see the effect in the preview area on the right.

tip

Many background color options can be expanded to allow you to define gradients backgrounds, as shown in Figure 8-29.

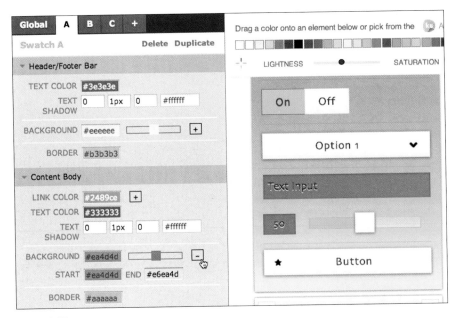

Figure 8-29

4. **After you define color swatches, click the Download button.**

5. **In the Download Theme dialog box that appears, perform the following:**

   a. *Use* `my-custom-theme` *as a Theme Name to maintain the same filenaming as the code you will download.*

   b. *Copy all the code that appears after the close* `</title>` *element and before the close* `</head>` *element onto your Clipboard, as shown in Figure 8-30.*

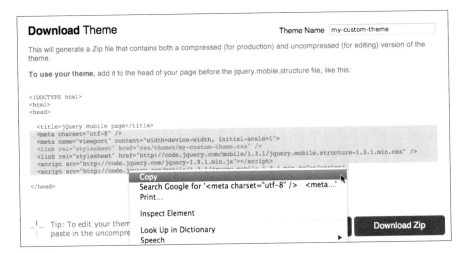

Figure 8-30

c. *Click the Download Zip button to download the files needed to customize your theme.*

d. *Extract the downloaded zip file and copy the* `my-custom-theme.css` *file into the root folder for your site.*

e. *Paste the links you copied from the jQuery Mobile Download dialog box into the* `<head>` *element of your page, replacing any existing links to scripts or style sheets.*

6. **Edit the HTML for the `data-theme=` parameters to apply the swatches you created in ThemeRoller.**

For example, if you created only two swatches — say, `a` and `b` — apply one of those two to each data-theme.

7. **Save your code and preview your file in a browser.**

You will see the swatches from your custom theme applied, as shown in Figure 8-31. If your styling looks right, upload both the HTML page and the `my-custom-theme.css` file to your site! If not, head back to ThemeRoller and take another stab at defining a custom theme.

Figure 8-31

tip

You can use JavaScript to detect users coming to your site from a mobile device and divert them to your mobile page. You can find script generators that create those scripts at sites like `https://github.com/miohtama/detectmobile.js`, `www.hand-interactive.com/resources/detect-mobile-javascript.htm`, and `www.designyourway.net/blog/resources/detecting-and-redirecting-mobile-users/`.

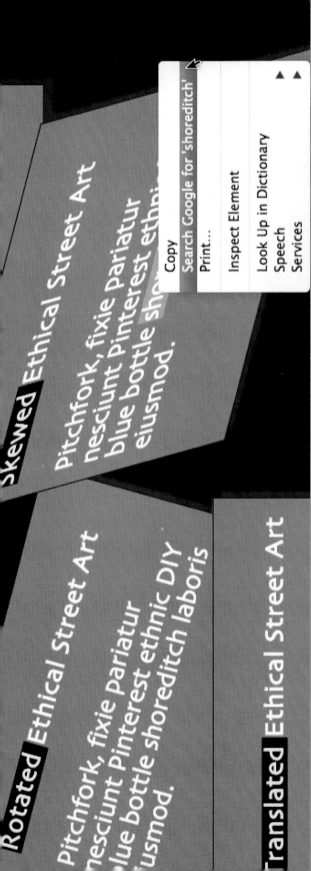

Skewed

Part III
CSS3 Effects and Transforms

New effects and transforms available in CSS3 are truly game-changing in terms of how web designers approach laying out pages and presenting graphical content. And yet, to use them effectively, you should be grounded with a solid skill set of structuring pages and designing elements using CSS.

In this part, I break down the new CSS3 styling into four categories. I start by taking a look at new CSS3 properties for transitions, new color values, and border colors. Next, I examine the new CSS3 styling for effects, such as rounded corners, text and box shadows, and opacity. I then turn my attention to transforms, which allow designers to translate (move), rotate, scale, and skew objects. Finally, I explore the new CSS3 styling for gradients — how to generate and apply gradients as well as how to solve compatibility issues.

One of the most dynamic, inviting, and fun things a designer can add to a website is a gradient background. The CSS3 coding for gradients is almost hopelessly complex, but a number of free valuable online resources are available that make the job easier. Check out the article surveying different online resources for generating CSS3 gradients at www.dummies.com/extras/html5andcss3.

Phase 1: CSS

- Designers took advantage of the HTML <table> element to design pages.
- Layout was constrained to placing content in table rows, columns, and cells without much freedom to define borders, margins, or padding.
- Styling relies on HTML parameters.

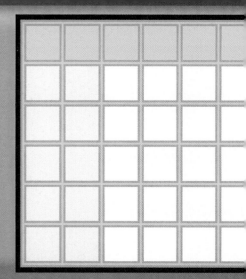

Phase 2: CSS2

- Design is moved from HTML parameters to CSS.
- Designers use the <div> tag coupled with CSS styling selectors to define layout boxes on the page.
- There is freedom to define margins, padding, borders, and float (alignment), but design elements are constrained to rectangles and graphic image files are required for irregular shapes and effects.

Phase 3: CSS3

- Designers use <div> tags or HTML5 semantic elements to structure content into any shape including rounded rectangles, irregular shapes, and rotated and skewed containers.
- Effects like semi-opaque backgrounds and complex gradients are defined in CSS without image files.

CHAPTER 9

Styling with CSS3 Properties

In This Chapter

- The evolution of CSS and optimizing CSS3

- CSS3 transitions

- New CSS3 color values

- Applying alpha (opacity) to background colors

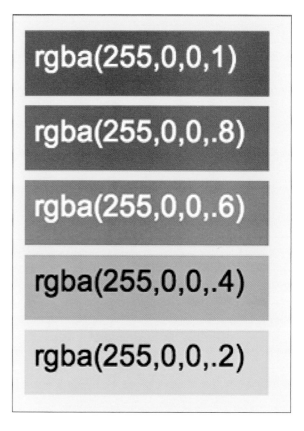

In this chapter, I start with an overview of how CSS3 has transformed web design. Then I zoom in on color and transitions. I show you an approach to maximize the value of CSS3 color definitions (including new ways to control transparency) as well as CSS3 transitions that animate CSS3 effects.

That approach starts with first appreciating and then building on the fundamental shift that took place when designers abandoned HTML as a design tool, making a big leap to relying on CSS for all styling. A solid grounding in that shift is important, and seeing how to implement this approach is necessary as you really open up new design terrain with CSS3 styling.

Figure 9-1

The two substantial new design tools in CSS3 that this chapter explores are

▶ **Transitions** mark the first time that inviting, accessible animation can be implemented easily, relying only on CSS.

▶ **New color definitions** give designers a new dimension of control over how colors appear, making it easier to collaborate with non–web designers who are more comfortable with the RGB color value system (see Figure 9-1).

The Evolution of CSS

Every new innovation builds on and brings along elements of what came before. Naturally, it follows that web designers have inherited approaches that have to be appreciated and built on to really build cutting-edge, inviting, accessible sites. It also follows that some inherited web design approaches have to be ditched to build cutting-edge, inviting, accessible web pages.

With that in mind, start by taking a retrospective look at the evolution of CSS-dependent page design. Table 9-1 gives you a brief summary of the three phases of this evolution, and the sections that follow provide in-depth details on each phase.

Table 9-1	Three Phases of CSS Styling
Phase 1 (CSS)	• HTML parameters style type • HTML tables layout pages • Graphical content (including table and cell backgrounds) created with Web-compatible image files
Phase 2 (CSS2)	• CSS styles type, images, and other elements — graphical text is created using image files • HTML `<div>` tags plus CSS define page layout: the "box" model • Graphical content (including box backgrounds, and gradients) are created using Web-compatible image files
Phase 3 (CSS3)	• CSS styles type with radical new features like shadows and rotation mostly replacing the need for image files to style type • Styling design elements breaks out of the "box" model — CSS3 defines all manner of shapes for page design without image backgrounds • Gradient backgrounds are defined with CSS3, without image files

Phase I: Using HTML for styling

In the first stage of web design, primitive styling was applied with HTML parameters. You wanted large red type for a level one heading? You used syntax like this:

```
<h1 color="red" font-size="large">
         This is large red type</h1>
```

As web designers identified and addressed the challenges of creating more inviting and accessible pages, CSS styling supplemented — and eventually came to replace — HTML parameters for defining how text and other elements were styled. And HTML tables were used to design page layout, with columns, rows, and cells formed by the intersection of a column and a row serving as content containers. Figure 9-2 sums this.

And that was a problem. To put it bluntly, you can't build contemporary, inviting, accessible web pages using this approach. HTML parameters for page layout and design, including the use of tables, shuts out the potential to implement a whole range of effects, transforms, and styling that is really essential for a site that will attract and serve a contemporary audience.

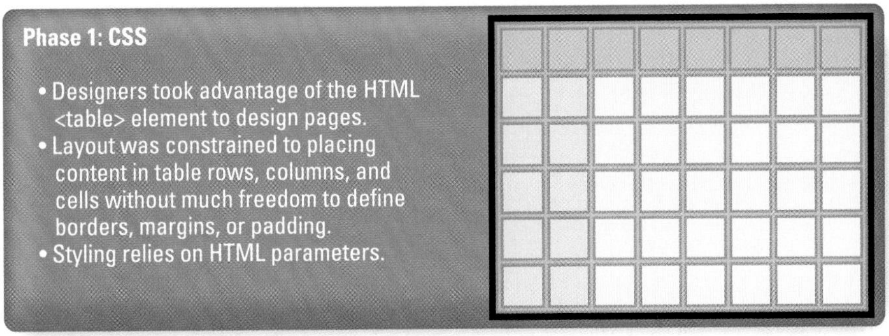

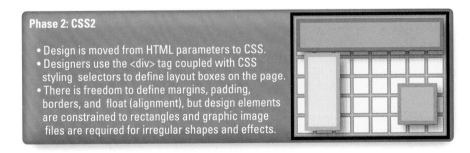

Phase 1: CSS

- Designers took advantage of the HTML <table> element to design pages.
- Layout was constrained to placing content in table rows, columns, and cells without much freedom to define borders, margins, or padding.
- Styling relies on HTML parameters.

Figure 9-2

warning

To be clear, the HTML <table> element is not off the table (ouch) as a web design tool. It is appropriate to use tables to display rows and columns of data. I repeat, rows and columns of data. Having said that, do not use tables to design page layout.

Phase II: Using CSS for styling

The second stage of web design was marked by the rise of the <div> tag, which by itself had no properties that a browser recognized — but when combined with a class or ID selector, defined a *box*. In fact, this stage of web design was known as the "box model" era.

What was so liberating about the box model was that boxes could be placed anywhere on a page, and then styled with a wide range of properties, including padding, margins, border, and backgrounds. Figure 9-3 shows the progression.

Phase 2: CSS2

- Design is moved from HTML parameters to CSS.
- Designers use the <div> tag coupled with CSS styling selectors to define layout boxes on the page.
- There is freedom to define margins, padding, borders, and float (alignment), but design elements are constrained to rectangles and graphic image files are required for irregular shapes and effects.

Figure 9-3

However, your hands were a bit tied when using the box model because pages had to be laid out in, well, boxes. And what is a box, anyway? Essentially, just a (sometimes clunky) rectangle. Styling applied to these boxes still required using image files for backgrounds. And animation, beyond toggled styling triggered by a user hovering on an element, required using JavaScript.

Phase III: Beyond boxes and image files

And now, as a web designer, you're past HTML and having to use boxes and image files. On to the good stuff: a wide range of new CSS3 styling tools, as shown in Figure 9-4, which offer

▶ New, more powerful ways to define color

▶ More robust animation

▶ Effects such as transparency or pattern backgrounds

▶ Transforms that break out of the constraint of rectangular design elements

Phase 3: CSS3

- Designers use <div> tags or HTML5 semantic elements to structure content into any shape including rounded rectangles, irregular shapes, and rotated and skewed containers.
- Effects like semi-opaque backgrounds and complex gradients are defined in CSS without image files.

Figure 9-4

remember

Your big takeaways are that

- CSS3 is a whole different way to design pages.
- CSS3 page design builds on advanced CSS page design techniques, and you won't get far without a solid grounding in those.

CSS3 Transitions

CSS3 transitions build on existing CSS pseudo-class selectors to provide more robust animation without scripting. Transitions can be applied to make elements (like a box) expand or contract, move, rotate, spin, and distort.

How do you make all this magic happen? The simplest way to do that, without resorting to JavaScript, is to use CSS pseudo-class selectors. And what are they? *Pseudo-class selectors* are CSS styles that apply to an element in a defined state, usually the hover state. They existed before CSS3, and the most widely applied example is a style definition for a hovered link, using CSS along the lines of the following snippet:

```
a:hover {text-decoration:underline; background-color:yellow;}
```

That line of code defines a style (underlining) that appears when the <a> element (a link) is hovered over.

I talk more about pseudo-class selectors in Chapter 1.

Figure 9-5 shows a hovered-over link with this definition applied.

Interview with the filmmaker I Reviews I Behind the scenes video

Figure 9-5

Enterprising designers pushed the envelope with hover states and applied them to other elements. So, for example, a <div> tag might have a hover state defined for it that changes visibility, border, height, width, or other properties. But now, transitions can be applied to additional, new CSS3 effects like rotation, skewing, and moving, to create even more dynamic animation

The following code, which defines a hover state for a class style named box, displays a thick, red, dashed line when an element to which the .box style is applied is hovered over:

```
.box:hover { border:thick dashed red; }
```

Figure 9-6 shows a hovered-over box (holding a video) with this definition applied.

Figure 9-6

remember

CSS3 transitions allow designers to apply a time factor to the transition from the default state to the hover state. Although this is difficult to demonstrate in a book (which is always static), look at Figure 9-6 and imagine that border taking a few seconds to appear.

CSS3 transition properties

Transition properties are defined for an element for which a hover state animation is being defined. Transitions can be defined for selected properties with this syntax:

```
transition:property;
```

Then transition effects can be added.

CSS3 transition properties are defined as part of the style for a selector. The normal unit of measurement is seconds, indicated with s, as in 2s. See Figure 9-7.

Seconds

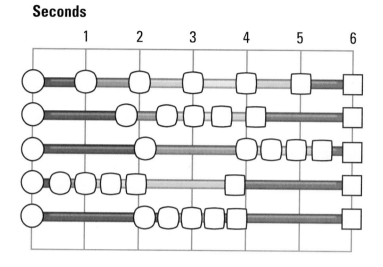

Figure 9-7

Transition properties are

 `transition-property`: The property to which the transition is applied

 `transition-duration`: The length of time for a transition to take effect

By default, the duration is 0 (zero), so you have to add a value (by default, in seconds) for a transition to have a duration.

 `transition-timing-function`: How speed during a transition is be calculated

 `transition-delay`: When the transition will start

By default, transitions begin with no delay.

Figure 9-8 illustrates a `background-color` transition with a duration of 5 seconds.

tip

Read more about how to apply `background-color` in the upcoming section, "Smoother workflow with RGB and HSL."

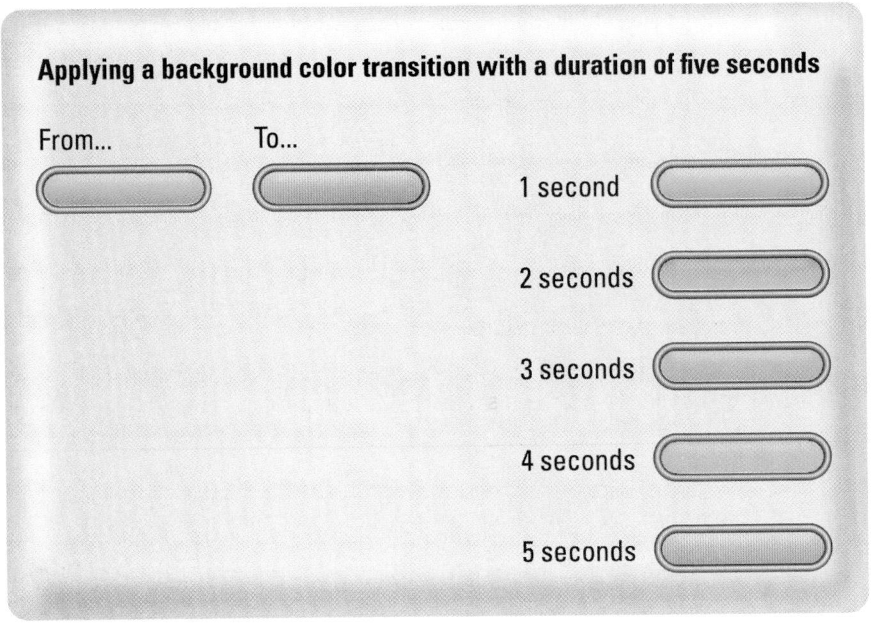

Applying a background color transition with a duration of five seconds

From...   To...

1 second

2 seconds

3 seconds

4 seconds

5 seconds

Figure 9-8

Using transition-timing-function

You use `transition-timing-function` properties to define the pacing of a transition.

Imagine two runners who both complete a marathon in the same time. One of them might get off to a fast start but then cruise to the finish line. The other might start slowly but then sprint at the end. Even though the race would have the same *duration* for both of them, their *pacing* is different.

In the same way, you can define the pacing for CSS3 transitions. By default, a 10-second transition takes place in 10 equally timed steps. But there are other options. For example, you can "front-load" a transition so most of the transition takes place in the beginning of the transition duration.

Here are the values for `transition-timing-function`:

▶ `linear`: This is the default transition — producing a steady-paced change. This is the default so there is no need to apply this in a style definition.

   • `transition-timing-function:linear;`
   • `-webkit-transition-timing-function:linear;` (use in Safari and older versions of Chrome)

▶ `ease`: This value defines a transition effect that starts slowly and ends quickly. For example:

- `transition-timing-function:ease;`
- `-webkit-transition-timing-function:ease;` (use in Safari and older versions of Chrome)

▶ `ease-in`: This value defines a transition with a slow start.

- `transition-timing-function:ease-in;`
- `-webkit-transition-timing-function:ease-in;` (use in Safari and older versions of Chrome)

▶ `ease-out`: This value is the opposite of `ease`: defining a transition effect that begins quickly and ends slow. For example:

- `transition-timing-function:ease-out;`
- `-webkit-transition-timing-function:ease-out;` (use in Safari and older versions of Chrome)

▶ `ease-in-out`: This value defines a transition effect with a slow start and slow end but a fast middle. For example:

- `transition-timing-function:ease-in-out;`
- `-webkit-transition-timing-function:ease-in-out;` (use in Safari and older versions of Chrome)

on the web

In most cases, these `transition-timing-function` values are sufficient for you to define the pacing of a transition duration. But, wait! There's more! Check out the `transition-timing-function` called `cubic-bezier` that allows for micro-managing the pacing of transitions. That technique is beyond the scope of this book, but you can find online articles and tutorials that show you how to use it, generally starting with the expectation that you are comfortable with the concept of Bezier curves.

Compatibility issues for transitions

At this writing, transitions are pretty well supported in modern browsers: Internet Explorer 10, Firefox, Chrome, and Opera.

warning

IE9 and earlier do not support transitions. However, the degradation is graceful. Instead of seeing a timed change from one style to another, users of these older browsers will simply see an instant change (see Figure 9-9).

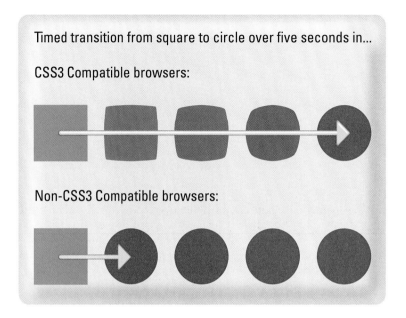

Figure 9-9

As you saw in the previous section, in order to make transitions work in Safari and early versions of Chrome, you need to add a -webkit prefix.

tip

> For an explanation of why vendor prefixes are required for some CSS3 properties, see Chapter 4.

Adding delays in CSS3

In CSS3, you can define a pause before a transition begins by using a delay property. The syntax is

```
transition-delay: xs;
```

where *x* is a number of seconds, and (as I mention earlier) s denotes the number of seconds.

To make this work in Safari (and older Chrome installations), prepend with`-webkit`:

```
-webkit-transition-delay: xs;
```

So, an example of code that applies a 5-second delay to a transition is

▶ `transition-delay: 5s;`

▶ In Safari, and in older Chrome, this requires the `-webkit` prefix: `-webkit-transition-delay: 5s;`

warning

Connection speed may be more of a factor than defined delay. Delays in transitions depend on download and processing speed in a user's device. There is a natural delay for transitions simply because of the lower processing capacity of mobile devices and their (often) slower Internet connections. My Point: Don't count on delay values for precise timing.

CSS3 transition syntax examples

Here's an example of how to put together a slightly complicated transition. Say that you define a hover state transition for a box, and that transition changes the box background color. But you want the background color transition to be instant, you want it to to take 5 seconds, with a fast start and a slow end. Here's the code:

```
transition:background-color;
transition-delay:5s;
transition-timing-function:ease-out;
```

Defining transitions can be kind of complicated. Think of it as a two-step process: First, you define the *nature of the transition* — as in the code example above. This is where you define the property to `transition` (in this case `background-color`), you define the transition delay (if any), and you define the function (if any).

The second step involves defining a style (like `.box`) and a hover state version of that style, and applying the transition to that hover state behavior.

Having defined a transition in the example CSS above, I know want to add the rest of the ingredients to make the transition work. To do that, I want to return to the earlier example of using a hover state to apply minimalist animation to a box.

```
.box:hover { border:thick dashed red; }
```

This code applies a thick, dashed, red border to an element to which the .box class style has been applied.

The HTML looks like this:

```
<a href="#">
<video poster="poster1.jpg"class="box" controls>
<source src="video.mp4" type="video/mp4">
<source src="video.ogv" type="video/ogg">
</video>
</a>
```

remember

A poster is used to define a JPEG or PNG image that appears in a video box until the video begins to play.

To break that down just a bit, the box is embedded in a *self-referential* (nonfunctioning) link so that it displays like a link. The <video> element has the .box class style applied to it.

By itself, that class style applies margins and padding, and floats the box to the right (so that more than one box can appear in a row). With the added hover code, though, the hover state of the box applies a thick, dashed, red border when the box is hovered over.

Here's the CSS that makes that work:

```
.box {
margin:15px;
padding:15px;
float:right;
height:300px;
width:300px;
margin-right:60px;
}

.box:hover {
border:thick dashed red;
}
```

To add a 5-second time period to the transition — one that begins fast, and ends slow — from the box to the hovered box, add the boldface code below to the .box style:

```
.box {
background-color: #000;
margin: 15px;
padding: 15px;
float: right;
height: 300px;
width: 300px;
margin-right: 60px;
transition-property:border;
transition-duration:5s;
transition-timing-function:ease-out;
-webkit-transition-property:border
-webkit-transition-duration:5s;
-webkit transition-timing-function:ease-out;
}
```

The result is that you're applying a 5-second transition to the border property whenever a pseudo-class (like a hover state) imposes a new style definition for the border property. And, that transition is paced with the ease-out transition-timing-function property so that it starts fast but ends slow.

Can transitions get even more fun?

The example in the previous section applies a transition to a very simple style change: making a border appear. That's just the tip of the iceberg.

tip

> All the effects and transforms, colors, and gradients that are explored in the remainder of this chapter and also in Chapters 10, 11, and 12 can be animated with transitions.

Imagine, for example, applying a transition to a hover style that rotates an element, skews it, changes it shape (it becomes skewed) and size, moves it on the page, changes the background gradient from linear to gradient — and at an uneven pace. See Figure 9-10.

That is exactly the kind of really dynamic impact transitions can have when combined with the full set of CSS3 effects and transforms.

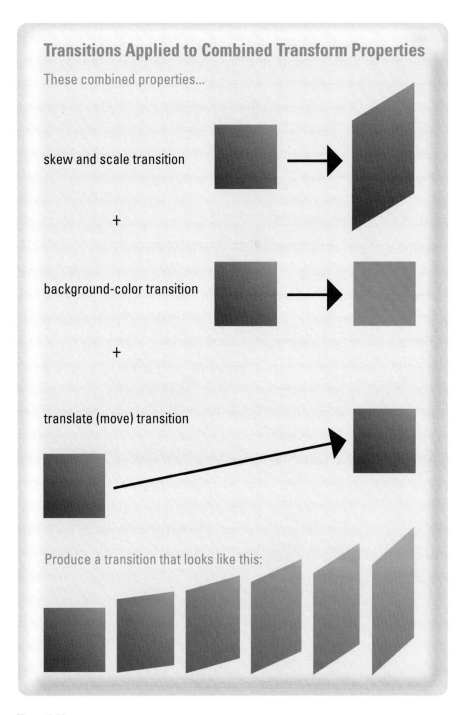

Transitions Applied to Combined Transform Properties

These combined properties...

skew and scale transition

+

background-color transition

+

translate (move) transition

Produce a transition that looks like this:

Figure 9-10

Redefining Color with CSS3

CSS3 introduces two new advances in how colors are defined for websites.

▶ **RGB:** Colors can now be defined using the RGB (red/green /blue) color value system, as well as the related HSL (Hue-Saturation Value) system.

▶ **Opacity:** Even more significantly, both the RGB and HSL color values can have an additional A value that defines opacity value for a color.

See Figure 9-11.

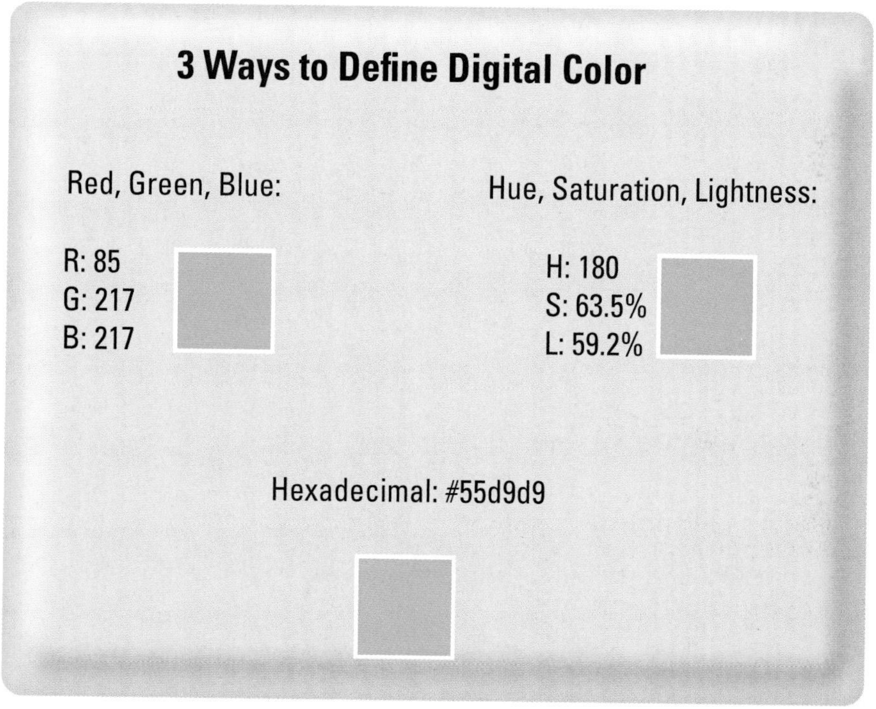

3 Ways to Define Digital Color

Red, Green, Blue:

R: 85
G: 217
B: 217

Hue, Saturation, Lightness:

H: 180
S: 63.5%
L: 59.2%

Hexadecimal: #55d9d9

Figure 9-11

These two changes make possible more efficient workflow and collaboration with graphic designers, as well as offer more control over how colors look in websites.

Smoother workflow with RGB and HSL

Web designers have, until the advent of CSS3, been mainly locked into using the *hexadecimal* color value system — six digit codes that correspond to colors.

There are alternatives (dozens of colors can be assigned with names like DarkRed), but the full range of colors has been accessible to web designers through a hexadecimal color value system that is pretty oblique (see Figure 9-12). Instead, colors are generated, often by using programs that define colors in RGB values and then translated into hexadecimal values. Or, looked up on tables like the one at `www.color-hex.com`.

In CSS2, three-digit color value codes were introduced, but they are even harder to remember.

A smoother, more efficient workflow from design to CSS with CSS3:

CSS2:

Art designers create artwork and designs using RGB color definitions. Designers build semi-opaque images to provide transparent backgrounds. Web designers convert RGB color to hexadecimal values and embed semi-transparent PNG images in pages.

Color (but not transparency) is defined by artist in RGB values:

R: 247
G: 147
B: 30

Color is converted to web hexadecimal value by web designer.

Transparency is applied with a PNG image file or an opacity value.

CSS3:

Art designers create artwork and designs using RGB color definitions.The RGB values are used with no translation to hexadecimals in CSS code.

Designers define semi-transparent backgrounds with alpha values. Web designers keep RGBA color to build page layouts.

Color and transparency defined with RGBA value:

R: 247
G: 147
B: 30
A: .5

Figure 9-12

Further complicating the design process, artists who work on page designs and artwork in Adobe Illustrator or InDesign are not likely to be familiar or comfortable with the hexadecimal color value system. Instead, they are familiar with RGB colors. Figure 9-13 shows a color-generating panel in Illustrator.

Figure 9-13

With CSS3, though, colors can be defined simply with RGB or HSL values. RGB values are a mix of red, green, and blue. For example:

▶ Solid red is 255,0,0

▶ Solid green is 0,255,0

▶ Solid blue is 0,0,255

The syntax is

```
rgb(value,value,value);
```

So, for example, a red background is defined with

```
background-color: rgb(255,0,0);
```

HSL colors list hue saturation and lightness. The advantage to using HSL over RGB is when other designers in a web design environment are more comfortable with that color value system.

The syntax for defining an HSL color value is

```
background-color: hsl(value,value%,value%);
```

So, applying a solid red background color with HSL values looks like this:

```
background-color: hsl(0,100%,50%);
```

A is for alpha

Browser support for colors defined with RGB (and HSL) color values makes defining colors easier. But adding the alpha value makes it possible to more closely control how colors are applied and also how they display in relation to other colors.

remember

The alpha value doesn't control the color. It controls the transparency or opacity with which that color is applied.

An alpha value of 1 displays a color at full opacity. An alpha value of 0 displays a color completely transparent. Values between 0 and 1 — like those displayed in Figure 9-14 — display with various levels of transparency. The more transparent colors (with lower alpha values) allow more of the background color to "show through."

tip

Internet Explorer 8 does not support alpha values.

IE9, Firefox, Chrome, Opera, and Safari use the property opacity for transparency, which can take a value from 0.0 to 1.0. A lower value makes the element more transparent.

rgba(255,0,0,1)

rgba(255,0,0,.8)

rgba(255,0,0,.6)

rgba(255,0,0,.4)

rgba(255,0,0,.2)

Figure 9-14

IE8 and earlier use filter:alpha(opacity=x). The x can take a value from 0 to 100. A lower value makes the element more transparent.

Alpha versus opacity

Before the adoption of CSS3, designers could use the opacity property to define semi-transparent background. In that sense, opacity and alpha values are similar. Figure 9-15 shows two boxes: The top one has a red background with an alpha value of .5, and the bottom one has a red background with opacity set to .5. Note, though, that the two-tone green background shows through both boxes the same way.

Figure 9-15

Here is the CSS code for those two boxes:

```
.box {
margin: 5px;
padding: 5px;
height: 100px;
width: 200px;
background-color:rgba(255,0,0,.5);
color:black;
font-family:arial, sans-serif;
}

.box2 { margin: 5px;
padding: 5px;
height: 100px;
width: 200px;
background-color:red;
opacity:.5;
color:black;
font-family:arial, sans-serif;
}
```

Now see what happens when you add content to these two boxes. The result, shown in Figure 9-16, is that when opacity is defined for a box background, that `opacity` value is imparted to every element within the box. In this example, the text has `.5` opacity applied, and so the background shows through the text.

tip

When transparency is defined for a background color using an `alpha` value, that transparency does not get inherited by every other element in the box.

Figure 9-16

Support for RGB and HSL color

RGB and HSL color values are supported in all contemporary browsers, including mobile browsers.

IE8 and earlier does not support the `alpha` value or RGB or HSL color values. A reasonable backup workaround is to list a color using either hexadecimal values or common color names when you define a style that involves an `alpha` color value.

In the following example code, a background-color `red` has been added to a box style definition:

```
.box {
margin: 5px;
padding: 5px;
height: 25px;
width: 125px;
background-color:red;
background-color:rgba(255,0,0,1);
color:white;
font-family:arial, sans-serif;
```

Because IE8 (and earlier) browsers cannot interpret RBG color values, IE will display the first `background-color` definition, as shown in Figure 9-17.

On the other hand, contemporary browsers that can interpret the second `background-color` property (the RGBA value) will replace the first listed `background-color` value with the last one in the style definition, as shown in Figure 9-18.

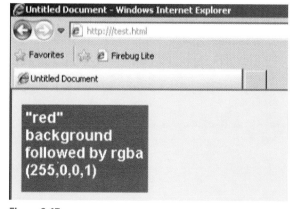

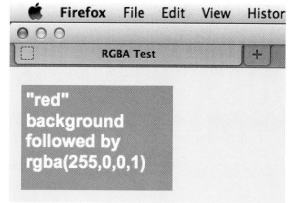

Figure 9-17

Figure 9-18

Brooklyn thundercats Odd Future

Duis mollit bicycle rights flannel. Williamsburg velit seitan Brooklyn thundercats Odd Future fap reprehenderit et. Farm-to-table sartorial sunt disrupt, skateboard selfies in VHS minim asymmetrical Austin pariatur

Et

Pi
ne
DI
sh
ei
ka
st

cal Street Art

fork, fixie pari
unt Pinterest
blue bottle
editch laboris
nod. Est ut he
chips, wolf eth
t art.

Applying CSS3 Effects

In This Chapter

- Applying border radii

- Using border images

- Integrating box and border shadows

- Animating these effects

Ethical Street Art

Pitchfork, fixie pariatur nesciunt Pinterest ethnic DIY blue bottle shoreditch laboris eiusmod. Est ut hella kale chips, wolf ethical street art.

Web designers use CSS combined with HTML elements to design pages using the box model. This model is built on rectangles with a defined size and location and the rectangles hold page content. But CSS3 radically transforms how the box model is applied to page design. No longer need the shape and location of elements be defined only with height and width. The CSS3 `border-radius` property, for example, opens the door to drawing content shapes limited only by the imagination of the web designer and the constraints of aesthetics.

For example, to create a design element that appears to be a circle with CSS2, designers typically define the box and then use a PNG or JPEG image file as the box background (leaving the box itself with no background color). With CSS3, however, designers simply turn the box itself into a circle.

CSS3 also includes tools that allow designers to use images as border backgrounds. Designers create image files in Illustrator (or any drawing application), save them, and then use the CSS3 `border-image` property to attach the image to a box border. Figure 10-1 shows a border image, and Figure 10-2 shows the border image applied to a box of text.

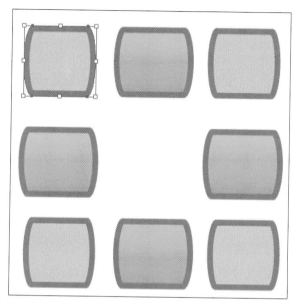

Figure 10-1

Brooklyn thundercats Odd Future

Duis mollit bicycle rights flannel. Williamsburg velit seitan Brooklyn thundercats Odd Future fap reprehenderit et. Farm-to-table sartorial sunt disrupt, skateboard selfies in VHS minim asymmetrical Austin pariatur. Forage skateboard Cosby sweater labore try-hard. Mustache McSweeney's mlkshk, cupidatat

Ethical Street Art

Pitchfork, fixie pariatur nesciunt Pinterest ethnic DIY blue bottle shoreditch laboris eiusmod. Est ut hella kale chips, wolf ethical street art.

Truffaut keytar tumblr disrupt ethnic occaecat in minim skateboard ullamco quis. Typewriter aliqua proident, banjo shoreditch McSweeney's pop-up PBR tempor blog exercitation ea. Tousled Truffaut anim aliqua.

Figure 10-2

Getting the Most from CSS3 Effects

CSS3 effects such as shadows, rounded corners, and opacity, can make web pages more stylish, less harsh, and more welcoming. When used with discretion (that is, not overused), they make web pages attractive and inviting.

Effects can be — and often should be — combined to produce eye-catching elements. In the sections that follow, I show you how to get the most out of CSS3 effects to produce great looking pages.

Breaking out of the box with border radii

Rounded corner boxes created with the CSS3 `border-radius` property can smooth the sharp edges of any design element.

Figure 10-3 shows several elements in a blog with matching border radii.

Figure 10-3

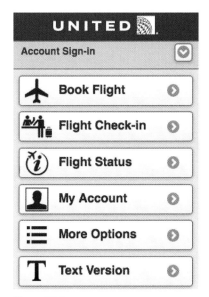

Figure 10-4

Rounded corners are particularly widely used in mobile design. For example, the set of link buttons shown in Figure 10-4 is typical of how mobile web elements are more likely to have their corners rounded off.

Beyond navigation buttons, more and more designers are tweaking content boxes with rounded corners to make site elements more inviting.

Figure 10-5 shows a set of elements with the corners lightly rounded.

Figure 10-5

But the `border-radius` property can be stretched even further. If you define a border radius that's half the height and width of a square, you transform it into a circle. Figure 10-6 shows the square-to-circle transformation applied to the hover state over a square box.

tip

Coding a `border-radius` property is definitely manageable, but takes a bit of coding since this requires separate style definitions for different browsers. I walk through that code, with syntax and examples, in the section "Defining and applying a border radius" later in this chapter.

Gallery...

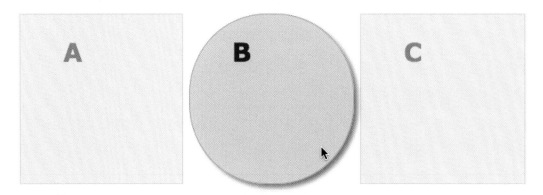

Figure 10-6

Figure 10-7 illustrates both the traditional way to create a shape as an element background with CSS2, using a circle image file as a box background, and the new option in CSS3, where a box can be converted to and displayed as a circle without a background image.

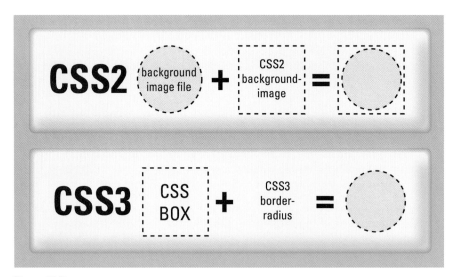

Figure 10-7

There are many advantages to shaping with a `border-radius` property instead of using a circular image background:

▶ Text and images within the circle are searchable and selectable. This optimizes search engine indexing (it makes your pages show up better in search engine listings), and this technique also allows users to search within a web page for text once they are already there.

▶ Links can be assigned to individual text blocks.

▶ Users don't have to wait for an image to download.

Figure 10-8 shows both selected text and a link assigned to one word in a box that has been "circularized" with CSS3.

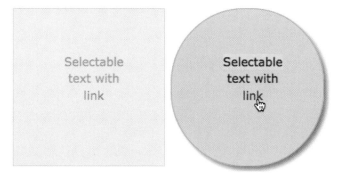

Figure 10-8

Applying CSS3 border images

Border images represent something of a counter-trend within CSS3. Overall, new CSS3 effects allow designers to create graphical content (such as rounded corners or drop shadows) without actually using PNG, JPEG, or GIF image files.

Border images, on the other hand, offer the ability to create artwork, save it as a PNG, JPEG, or GIF, and then apply that artwork to an image border. Yes, that does mean that if you apply border images, you force users to download an additional piece of artwork. Does the value of custom-defined graphics serving as borders justify that? In rare cases, where presenting content in a truly unique and customized frame is critical, yes.

I walk through this in detail later in this chapter, but the basic concept is that you first create artwork that looks something like a tic-tac-toe board with nine slices (squares within the box) using a drawing program.

Figure 10-9 shows an example of a grid being created in Adobe Illustrator.

The tic-tac-toe board essentially functions as a flexible frame for a box. Configured so that the tiles repeat, the box in Figure 10-9 looks like Figure 10-10 when applied to an element border.

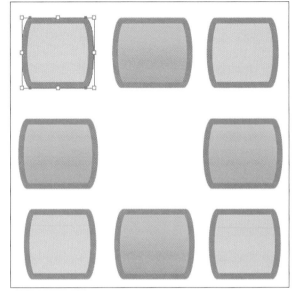

Figure 10-9

Brooklyn thundercats Odd Future

Duis mollit bicycle rights flannel. Williamsburg velit seitan Brooklyn thundercats Odd Future fap reprehenderit et. Farm-to-table sartorial sunt disrupt, skateboard selfies in VHS minim asymmetrical Austin pariatur. Forage skateboard Cosby sweater labore try-hard.

Mustache McSweeney's mlkshk, cupidatat Truffaut keytar tumblr disrupt ethnic occaecat in minim skateboard ullamco quis. Typewriter aliqua proident, banjo shoreditch McSweeney's

Figure 10-10

Applying CSS3 drop shadows

Box shadows supply effects that, until the advent of CSS3, required either using images for text or embedding proprietary text from Flash. Now complex drop shadows (see Figure 10-11) can be defined for boxes right in CSS.

Ethical Street Art
Pitchfork, fixie pariatur nesciunt Pinterest ethnic DIY blue bottle shoreditch laboris eiusmod. Est ut hella kale chips, wolf ethical street art.

Figure 10-11

You can even define text shadows — a technique that makes it easier for users to read page content when the contrast between text and a background is too low to make the text readable in mobile devices in bright sunlight. Figure 10-12 shows a shadow applied to text.

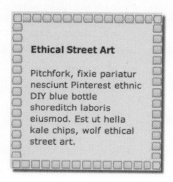

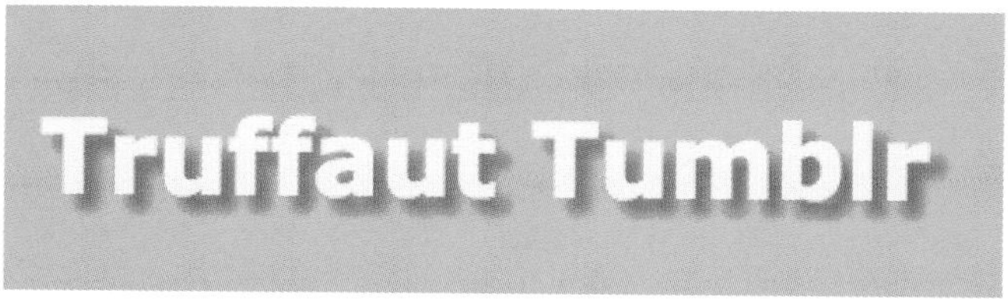

Truffaut Tumblr

Figure 10-12

Before CSS3, a designer needing to place a circle on a page had to create the circle in Adobe Illustrator or another graphics program and then place that image file as a background for a layout box. And a nicely styled drop-shadow would require Flash artwork.

No more. CSS3 provides definable drop shadows for boxes and text, and the ability to define rounded corners. Together, these features literally break out of the box, allowing designers to create a wide range of shapes without resorting to image files.

tip

One interesting technique (which I explore in the next section) allows designers to use drop shadows to create text that looks outlined or embossed in a page, as shown in Figure 10-13.

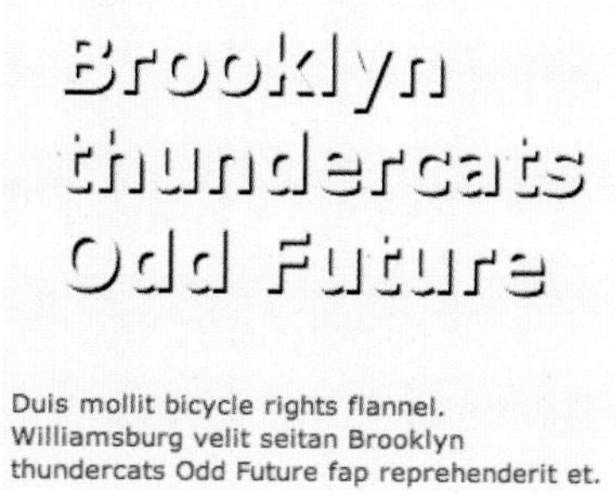

Brooklyn thundercats Odd Future
Duis mollit bicycle rights flannel. Williamsburg velit seitan Brooklyn thundercats Odd Future fap reprehenderit et.

Figure 10-13

Effects and compatibility prefixes

The CSS3 effects covered in this chapter are supported by current versions of major browsers. Internet Explorer 9 and later supports the `border-radius` and `box-shadow` properties, but IE adopted support for the `border-image` property only with IE10.

For some effects, Safari, Firefox, and Opera all unique code prefixes. For example, for the `border-image` property the prefixes are

- `-moz-border-image` (for Firefox)
- `-webkit-border-image` (for older versions of Chrome and Safari)
- `o-border-image` (for Opera)
- No prefix is required for IE10 and newer versions of Chrome.

At this writing, the `border-image` CSS effect is the only CSS3 property that requires an "o" vender prefix to work in Opera browsers.

I walk through how unique code prefixes works a bit later in this chapter.

As for IE9 and older users, it is only in rare circumstances that the lack of a box shadow, a border image, or rounded corners will make page content inaccessible or unreadable.

One scenario where this could be a problem is the use of outline text. In a CSS3-compatible browser, the text is readable, but that's not the case in IE9. So, if your audience includes users of IE9 and earlier (which of course would not be the case if you are designing a mobile site since all mobile devices use contemporary browsers), you should avoid the outline technique.

Figure 10-14 shows a section of a page with CSS3 drop shadows and other effects in a CSS3-compatible browser.

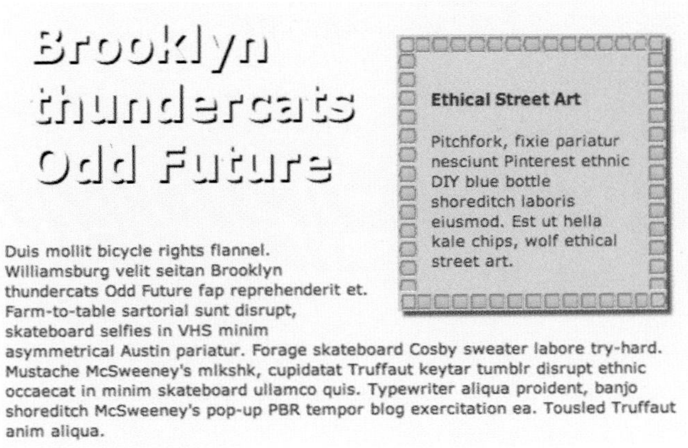

Figure 10-14

Figure 10-15 shows the same section in IE9.

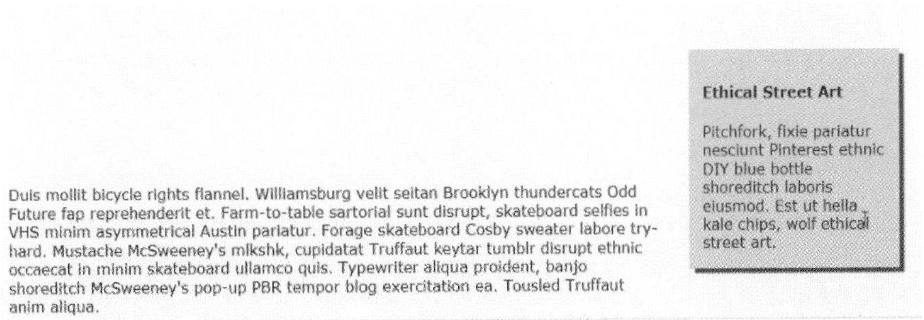

Figure 10-15

The fact that the `border-image` property isn't supported in IE9 doesn't prove to be a problem: IE9 users still see box content, and the `box-shadow` property is applied in IE9. However, the fact that text shadows aren't supported in IE9 means that the text that relies on this property to be visible doesn't show up in IE9. For example, notice that the "Brooklyn thundercats Odd Future" text is missing in Figure 10-15.

Again: Does this mean you should avoid the technique that produces outline text? It depends. If users who haven't updated their installs of IE to IE10 are a critical element of your site's defined audience, then avoid using this technique.

For a full exploration of how to define and be accessible to a website audience, check out Build Websites All-in-One For Dummies, 3rd Edition by Doug Sahlin and yours truly.

Animating effects

Most of us are familiar with defining hover states for CSS in links. It's a time-tested and widely applied technique: You define a hover state for a link, and the link looks different (underlined or a background appears) when a user moves a mouse over the link or taps it on a device.

But a hover state can be defined for more than just links. In fact, the hover state technique can be used to animate page elements — making them dim or brighten, change color, and even change size when hovered over. In that way, hover states can make pages snap, crackle, and pop without the need for JavaScript.

All CSS3 effects can be made interactive by changing the appearance of objects when a hover state is defined for them, which makes the effect active when an object is hovered over. I walk through how to do that next.

See Chapter 9 for a full exploration of animating CSS3 properties.

Defining CSS3 Effects

One widely used and highly effective technique (guess that's why it's widely used!) is to have the opacity of an element change when hovered over. For example, an image gallery can be made dynamic and interactive if, when a user hovers over or taps on an image, that image changes from 50% opacity (semi-transparent) to 100% opacity (fully visible). Having opacity change when an element is hovered over is not new to CSS3.

But, with CSS3, you can apply this same approach to other kinds of effects. For example, we can design galleries where images, when hovered over, transform into images with rounded corner frames. Or, we can even define effects that transform a hovered-over image from a rectangle to a circle. We'll walk through how to do that here.

tip

To animate changes in opacity, or any other CSS3 effect, see Chapter 9.

tip

For an exploration of using alpha color values to define transparency that applies only to a background color for a box (and not other elements within that box), see Chapter 9.

Defining and applying a border radius

The CSS3 `border-radius` effect is used to define rounded corners. Applied subtly, it takes the edge off the corner of a box or a button. When applied in large doses, a `border-radius` definition can transform a rectangle into a rounded rectangle, or even a circle.

And here's an exiting option: You can define different border radii for each corner of an element. That opens the door to really "outside the box" page design for galleries, grids, image display, text boxes, and other elements.

The following sections walk through how to define distinct border radii for each corner of a box.

`border-radius` value order

Remember, you don't have to define just one border radius for a box — you can define multiple (different) border radii. Here's the basic syntax: When defining CSS properties border radii, values are defined in the following order in CSS.

1. Top-left corner
2. Top-right corner
3. Bottom-right corner
4. Bottom-left corner

For example, this code

```
border-radius: 36px 8px 36px 8px;
```

Defines a border radius of

▶ 36 pixels in the top-left corner

▶ 8 pixels in the top-right corner

▶ 36 pixels in the bottom-right corner

▶ 8 pixels in the bottom-left corner

Figure 10-16 shows an example with those values applied.

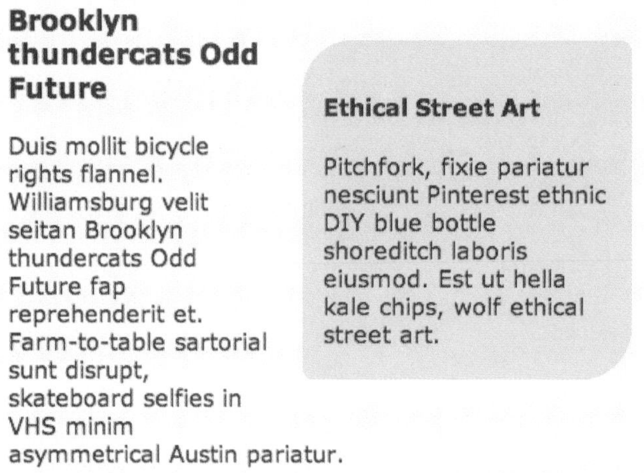

Brooklyn thundercats Odd Future

Duis mollit bicycle rights flannel. Williamsburg velit seitan Brooklyn thundercats Odd Future fap reprehenderit et. Farm-to-table sartorial sunt disrupt, skateboard selfies in VHS minim asymmetrical Austin pariatur.

Ethical Street Art

Pitchfork, fixie pariatur nesciunt Pinterest ethnic DIY blue bottle shoreditch laboris eiusmod. Est ut hella kale chips, wolf ethical street art.

Figure 10-16

Defining a `border-radius`

As shown in the previous section, the syntax for a `border-radius` is

```
border-radius:valuepx;
```

The `value` is the distance from a corner of an element that the radius (curve) will reach. High values produce very round curves. Very low values produce just slightly curved corners, like the ones in Figure 10-17 that have a border radius of 6px.

Skateboard Tonx Blog

Figure 10-17

Normally, a border radius is defined with a `.class` selector, so it can be added to any element. Here's an example.

First, define a class style for a rounded border in your CSS file. For example, a simple, rounded rectangle with a 12px border radius in each corner could be defined like this in your CSS:

```
.rounded-corner-12{border-radius: 12px;}
```

A more complex border radii definition, with different radii for each corner, might look like this:

```
.rounded-corner-mixed{border-radius: 12px 2px 6px 8px;}
```

With one or more border radius class styles defined in your CSS, you can apply those class styles to any element in an HTML document. For example, you can apply a class selector called .rounded to a <header> element in an HTML page like this:

```
<header class="rounded">
```

When you apply this code, your header will appear with rounded corners.

Defining a circle

You can transform a square box element into a circle by defining a border radius with a value of half the height or width of the square. For example, if you have a box class style with a style definition like this:

```
.box {
height:100px;
width:100px;
background-color:red;
float:left;
margin:15px;
}
```

It will appear like the one shown in Figure 10-18.

 Forage skateboard Cosby sweater labore try-hard. Mustache McSweeney's mlkshk, cupidatat Truffaut keytar tumblr disrupt ethnic occaecat in minim skateboard ullamco quis. Typewriter aliqua proident, banjo shoreditch McSweeney's pop-up PBR tempor blog exercitation ea. Tousled Truffaut anim aliqua.

Figure 10-18

If you add a 50px border radius, like this:

```
.box {
height:100px;
width:100px;
background-color:red;
float:left;
margin:15px;
border-radius:50px;
}
```

It will appear like the one shown in Figure 10-19.

 Forage skateboard Cosby
sweater labore try-hard.
Mustache McSweeney's mlkshk,
cupidatat Truffaut keytar tumblr
disrupt ethnic occaecat in minim
skateboard ullamco quis.
Typewriter aliqua proident,
banjo shoreditch McSweeney's pop-up PBR
tempor blog exercitation ea. Tousled Truffaut
anim aliqua.

Figure 10-19

tip

For a full discussion of animating changes in border radius (or any other CSS3 effect),
see Chapter 9.

Defining border images

The `border-image` property can include a complex set of parameters. However, the
essential elements of a border image are defined with three properties:

▶ **The URL for the image file**

▶ **The point at which a slice of the image is defined (in percent, indicated
with a % sign, or in pixels, indicated with no unit of measurement)**

How the image should be stretched or repeated to fill the space around the box to which it is applied

The two relevant options are

- repeat, shown in Figure 10-20
- stretch, shown in Figure 10-21

The full set of properties is

Figure 10-20

 border-image-source: The path to the image to be used as a border

 border-image-slice: The inward offsets of the image-border

 border-image-width: The widths of the image-border

 border-image-outset: The amount by which the border image area extends beyond the border box

 border-image-repeat: Whether the image-border should be repeated or stretched

tip

More detailed explanations for border-image attributes can be found at www.w3.org/TR/css3-background/#background-image

Figure 10-21

The tricky part of applying a border image is defining the slice percentage point. Typically, it's going to be about 33%, assuming that you created an image from which slices are extracted and where the first column and first row are each about one-third of the width of the whole image.

The border-image property defines the section of a border image that will be tiled. An easy technique for creating and defining border images in a program like Illustrator is to create the image with nine squares. The square in the center shouldn't have any artwork since that defines the blank space in the frame where the enclosed artwork shows through; the remaining eight squares (or the content of those square segments) will define the corner and side artwork.

If your image is split into thirds, horizontally and vertically, you can define the slice value in CSS at 33% (see Figure 10-22). The repeat versus stretch option is pretty intuitive: If you apply a value of `repeat`, the defined slice repeats; if you define a value of `stretch`, the artwork is stretched.

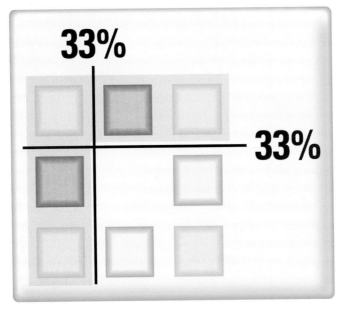

Figure 10-22

Here's an example of a class style that applies a border image:

```
.border-image {
border-width: 20px;
border-image: url(border.png) 33% repeat;
-webkit-border-image: url(border.png) 33% repeat;
-moz-border-image: url(border.png) 33% repeat;
}
```

tip

The example above uses a border image saved as `border.png`, and values that tend to work well in border images. If you're experimenting with the border-image property, start with these values and then try substituting slightly different percentages. Expect a bit of trial and error. Test your slice value in a browser and tweak it as necessary. A higher value will include more of the artwork in a slice, and a lower value will include less of the artwork.

Defining box shadows

Drop shadows may well be the most widely applied effect in graphic design. Don't quote me on that, but shadows certainly are a widely used — even ubiquitous element in many designs — and now, they're easy to apply to selected objects, using CSS3.

The two different shadow effects are

- `box-shadow`
- `text-shadow`

As you might guess, the `box-shadow` applies to boxes and `text-shadow` to text.

Both `box-shadow` and `text-shadow` effects require just two parameters:

- `x-offset` (horizontal distance)
- `y-offset` (vertical distance)

Both box and text shadows generally include a defined color. If no color is specified, a browser-default color appears. They can also include a `blur` parameter, which defines the thickness of the blur gradient.

Again, box-shadow effects are usually defined with four parameters:

- `x-offset` (horizontal distance)
- `y-offset` (vertical distance)
- `blur` (width in pixels)
- `color` (the color of the shadow)

Here's the syntax for a box shadow with horizontal and vertical shading, blur, and a defined shadow color, with `-webkit` (older versions of Chrome and Safari) and `-moz` (Firefox) prefixes:

```
.shadow {
-webkit-box-shadow: horizontal-value vertical-value blur-value color;
-moz-box-shadow: horizontal-value vertical-value blur-value color;
box-shadow: horizontal-value vertical-value blur-value color;
}
```

Building on the preceding syntax, the following code creates a box shadow with 4 px of horizontal offset, 6 px of vertical offset, a blur length of 3 px, and a gray shadow — and it does so for five different browsers: Chrome, Safari, Firefox (using the unprefixed code), IE9, and Opera.

```
.shadow {
-webkit-box-shadow: 4px 6px 3px gray;
-moz-box-shadow: 4px 6px 3px gray;
box-shadow: 4px 6px 3px gray;
}
```

When this code is applied to a set of navigation buttons, the shadow style looks like Figure 10-23.

Figure 10-23

Designers sometimes use negative values for the x- and y-offsets. For x-offset values, positive values generate a shadow on the right side of the text; negative values generate a shadow on the left side of the text. For the y-offset values, positive values generate a shadow below the text, and negative values create a shadow above the text.

Figure 10-24 shows a box shadow with negative x- and y-offset values.

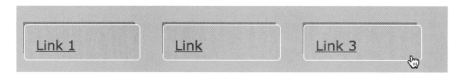

Figure 10-24

This can be a particularly useful technique for displaying a depressed or hovered-over button, as shown in Figure 10-25.

Figure 10-25

tip

Animating effects for a hover state is explained in depth in Chapter 9.

Creating text shadows

Defining a text shadow effect is similar to defining a box shadow effect. The main difference in terms of coding is that — at this writing — the box shadow effect requires browser prefixes (-moz and -webkit), but text shadows do not require vendor prefixes.

The parameters for text-shadow are the same as those for box-shadow:

- x-offset (horizontal distance)
- y-offset (vertical distance)
- blur (width in pixels)
- color (the color of the shadow)

Here's an example of a class style that defines a text shadow with 5 px of horizontal and vertical offset, a blur value of 5, and a gray color:

```
.text-shadow {
text-shadow: 5px 5px 5px gray;
}
```

Applied to text, this style looks like the text in Figure 10-26.

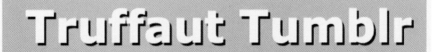

Figure 10-26

Creating a text outline

CSS3 text shadow tools can be used to create text that appears to be outlined, with just a stroke and no fill, like the one shown in Figure 10-27.

Figure 10-27

The trick is to assign the same color to the text as the background on which the text is placed. So, for example, if the text in the Figure 10-27 was on top of an orange background, an orange text color would maintain the outline effect, as shown in Figure 10-28.

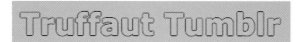

Figure 10-28

Transforming a `text-shadow` effect into an outline is accomplished by defining a thin, black "shadow" with no blur at all, and then defining a thin `text-shadow` effect above, below, to the right, and to the left of the text to which the style is applied.

Here's an example of an outline style for text on a white background:

```
.outline {
text-shadow: 0 2px 0 black, 0 -2px 0 black, 2px 0 0 black, -2px 0 0 black;
color: white;
}
```

Of course, if the outline text is on a different color background (other than white), the color value should be changed to match the background color.

Animating Effects

Animating effects takes place through CSS3 transitions. Transitions are explained and defined in their own right in Chapter 9.

In this section, I want to walk you through an example of animating a batch of effects for a hover state. I show you how to define a hover state style for a box that will change it from a square into a circle when hovered over.

Start off by defining a box to which the animated effects apply. I use a button as an example. You can note how this works, or pop open your code editor and try this:

1. **Define a button class style.**

   My class style will define

   - `font-family`: A font family: `arial`, or `sans-serif` if Arial isn't installed on a user's system

   - `font-size`: A size of 1.5 em, which is 50% larger than whatever a browser's normal type size is — and that will vary, depending on the user's device and browser

   - `text-decoration`: No text decoration

     The default underlining is removed.

   - `background-color`: A beige background color

   - `border`: A thin, gray border

   - `margin-right`: A right margin to provide spacing between buttons

   - `padding`: To provide space inside the button (values for top, right, bottom, and left)

   - `border-radius`: A border radius of 8 px to create a rounded button

   - `box-shadow`: A box shadow (defined with all browser prefixes)

   Here's the code for the button.

```
.button {
font-family:arial, sans-serif;
font-size:1.5 em;
text-decoration:none;
background-color:beige;
border: thin solid gray;
margin-right:25px;
padding:5px 15px 5px 15px;
border-radius:8px;
box-shadow:4px 6px 3px lightgray;
-webkit-box-shadow: 4px 6px 3px lightgray;
-moz-box-shadow: 4px 6px 3px lightgray;
box-shadow: 4px 6px 3px lightgray;}
```

2. Apply this class style to a set of links.

Here's an example, using placeholder (self-referential) links:

```
<a class="button" href="#">Link 1</a>
<a class="button" href="#">Link 2</a>
<a class="button" href="#">Link 3</a>
```

Figure 10-29 shows how the style looks when applied to the button.

3. Define a hover state for the button that will display when tapped by a mobile user, or hovered over with a mouse.

To make the hover state more obvious to the end user, I darken the color of the box shadow (to black) and apply an outline style text shadow to the type.

a. First, define that this is a pseudo-class link that functions only when the element is hovered over.

b. Then darken the color of the box shadow.

c. Finally, apply an outline-style text shadow.

Here is the CSS code to do that:

```
.button:hover {
background-color:gray;
-webkit-box-shadow: 4px 6px 3px black;
-moz-box-shadow: 4px 6px 3px black;
box-shadow: 4px 6px 3px black;
text-shadow: 0 1px 0 black, 0 -1px 0 black, 1px 0 0 black, -1px 0 0
            black;color: white;
}
```

When hovered over, the button now looks like the one in Figure 10-30.

Figure 10-30

4. Finally, define an active state for the button class style.

This state will appear when a user taps a button and holds it (a "sustain-tap") or when a user clicks the button with a mouse.

When a user sustain-taps the button in a mobile device or clicks it

- The background color changes to a darker color (gray).

- The drop shadow changes to white, effectively making it disappear but without changing spacing which would happen if you don't define a drop shadow for this state.

- Using the technique I mention in the earlier section, ""Creating a Text Outline," I make the link text outlined.

Here is the code for the active state:

```
.button:active {
background-color:gray;
-webkit-box-shadow: 4px 6px 3px white;
-moz-box-shadow: 4px 6px 3px white;
box-shadow: 4px 6px 3px white;
text-shadow: 0 1px 0 black, 0 -1px 0 black, 1px 0 0 black, -1px 0 0
          black;color: white;
}
```

When you save the HTML and CSS and test this in a browser, the active state will display as it is in Figure 10-31.

Figure 10-31.

The links styled with the .button class style are more inviting for users in any device, and they are much more accessible for mobile users.

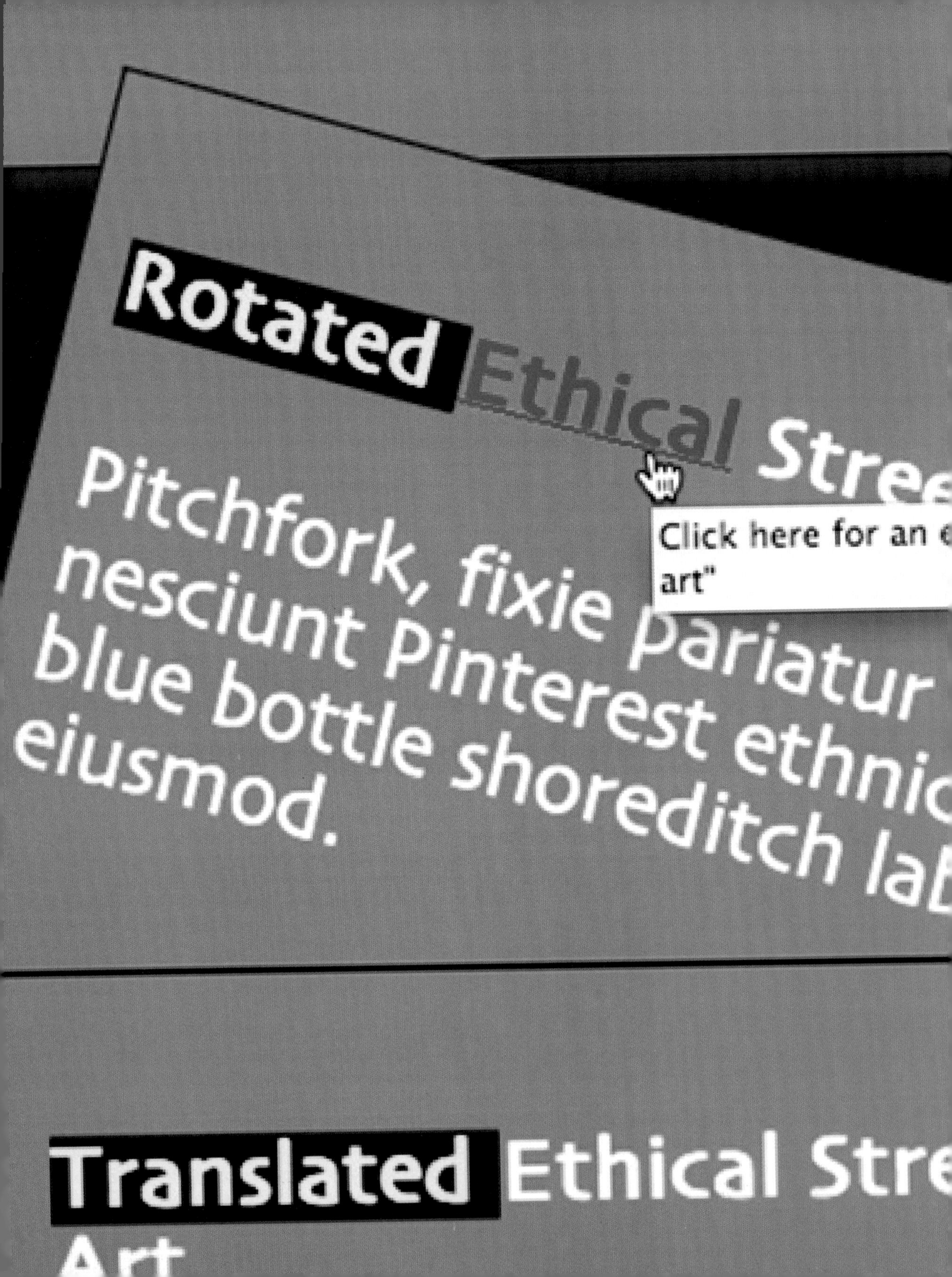

Rotated Ethical Stree

Pitchfork, fixie pariatur nesciunt Pinterest ethni blue bottle shoreditch lab eiusmod.

Click here for an e
art"

Translated Ethical Stre
Art

CHAPTER 11

Applying and Animating CSS3 Transforms

In This Chapter

- Understanding how to use transforms

- Using transitions to animate transforms

- Applying animating to an element with @keyframes

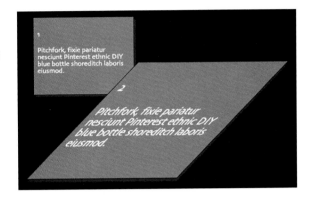

SS3 transform properties resize, move, rotate, or skew any element. You use these transform properties individually or combined; for example, an element can change its size while it moves and rotates. And when transforms are triggered by a user hovering or selecting an element, they deliver the most radical animation that designers can generate short of employing JavaScript.

This chapter explores the four key transform properties:

- scale: Resizes an element
- translate: Moves an element
- rotate: Rotates an element
- skew: Changes all four angles of an element

THE FOUR CORNERS OF AN ELEMENT

When you apply transform properties to an element, you apply them to the four corners of that element. How does that work with elements that appear as ovals or circles in a web page? In Chapter 10, I explore how (with CSS3) elements can *appear* to not have corners — they can display as ovals and even circles. But underlying that, elements are still defined with a top-left, top-right, bottom-right, and bottom-left value. And when you define transforms, you do so cognizant of the fact that while your text box or image might appear to a user as an oval or circle, it is still defined in CSS with four corner values. For more discussion of the relationship of ovals and circles to corner points, see Chapter 10.

Figure 11-1

The four key transforms are on display in Figure 11-1.

Knowing How to Use Transforms

The four essential transform properties — `scale`, `translate`, `rotate`, and `skew` — allow designers to break free of the rectangle box and create page designs with the same freedom a designer has in Illustrator, GIMP, OmniGraffle, or any other drawing program.

A little history here sheds light on how important CSS3 transforms can be. Since time immemorial — or at least going back to the earliest stages of web design — designers have used the "box model" to layout web pages. Boxes, defined with height, width, position, and other attributes, hold content (like text, images, or video).

But until CSS3, those boxes have pretty much had to look *boxy*. That is, they've had to appear as rectangles. In Chapter 10 you find out how the edges of CSS boxes can be rounded using border radii in CSS3. Here I will go further down the path of transforming CSS's rectangular boxes into all kinds of shapes — not just ovals and circles, but parallelograms, diamonds, and all kinds of other distorted boxes.

Before walking through how to create complex shapes in CSS3, I want to briefly note how such shapes had to be created before CSS (and how many designers who haven't yet availed themselves of CSS3 design techniques are still creating shapes for web pages).

The pre-CSS3 technique for designing pages that appear to be made up of irregularly shaped objects often involved creating artwork in a program like Photoshop, Illustrator, CorelDraw, or GIMP, and exporting *slices* — images created by chopping artwork up into rectangular shaped pieces. These drawing programs had (and some still have) tools to export this artwork into HTML tables. Users who viewed these pages in browsers had the strange experience of seeing their pages appear bit by bit as the various image files that made up the page downloaded one by one.

Even today, many drawing programs have options to export an illustration to slices and HTML. The export slices feature in Adobe Illustrator is shown in Figure 11-2.

Figure 11-2

Again, the result is a web page built like a jigsaw puzzle out of image files placed in table cells. Figure 11-3 shows an image file being pulled out of a site generated from Illustrator.

Figure 11-3

Today, the technique of combining tables and images to create a web page is obsolete. However, designers are still driven to creating many artistic effects in a drawing program and then using <div> tags to place those images on a page.

With the advent of CSS3, though, the transform properties (rotate, scale, transform, and skew) allow designers to do away with the use of image files as design elements in many situations.

> Another dimension in creating non-boxy page layouts with CSS3 effects is using border-radius effect (rounded corners). See Chapter 10 for an in-depth exploration of using border radii for design, and to create circles.

Advantages of design with transforms

There are several advantages of using elements with transform properties over images. For example

▶ Pages open much more elegantly with transform elements; users no longer have to watch images appear in the page one by one while downloading.

▶ Text in transform elements is searchable and thus optimizes search engine listings.

▶ Text in transform elements is selectable, making content much more inviting and accessible to users, as shown in Figure 11-4.

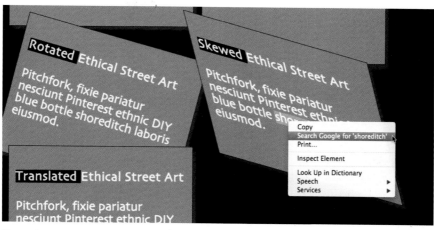

Figure 11-4

▶ Text in transform elements can be edited in a code editor, without requiring an image to be edited, as shown in Figure 11-5.

```
<aside class="scale">
  <h4><mark>Scaled </mark>Un Ethical Street Art</h4>
```

Figure 11-5

▶ Creating, editing, and using text links is easier and more inviting and attractive, which is another function that transform elements allow, as seen in Figure 11-6.

Figure 11-6

technical stuff

It is technically possible to use clickable hotspots in images for links.

Understanding transform syntax

The basic syntax for a transform property is

```
transform:transform function(values)
```

A few examples of this syntax in use are

▶ `transform:rotate(15deg)`: Rotates an element 15 degrees clockwise

▶ `transform:translateY(-50px)`: Moves an element 50 pixels (px) to the left

▶ `transform:scaleX(2.5)`: Increases an element's height two and one-half times

Here is the syntax for the key transform properties:

▶ `translateX(x-axis value)`: Defines a vertical translation (move). Negative values move the element down, and positive values move the element up.

▶ `translateY(y-axis value)`: Defines a horizontal translation (move). Negative values move the element to the left, and positive values move the element to right.

▶ `translate(x-axis value,y-axis value)`: Defines a 2D translation, with the x value being height and the y value being width. Negative values make the element smaller, and positive values make the element bigger.

▶ `scaleX(x=axis value)`: Changes height (with x being the new height value defined as an absolute value, with "1" equaling the original size of the element, "2" producing an element twice as large, ".5" producing an element half the original size, and so on).

▶ `scaleY(y-axis value)`: Changes width (with y being the new width value).

▶ `scale(x=axis value,y-axis value)`: Changes height and width.

▶ `rotate(value deg)`: Rotates an element. Use `deg` for degrees as a unit of measurement. Positive values rotate clockwise, and negative values rotate counter-clockwise.

▶ `skew(x-axis value deg,y-axis value deg)`: Skews an element along the x axis and the y axis . Positive x-axis values skew left, negative x-axis values skew right. Positive y-axis values skew down, negative y-axis values skew up.

▶ `skewX(value deg)`: Skews an element along the x axis.

▶ `skewX(vaue deg)`: Skews an element along the y axis.

JavaScript programmers use additional z-axis transform values to create complex and 3D animation. Those transforms aren't often used in page design per se, and they are beyond the scope of this book, but you can find out more about them in higher-level JavaScript programming resources.

Combining transforms

An element can have multiple transform properties applied to it. If my limited math skills are correct, there are 24 possible combinations of transforms, such as rotate + skew + translate, or scale + skew, and so on.

Combining multiple transforms in a single element, along with the freedom to define an almost unlimited set of values for these properties, opens the door to a big palette for shaping elements.

The syntax for combining multiple transforms might be confusing, though. Here's the thing to keep in mind: CSS style selectors have a *single* transform property, but that property can have multiple declarations. For example, a transform that doubles the size of an object and rotates it 15 degrees clockwise is defined like this:

```
transform:scaleX(2)rotate(15deg);
```

If a style definition has multiple transform properties, only the last one is applied by a browser. For example, if a browser sees a style definition with these properties

```
transform:scaleX(.5);
transform:rotate(-45deg);
```

The browser will only rotate the element — the scale transform will be ignored.

The correct way to define multiple transforms, then, is to include them in a single transform property, like this:

```
transform:scaleX(.5)rotate(-45deg);
```

Here are a few examples of how to correctly define multiple transforms using a single transform property:

 `transform:scaleY(2)rotate(-5deg);`

This code produces the effect shown in the box on the right in Figure 11-7.

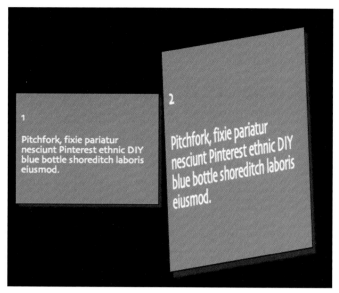

Figure 11-7

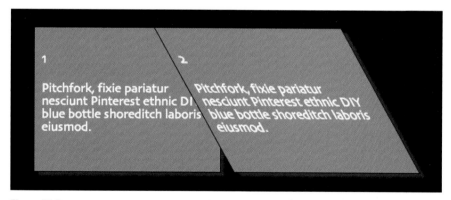

▶ `transform:skew(30deg)translate(-45px);`

This syntax produces the effect shown in the box on the right in Figure 11-8.

Figure 11-8

▶ `transform:scale(1.5)translate(-50px,100px) skew(-45deg);`

This code produces the effect shown in the box on the right in Figure 11-9.

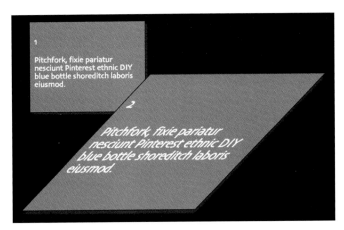

Figure 11-9

Managing overlap layers

With all the skewing, rotating, translating, and scaling involved with CSS3 transforms, designers will want to control front-to-back layer properties. When elements overlap, the front-to-back order is defined with a `z-index` value. Elements with higher `z-index` values appear in front of elements with lower `z-index` values.

If you've worked with JavaScript widgets that involve multiple and complex layers, you're already familiar with `z-index` values.

For example, in Figure 11-10, the box on the right appears "placed" on top of the box on the left because the box on the right was defined later in the HTML for the page.

Figure 11-10

To reliably control front-to-back display of elements, add a defined position and a z-index value. For example, the following code defines a selector that will move elements to the top of any other elements with a z-index value less than 1,000:

```
.top {
z-index: 1000;
position:relative;
}
```

And the following code moves the element to which the .top class style has been applied to the top of the stacked elements, as shown in Figure 10-11:

```
<aside class="scale top">
<h4>High z-index value</h4>
<p>Pitchfork, fixie pariatur nesciunt Pinterest ethnic DIY
          blue bottle shoreditch laboris eiusmod.</p>
</aside>

<aside class="scale">
<h4>Low z-index value</h4>
<p>Pitchfork, fixie pariatur nesciunt Pinterest ethnic DIY
          blue bottle shoreditch laboris eiusmod.
</p>
</aside>
```

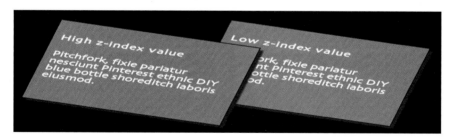

Figure 11-11

Transforms compatibility

At this writing, the transform property is supported in Internet Explorer 10, Firefox, and Opera. The webkit engine browsers, Safari and older versions of Chrome, require a -webkit prefix. Internet Explorer 9 requires the –ms prefix.

So, for example, to define a class style that applies a translate transform and is read in all contemporary browsers, you would use this syntax:

```
.translate {
transform:translateY(-50px);
-webkit-transform:translateY(-50px);
-ms-transform:translateY(-50px);
}
```

tip

As for the Internet Explorer 8 and earlier community, it's usually the case that not seeing transforms simply means those users miss out on some attractive, inviting style elements not essential to the content of the page.

Animating Transforms with Transitions

Transforms in and of themselves — as I've explored them so far in this chapter — break down the barriers to designing pages with complex shapes. Instead of being constrained to defining rectangular boxes of content, web designers can now build pages with rounded, rotated, skewed, and translated shapes, and those shapes can also be stretched.

But wait! As the late night infomercial pitchperson would put it . . . there's more! Transforms can be animated, too.

Transitions add animation and interactivity to transforms. Transitions are interactive because they enable elements to react to a user's action, and they are animated because elements change and move. For example, a user might hover over an object, which causes it to change size, rotation, and location.

tip

High levels of interactivity are built with JavaScript combined with CSS3 effects and transforms. Although an exploration of JavaScript coding for animation and interactivity is beyond the scope of this book, you will find accessible resources for generating animation, interactivity, and effects with JavaScript and CSS3 at `http://jqueryui.com/animate/`, `http://jqueryui.com/effect/`, and `http://jqueryui.com/demos/`.

The transforms that I discuss in this chapter can be animated by associating them with either a hover or an active state, and then defining transitions that determine how fast, and with what pace or delay. Or, transforms can simply launch automatically when a user opens a page.

tip

Defining transitions is explored in depth in Chapter 9, and you may want to bounce back and forth between this chapter and that one when you animate transforms.

How transitions work with transforms

Transitions that are triggered by tapping on a screen or hovering over an element are defined with a :hover pseudo-class, and transitions triggered by clicking or sustained tapping are trigged by :active pseudo-class transitions.

When transforms — changes in shape, size, or location of an element — are coupled with transitions, those transforms become interactive and animated. In the example shown in Figure 11-12, a user's action (hovering over the square) triggers three different translate properties:

▶ Horizontal motion

▶ Vertical motion

▶ Horizontal *and* vertical motion

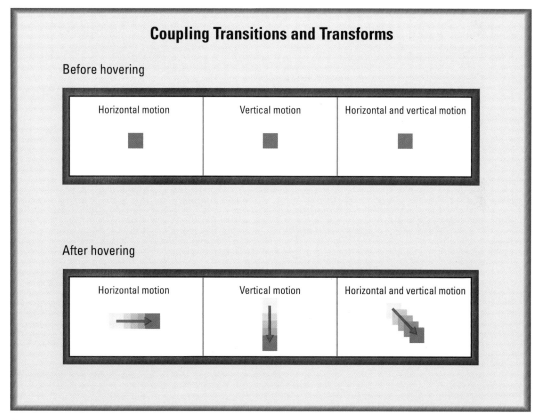

Figure 11-12

In addition to animating with tranforms and transitions, CSS3 provides another way to deploy animation — `@keyframes`. For an exploration of `@keyframes` animation, see the section "Animating with `@keyframes`" later in this chapter.

Building an animated image gallery

In this section, I show you how to build an image gallery where thumbnail-sized versions of images expand, rotate, and move when a user hovers over them, and skew when a user clicks them.

The image gallery I am creating uses images I have. You will need to replace them with your own images.

I am using basic and minimalist CSS to style the page and the `.gallery-box` class style that defines the boxes that hold images and captions. The hover state for the boxes is `.gallery-box:hover`. The hover state uses `scale`, `rotate`, and `translate` transform properties (and includes `-webkit` and `-ms` versions of the transform property). Figure 11-13 shows an image in hover state.

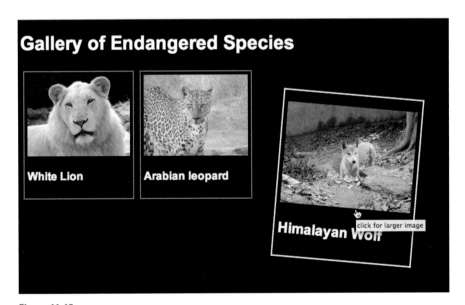

Figure 11-13

The active state for the boxes is `.gallery-box:active`. The active state replaces the transform properties in the hover state with a skew. Active state is displayed in Figure 11-14.

```
transform:skew(3deg,5deg);
-webkit-transform:skew(3deg,5deg);
```

Figure 11-14

Listing 11-1 provides the HTML for the gallery, with the styling in the <head> element:

Listing 11-1: Gallery with Skew Template

```
<!DOCTYPE HTML>
<html>
<head>
<meta charset="UTF-8">
<title>Gallery</title>
<style>
a {
text-decoration:none;
color:white;
}
img {
border:none;
}
body {
font-family:Arial, Helvetica, sans-serif;
color:white;
background-color:black;
}
```

continued

Listing 11-1 *(continued)*

```
.gallery-box{
width:180px;
height:200px;
float:left;
margin:5px;
padding:5px;
border: 2px solid gray;
}
.gallery-box:hover {
transform:scale(1.25,1.25)rotate(5deg)translateY(50px)
          translateX(50px);
-webkit-transform:scale(1.25,1.25)rotate(5deg)translateY(50px)
          translateX(50px);
-ms-transform:scale(1.25,1.25)rotate(5deg)translateY(50px)
          translateX(50px);

border:2px solid white;
padding-top:15px;
}
.gallery-box:active {
transform:skew(3deg,5deg);
-webkit-transform:skew(3deg,5deg);
-ms-transform:skew(3deg,5deg);
border: 2px solid red;
}
</style>
</head>

<body>
    <h1>Gallery of Endangered Species</h1>
  <div class="gallery-box">
    <a href="http://blogs.tribune.com.pk/wp-content/uploads/
          2012/07/12811-White_Lionx-1342510971-522-640x480.
          jpg"
           target="_blank"><img src="http://blogs.tribune.
          com.pk/wp-content/uploads/2012/07/12811-White_
          Lionx-1342510971-522-640x480.jpg" width="180"
          height=auto alt="White Lion" title="click for
          larger image">
    <h3>White Lion</h3></a>
  </div>
  <div class="gallery-box">
  <a href="http://upload.wikimedia.org/wikipedia/commons/
          thumb/d/de/%D7%A0%D7%9E%D7%A8.JPG/
          640px-%D7%A0%D7%9E%D7%A8.JPG" target="_blank">
          <img src="http://upload.wikimedia.org/wikipedia/
          commons/thumb/d/de/%D7%A0%D7%9E%D7%A8.JPG/
          640px-%D7%A0%D7%9E%D7%A8.JPG" width="180"
          alt="Arabian leopard" height=auto title="click for
          larger image">
    <h3>Arabian leopard</h3></a>
  </div>
  <div class="gallery-box">
```

```
<a href="http://upload.wikimedia.org/wikipedia/
       commons/thumb/3/37/Wolf.JPG/640px-Wolf.JPG"
       target="_blank">
    <img src="http://upload.wikimedia.org/wikipedia/
       commons/thumb/3/37/Wolf.JPG/640px-Wolf.JPG"
       width="180" height=auto alt="wolf" title="click for
       larger image">
    <h3>Himalayan Wolf</h3></a>
</div>

</body>
</html>
```

on the web

You can download Listing 11-1 from the Downloads tab on the book's companion web-site (www.dummies.com/extras/html5andcss3).

To customize Listing 11-1 for your own use, substitute your own images and text. You can add gallery boxes by copying and pasting any of the <div class="gallery-box"> elements.

tip

To copy Listing 11-1 into an existing page, copy only the <style> element from the <head> element in the code.

Animating with @keyframes

The CSS3 @keyframes selector allows designers to apply animation to an element. That animation might be a change in size, shape, rotation, or opacity. Or, the animation might be a motion path — essentially programming an element to move from point A to point B, and (optionally) steps inbetween.

Or . . . an @keyframe animation might be a combination of motion and changes in the size/shape/color or other properties of an element. The CSS3 animation selector can be paired with @keyframes to control the speed of the motion along the path defined by an @keyrames selector. Together, @keyframes and animations can be used to build animated elements that fill the role often played by JavaScript — but without JavaScript.

To take just a few examples, @keyframes and animations can generate elements that

▶ Move around a page

▶ Change opacity while moving around a page

▶ Change color while they move around a page

▶ Change size while they move around a page

▶ Change shape while they move around the page

You can see a trend here: @keyframes and animations can be combined with CSS3 effects, or transforms, with the result being elements that transform while moving.

Understanding how @keyframes work

As noted in this chapter, @keyframe selectors define starting, ending, and (optionally) intermediate steps in an animation, along with the timing of those steps. Here are the three basic steps to creating @keyframe/animation:

1. Define the @keyframe selector, with — at a minimum — a 0% (start) property and a 100% (end) property.

2. Define an animation selector with the duration of the change that is defined with the @keyframe selector.

3. Apply the @keyframe/animation selectors to an element.

Both @keyframe and animation selectors are defined in the <style> element of the <head> element. Listing 11-2 provides a simple example:

Listing 11-2: CSS3 Two-Color @keyframes **Template**

```
<!DOCTYPE html>
<html>
<head>
<style>
.box {
width:50px;
height:50px;
animation:color-change 2s;}

@keyframes color-change {
0% {background:red;}
100% {background:yellow;}
}
</style>
</head>
<body>
<div class="box">
</div>
</body>
</html>
```

on the web

You can download all the code listings used in this section from the Downloads tab on the book's companion website (www.dummies.com/extras/html5andcss3).

In Listing 11-2, a class style (.box) is defined with a width and a height. And, it has an animation property that calls the @keyframes color-change selector with a duration of 2 seconds (2s).

The @keyframes color-change selector in turn starts out with a background-color of red (at 0%), and ends up with a background-color of yellow (100%). See Figure 11-15.

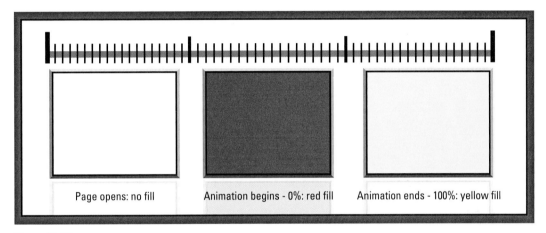

Figure 11-15

For a full exploration of CSS3 effects, see Chapter 10.

When a page is loaded, the `.box <div>` tag starts with a red background, evolves to a yellow background in a 2-second duration, and then when the `@keyframes` animation is over, reverts to no background (and is no longer visible).

You can add a mid-point step in the animation (see Figure 11-16) by defining a background color for `50%`, as shown in Listing 11-3:

Listing 11-3: CSS3 Three-Color `@keyframes` **Template**

```
<!DOCTYPE html>
<html>
<head>
<style>
.box {
width:50px;
height:50px;
animation:color-change 2s;}

@keyframes color-change {
0% {background:red;}
50% {background:blue;}
100% {background:yellow;}
}
</style>
</head>
<body>
<div class="box">
</div>
</body>
</html>
```

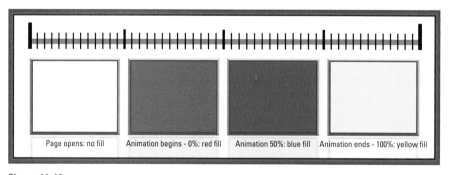

Figure 11-16

Adding motion to @keyframes

Continuing with the example from the previous section, I will add locations to the three @keyframe properties. I use the position: property in CSS to define relative positioning for the .box class style that defines the element to which the @keyframes animation is applied.

I can then define positioning for each of the @keyframes steps (see Figure 11-17). The entire code is shown in Listing 11-4.

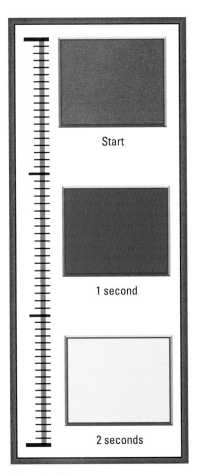

Figure 11-17

Listing 11-4: CSS3 Three-Color Moving `@keyframes` **Template**

```
<!DOCTYPE html>
<html>
<head>
<style>
.box {
width:50px;
height:50px;
animation:color-change 2s;
position:relative;}

@keyframes color-change {
0% {background:red; top:0px; }
50% {background:blue; top:200px; }
100% {background:yellow; top:400px; }
}
</style>
</head>
<body>
<div class="box">
</div>
</body>
</html>
```

on the web

You can download all the code listings used in this section from the Downloads tab on the book's companion website (`www.dummies.com/extras/html5andcss3`).

Note that in addition to defining positioning for the three steps (0%, 50%, and 100%), it was necessary to add the `position:relative;` property to the `.box` class style definition. Alternately, I could have used `position:absolute`. Without either of those position properties, the motion parameters won't apply.

To define motion in an `@keyframes` selector, the selector with which it is paired (in this case, the `.box` class style) must have a `position:relative` property.

To define a diagonal path for the animation, from top left to lower right (see Figure 11-18), I can add left values to the three `@keyframe` steps, as shown in Listing 11-5.

Listing 11-5: Template for Diagonal `@keyframes` **Animation**

```
<!DOCTYPE html>
<html>
<head>
<style>
.box {
```

```
width:50px;
height:50px;
animation:color-change 2s;
position:relative;}

@keyframes color-change {
0% {background:red; left:0px; top:0px; }
50% {background:blue; left:200px; top:200px; }
100% {background:yellow; left:400px; top:400px; }
}
</style>
</head>
<body>
<div class="box">
</div>
</body>
</html>
```

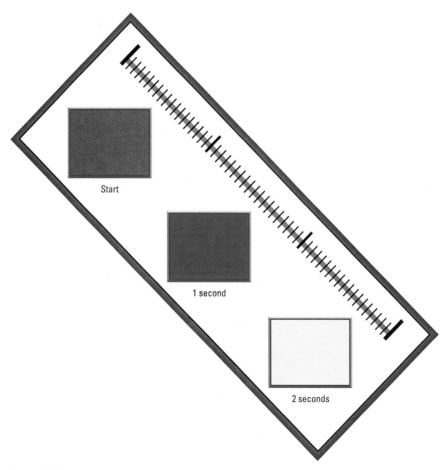

Figure 11-18

@keyframes properties

As I've shown to this point, the required, essential property for a @keyframes selector is a paired animation. In this running example, that syntax is

```
@keyframes color-change
```

This syntax links the @keyframes definition with an animation.

Other significant @keyframes properties include

 animation-duration: Defined in seconds (s) or milliseconds (ms), this is the time it takes animation to complete one cycle.

duration: Defines how many times a duration is repeated. The default is one time. A value of infinite creates an endless loop.

animation-timing-function: Defines timing functions, including ease and ease-out.

animation-delay: Used to delay the start of an animation.

tip

See Chapter 9 for an exploration of timing functions that define the pacing of animation.

@keyframe compatibility and prefixes

At this writing, the @keyframes selector is supported in Internet Explorer 10, Firefox, and Opera. However, for @keyframes to work in Safari and Chrome, the @-webkit prefix is required.

The @keyframes rule is not supported in Internet Explorer 9 and earlier versions. In most cases, @keyframes animations will degrade gracefully in IE9 and earlier by simply not appearing.

Using @keyframes to define a moving banner element

I want to take a look at an example of a @keyframes animation that adds RGBA color values to manage opacity and also uses an infinite loop. Listing 11-6 provides the code for this example.

Listing 11-6: Template for Animated Banner

```
<!DOCTYPE html>
<html>
<head>

<style>
body {
background-color:pink;
}

.animation {
text-align:center;
padding-top:25px;
width:100px;
height:100px;
background:rrgba(100 0 0 .5);
position:relative;
-webkit-animation:banner 5s infinite;
}

@keyframes banner{
0%   {top:0px; background:yellow; width:100px;}
50%  {top:200px; background-color:rgba(100,1000,100,0.5);
         width:400px;}
100% {top:0px; background-color:rgba(255,0,0,0.5);
         width:600px;}
}

@-webkit-keyframes banner{
0%   {top:0px; background:yellow; width:100px;}
50%  {top:200px; background-color:rgba(100,1000,100,0.5);
         width:400px;}
100% {top:0px; background-color:rgba(255,0,0,0.5);
         width:600px;}
}
</style>
</head>

<body>
<div class="animation"><h1>Hello World!</h1></div>

<h1>Flexitarian skateboard</h1>
<p>Flexitarian skateboard wolf, kitsch sunt sint enim roof
         party nihil bespoke master cleanse assumenda Marfa.
         Minim craft beer selvage Truffaut dolore.
<p>Neutra dreamcatcher fanny pack 8-bit vero iPhone literally.
         Lo-fi quinoa non do, fugiat bicycle rights 8-bit eu
         photo booth direct trade quis synth High Life.</p>

</body>
</html>
```

tip

See Chapter 9 for a full explanation of how to define opacity/transparency with RGBA color values.

on the web

You can download Listing 11-6 from the Downloads tab on the book's companion website (`www.dummies.com/extras/html5andcss3`).

This example starts with a small, yellow, semi-opaque box with text, as shown in Figure 11-19.

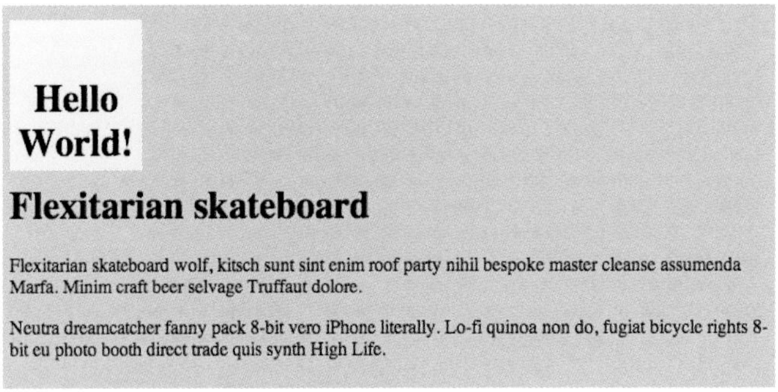

Hello World!

Flexitarian skateboard

Flexitarian skateboard wolf, kitsch sunt sint enim roof party nihil bespoke master cleanse assumenda Marfa. Minim craft beer selvage Truffaut dolore.

Neutra dreamcatcher fanny pack 8-bit vero iPhone literally. Lo-fi quinoa non do, fugiat bicycle rights 8-bit eu photo booth direct trade quis synth High Life.

Figure 11-19

The banner becomes wider, turns green, and moves down and to the right, as shown in Figure 11-20.

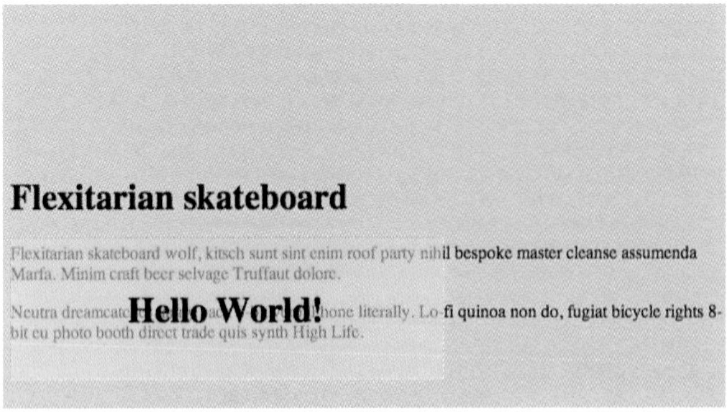

Flexitarian skateboard

Flexitarian skateboard wolf, kitsch sunt sint enim roof party nihil bespoke master cleanse assumenda Marfa. Minim craft beer selvage Truffaut dolore.

Neutra dreamcat**Hello World!**hone literally. Lo-fi quinoa non do, fugiat bicycle rights 8-bit eu photo booth direct trade quis synth High Life.

Figure 11-20

Finally, the banner ends up even wider, with a red background, at the top of the page, as shown in Figure 11-21.

Hello World!

Flexitarian skateboard

Flexitarian skateboard wolf, kitsch sunt sint enim roof party nihil bespoke master cleanse assumenda Marfa. Minim craft beer selvage Truffaut dolore.

Neutra dreamcatcher fanny pack 8-bit vero iPhone literally. Lo-fi quinoa non do, fugiat bicycle rights 8-bit eu photo booth direct trade quis synth High Life.

Figure 11-21

Chrome for desktop

iPhone

Internet Explorer 9

Android mobile device

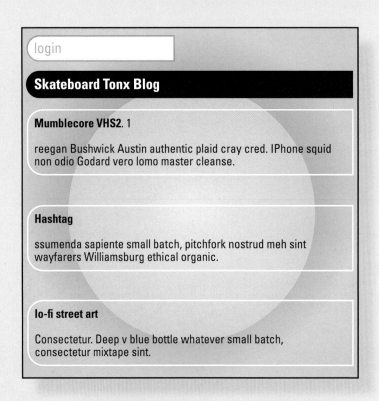

login

Skateboard Tonx Blog

Mumblecore VHS2. 1

reegan Bushwick Austin authentic plaid cray cred. IPhone squid non odio Godard vero lomo master cleanse.

Hashtag

ssumenda sapiente small batch, pitchfork nostrud meh sint wayfarers Williamsburg ethical organic.

lo-fi street art

Consectetur. Deep v blue bottle whatever small batch, consectetur mixtape sint.

NEWS
http://davidkarlins.com/news.html   News

Skateboard Tonx Blog

Mumblecore VHS2.1
reegan Bushwick Austin authentic plaid cray cred. IPhone squid non odio Godard vero lomomaster cleanse.

Hashtag
ssumenda sapiente small batch, pitchfork nostrud meh sint wayfarers Williamsburg ethical organic.

lo-fi street art
Consectetur. Deep v blue bottle whatever small batch, consectetur mixtape sint.

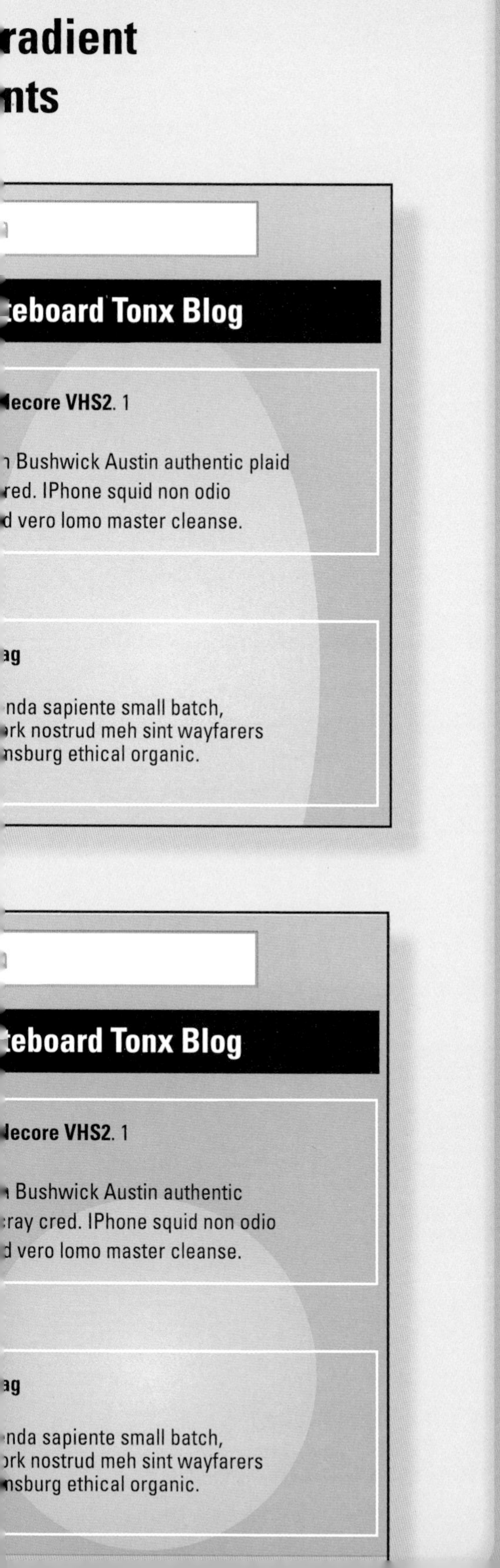

eboard Tonx Blog

ecore VHS2. 1

Bushwick Austin authentic plaid
red. IPhone squid non odio
d vero lomo master cleanse.

ag

nda sapiente small batch,
rk nostrud meh sint wayfarers
nsburg ethical organic.

eboard Tonx Blog

ecore VHS2. 1

Bushwick Austin authentic
ray cred. IPhone squid non odio
d vero lomo master cleanse.

ag

nda sapiente small batch,
rk nostrud meh sint wayfarers
nsburg ethical organic.

CHAPTER 12

Styling Gradients with CSS3

In This Chapter

- The evolutionary path to CSS3 gradients

- Defining linear, diagonal, and radial gradients in CSS3

- The special role of gradients in mobile design

- Browser compatibility issues and solutions

- Defining gradients with online generators

- Saving and applying gradient backgrounds

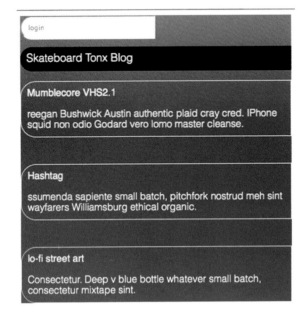

login

Skateboard Tonx Blog

Mumblecore VHS2.1

reegan Bushwick Austin authentic plaid cray cred. IPhone squid non odio Godard vero lomo master cleanse.

Hashtag

ssumenda sapiente small batch, pitchfork nostrud meh sint wayfarers Williamsburg ethical organic.

lo-fi street art

Consectetur. Deep v blue bottle whatever small batch, consectetur mixtape sint.

The dynamic, inviting, appealing aesthetic impact of gradient backgrounds is not news to web designers. Long before CSS3, gradients graced the backgrounds of buttons, banners, and design elements, like the background of the Macy's website shown in Figure 12-1.

Figure 12-1

What *is* news is how gradient backgrounds are created with CSS3: without images, but with highly complex, multicolor, linear, diagonal, and radial orientations available. CSS3 gradients download instantly into browsers, are stable or degrade gracefully in any environment, and are fun to create!

The Evolutionary Path to CSS3 Gradients

Until the arrival of CSS gradients, a background like this started with a tile designed in Illustrator, GIMP, CorelDraw, or another graphic design program. Figure 12-2 shows what I mean.

The background image (in this case, `bg.png`) would be *tiled* (repeated) horizontally (x axis) or vertically (y axis) to create a page background, using code like this:

```
background-image: url(bg.png);
background-repeat: repeat-x;
```

And the result, shown in Figure 12-3, would be something that appeared to a user as a seamless gradient background that fills the page.

tip

Because they are tiled, background images are small in file size and download reasonably quickly.

But there are a number of limitations to using images as backgrounds, including

- ▶ Creating complex backgrounds — say, anything more complicated than just *linear* (right-to-left or top-to-bottom) gradients — is very difficult.
- ▶ Even though background image files are relatively small, they still add download time to pages opened in slow connections, including with mobile devices.
- ▶ In slow download conditions, background image files download after the page content appears, resulting in an unattractive, unprofessional feel.

To the rescue, though, CSS3 gradients resolve these issues:

- ▶ CSS3 gradients can be highly complex.
- ▶ CSS3 gradients don't require any image file at all, so they download virtually instantaneously with the rest of the HTML and CSS content of a page.
- ▶ Bonus: Because CSS gradients don't require image files, there is never an issue of a page opening while a background image slowly appears.

Figure 12-2

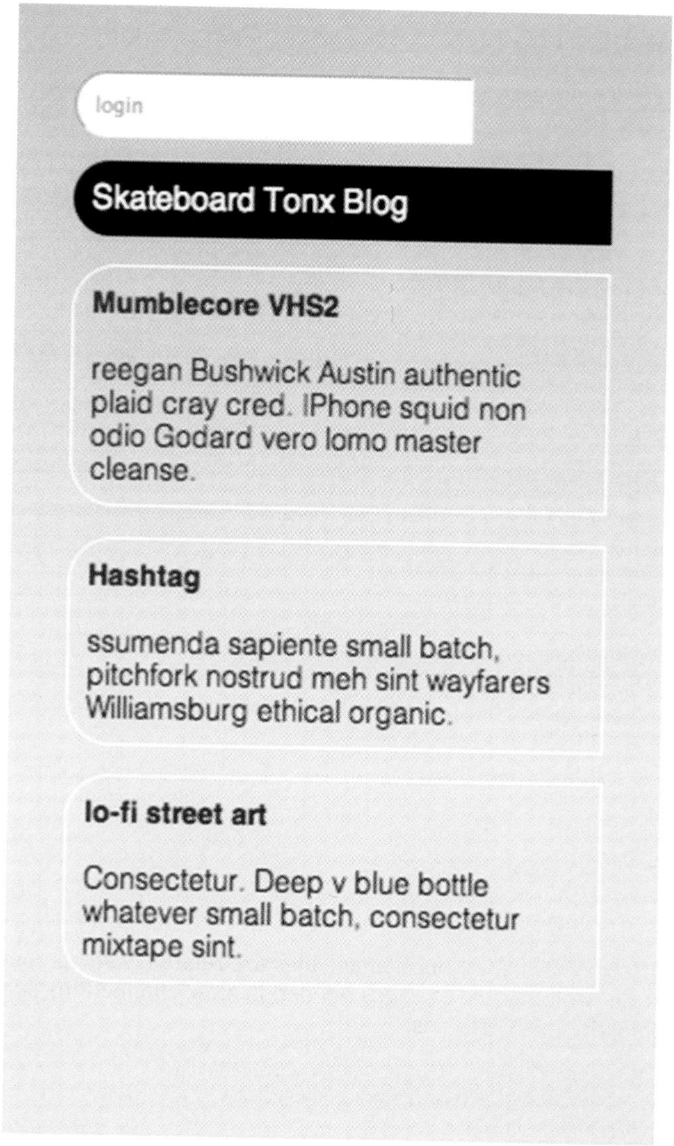

Figure 12-3

remember

CSS3 linear gradients perform much the same task as traditional tiled-image gradient backgrounds, but (again) with the advantages of smooth, fast loading because they don't rely on images.

Rotated and radial

And there's more! CSS3 linear gradients can also be *rotated:* that is, they can start not just at the top of a box, but — for example — a gradient can start in the upper-left corner of a box and end in the lower-right corner.

And background gradients can be radial — starting in the middle of a box and gradating out to the edges of the box. Figure 12-4 demonstrates a radial gradient background.

login

Skateboard Tonx Blog

Mumblecore VHS2

reegan Bushwick Austin authentic plaid cray cred. IPhone squid non odio Godard vero lomo master cleanse.

Hashtag

ssumenda sapiente small batch, pitchfork nostrud meh sint wayfarers Williamsburg ethical organic.

lo-fi street art

Consectetur. Deep v blue bottle whatever small batch, consectetur mixtape sint.

Figure 12-4

And CSS3 gradients can also be *radial,* radiating and changing color from the center to the edges of an element, as shown in Figure 12-5.

Figure 12-5

Gradients and mobile: A nice fit

Mobile design presents specific challenges. One of them is how to make pages attractive and inviting without taking up precious viewport space with images. A widely used design strategy is to load up mobile sites with gradients.

Take a good look at a nicely designed mobile site, such as Travelocity Mobile (www.m.travelocity.com). (If you don't have a mobile device handy, go to www.travelocity.com for links to screenshots of the Travelocity site in different mobile devices.) Figure 12-6 zooms in on the banner at the top of the mobile page.

HAVE A TRAVELOCITY ACCOUNT?

Figure 12-6

On close inspection, you can see that the background for the heading is a gradient blend from light blue to darker blue.

A slightly different treatment is the Kayak mobile site (the site you see when you go to kayak.com on a mobile device, or you can display the page in a laptop/desktop by going to m.kayak.com). Here the heading has a gradient blend background, as shown in Figure 12-7.

Figure 12-7

The more you study mobile page designs, the more you'll note how widespread gradient backgrounds are used. You'll find them behind headings and page content as well as almost universally as button backgrounds, like the one in Figure 12-8.

Figure 12-8

CSS3 GRADIENTS AND MOBILE SITES: A PERFECT FIT

CSS3 Gradients are a perfect fit for mobile sites for a number of reasons:

- For starters, gradients look good!
- Gradients create graphical elements without requiring a user to download an image over a slow mobile connection.
- Almost all mobile devices support CSS3 gradients, including iOS Safari, Android Browser, Blackberry Browser, Chrome for Android, and Firefox for Android.

tip

As of this writing, Opera Mini does not support CSS3 gradients.

Compatibility solutions

There are two compatibility issues associated with CSS3 gradients. One —as you might expect — is that support in Internet Explorer 8 is limited. Note I didn't say there is *no* support for CSS gradients in IE8; IE8 does support linear gradients, as shown in Figure 12-9.

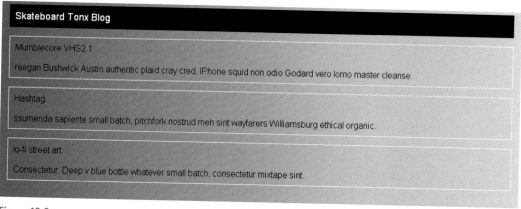

Figure 12-9

The other compatibility issue is that different browsers have different syntax for defining complex gradients. For example, the IE8 user base can't see radial CSS3 gradients. IE8 will translate radial gradients (read about those earlier in this chapter) into linear gradients, which can present serious readability issues — for example, when text is colored in a way that requires a complementary (highly contrasting) background color (see Figure 12-10). As you can see in the bottom image (IE8), the white text falls atop a very light blue background, making it difficult to read. The top image (current browser), using the same white text, is very readable on the darker blue background.

IE8 Does Not Support Radial Gradients

A CSS3 radial background in a current generation browser.

The same page viewed in Internet Explorer 8. IE8 displays a linear gradient, resulting in loss of functionality because white text is now displayed against a very light background.

Figure 12-10

Competing CSS3 Gradient Syntax

In many instances of CSS3 styling, browser prefixes are required to make a style work in all contemporary browsers. For example, the @keyframes selector, which I discuss in Chapter 11, has a syntax that begins with @keyframes, but a duplicate style definition that begins with @-webkit-keyframes is required for @keyframes animation to work in browsers using WebKit standards (older versions of Chrome and current versions of Safari).

Defining duplicate CSS styling for different browser prefixes is a bit of a hassle, but not that bad. The situation is worse, though, when it comes to the syntax for CSS3 gradient backgrounds.

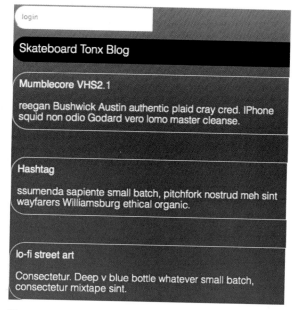

Figure 12-11

Take, for example, a class style (here named .green-blue) that applies a gradient background that blends from green to blue, as shown in Figure 12-11.

The syntax for this relatively simple background style is

```
.green-blue {
   color:white;
background: -moz-linear-gradient(top, green 0%, blue 100%);
background: -webkit-gradient(linear, left top, left bottom,
         color-stop(0%,green), color-stop(100%,blue));
background: -webkit-linear-gradient(top, green 0%,blue 100%);
background: -o-linear-gradient(top, green 0%,bluef 100%);
background: -ms-linear-gradient(top, green 0%,blue 100%);
background: linear-gradient(to bottom, green 0%,blue 100%);
```

The prefixes and syntax apply this way:

- ▶ `-moz-linear-gradient`: Firefox
- ▶ `-webkit-gradient` and `-webkit-linear-gradient`: Different versions of Chrome and Safari
- ▶ `-o-linear-gradient`: Opera
- ▶ `-ms-linear-gradient`: Internet Explorer 10 and newer
- ▶ `linear-gradient`: The supposedly standard syntax set by the World Wide Web Consortium (W3C)

A SIMPLER WAY TO GENERATE COMPLEX GRADIENTS

As you can infer, there is a bigger problem here than simply creating a bunch of duplicate styles and putting different browser prefixes at the beginning of the style definition. The actual syntax and even the names of the properties are different. Some browsers use the `-gradient` property and define the linear direction as part of the property value. In other cases, the property parameter is `linear-gradient`.

Insane, right?

So, here comes a bad news/good news announcement. At least the good news trumps the bad news.

Bad news: Gradient syntax, even for simple, two-color linear gradients — let alone complex, multicolored, diagonal, or radial gradients — is too confusing to try to learn.

Good news: A number of very powerful, free, easy-to-use gradient generator resources are online that allow you to define gradients as easily as you would in a drawing program such as Illustrator, GIMP, CorelDraw, and so on.

Defining Gradients with Free Online Generators

Here are two very valid and important arguments for generating CSS code for gradients:

- ▶ Doing it yourself is too hard.
- ▶ There's no need to do it yourself.

You can easily find a number of very effective and intuitive online resources for generating CSS for gradients. All these resources allow designers to generate CSS gradients with WYSIWYG (what you see is what you get) graphical interfaces, meaning that you can see the gradient while you tweak settings. Many of these resources include very valuable extras, such as generating SVG (scalable vector graphic) image files for browsers with no support for CSS3 gradients, or generating workaround coding that allows IE9 to display nonlinear gradients.

In the next section, I walk you through using Ultimate CSS Gradient Generator (www. colorzilla.com/gradient-editor), created by Alex Sirota.

Before I do that, though, here are some free alternatives:

▶ **CSS3 Gradient Generator**

> http://gradients.glrzad.com

Created by Damian Galarza, this generator (see Figure 12-12) provides a clear, easy-to-use interface. It's not quite as loaded with features as Ultimate CSS Gradient Editor, but it sports nearly all the gradient generating tools anyone will ever need.

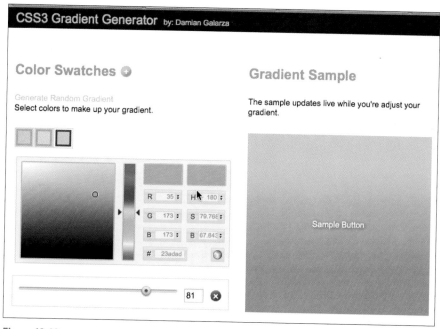

Figure 12-12

Figure 12-13

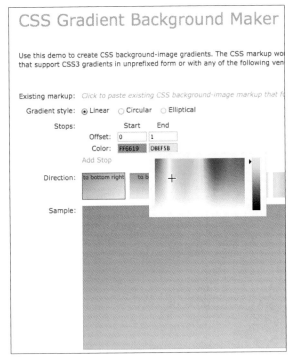

Figure 12-14

▶ CSS Gradient Generator

`www.display-inline.fr/ projects/css-gradient/`

This generator is as full-featured as gradient generators come with options for workaround display in legacy browser versions (see Figure 12-13). CSS Gradient Generator creates a downloadable PNG image as a backup. Designers can use Chrome, Firefox, or Safari to generate background gradients.

▶ CSS Gradient Background Maker

`http://ie.microsoft.com/testdrive/graphics/cssgradient backgroundmaker`

This generator, provided by Microsoft, isn't quite as full-featured as the other generators when it comes to legacy browsers, but (as you might imagine) designers can use IE10 here to generate gradients. See Figure 12-14.

Using Ultimate CSS Gradient Generator

Ultimate CSS Gradient Generator isn't the easiest CSS generator to use, but it is the most powerful. And it's way *way* easier to use than trying to create multiple CSS definitions for complex gradients.

Ultimate CSS Gradient Generator is an online resource with tools to create highly tuned gradient blends with multiple colors. It generates solid backup code for legacy browsers. And it comes with a substantial palette of preset backgrounds. The URL: www.colorzilla.com/gradient-editor/. The cost of accessing this site: free.

Using preset gradients and the preview feature

A good way to get your feet wet with Ultimate CSS Gradient Generator is to explore its palette of presets (on the left of the workspace). After you choose a preset in the panel, you can its effect on the right in the Preview area. See Figure 12-15.

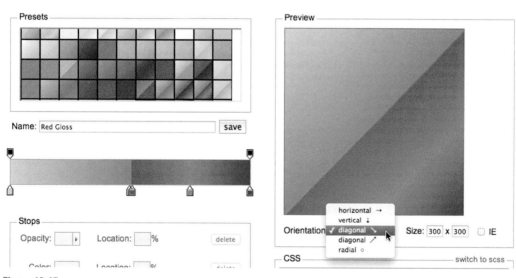

Figure 12-15

Once you've chosen a preset, here are some additional things you can do:

▶ Use the Orientation option menu (shown open in Figure 12-15) to experiment with displaying the gradient in a horizontal, vertical, diagonal upper left-to-lower right, diagonal upper right-to-lower left, or radial orientation.

▶ Use the Size fields to define width (left field) and height (right field) in pixels. This way, you can see how the generated gradient will look in a box with a specific size, as shown in Figure 12-16.

▶ The IE check box in the Preview area shows how the defined gradient will look in IE9. Figure 12-17 shows how a defined gradient looks in IE9, which does not support non-linear gradients.

Figure 12-16

Defining gradient color stops

Starting either from scratch or from a preset that's close to your intended background, you can add, subtract, and move color stops on the intuitive color bar under the Presets palette.

Figure 12-17

technical stuff

A color stop for a gradient is the position at which one color changes to another. The space between stops is the area in which a transition takes place between color defined by stops.

▶ **Move a color stop** by dragging it on the color bar, as shown in Figure 12-18.

▶ **Remove a color stop** by dragging it off the color bar.

▶ **Add a color stop** by hovering over the edge of the color bar and clicking, as shown in Figure 12-19.

Figure 12-18

Figure 12-19

tip

Another option for generating gradients is to extract colors from an image. Do that by using the Import from Image button at the bottom of the generated code (which I talk about next).

Saving and applying gradient backgrounds

As you edit the color stops, orientation, and other elements of a gradient, the generated code updates. At any time, you can copy the code onto your Clipboard and paste it into a selector definition in your CSS style sheet.

Here's how to save and apply a gradient:

1. **Select the Comments check box (see upcoming Figure 12-20).**

tip

> I recommend generating code with comments as a good way to learn to understand, and even home-cook, gradient CSS.

2. **To generate additional code to make nonlinear gradients work in IE9, select the IE Support check box.**

   Both the Comments and IE Support options are selected in Figure 12-20.

```
CSS _____  switch to scss

  background: #1e5799; /* Old browsers */
  background: -moz-linear-gradient(top, #1e5799 0%,
     #7db9e8 100%); /* FF3.6+ */
  background: -webkit-gradient(linear, left top, left
     bottom, color-stop(0%,#1e5799), color-
     stop(100%,#7db9e8)); /* Chrome,Safari4+ */
  background: -webkit-linear-gradient(top, #1e5799
     0%,#7db9e8 100%); /* Chrome10+,Safari5.1+ */
  background: -o-linear-gradient(top, #1e5799 0%,#7db9e8
     100%); /* Opera 11.10+ */
  background: -ms-linear-gradient(top, #1e5799 0%,#7db9e8
     100%); /* IE10+ */
  background: linear-gradient(to bottom, #1e5799
     0%,#7db9e8 100%); /* W3C */
  filter: progid:DXImageTransform.Microsoft.gradient(
     startColorstr='#1e5799',
     endColorstr='#7db9e8',GradientType=0 ); /* IE6-9 */
```

Color format: [hex ‡]   ☑ Comments ☐ IE9 Support (?)

Figure 12-20

3. **Choose a color value type from the Color Format option menu, as shown in Figure 12-21.**

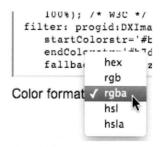

Figure 12-21

tip

For an explanation of CSS3 colors, including RGBA, see Chapter 9.

4. **Hover over the generated code in the CSS box and then click the Copy link that appears in the lower left of the box, as shown in Figure 12-22.**

```
background: -ms-radial-gradient(center, ellipse
    cover, rgba(183,222,237,1)
    0%,rgba(113,206,239,1) 50%,rgba(33,180,226,1)
    51%,rgba(183,222,237,1) 100%); /* IE10+ */
background: radial-gradient(ellipse at center,
    rgba(183,222,237,1) 0%,rgba(113,206,239,1)
    50%,rgba(33,180,226,1) 51%,rgba(183,222,237,1)
    100%); /* W3C */
                                                    copy
```

Figure 12-22

5. **Toggle out of your browser window and into your code editor.**

6. **Add the background gradient to an element by pasting the copied CSS into the style definition for an element.**

warning

You will be pasting a fair amount of code — a couple dozen lines of complex code, at that — so make sure all the generated code is added to one of your style definitions. For example, the place where the copied gradient style goes in the following class style definition for a box is indicated with a comment:

```
.box {
width:50px;
height:50px;
<!--copied gradient CSS goes here -->
}
```

7. **Save your CSS file and preview your HTML page.**

tip

Test the gradient in multiple browsers if possible.

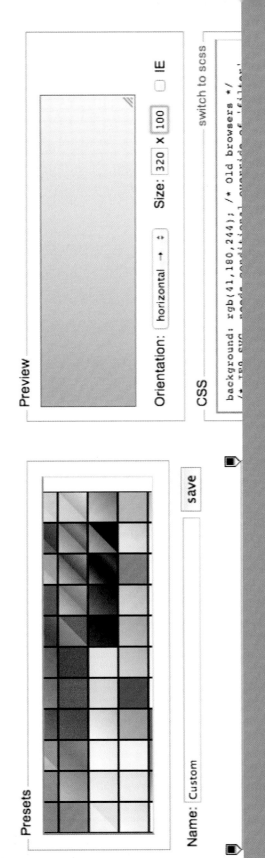

A powerful Photoshop-like CSS gradient editor from ColorZilla.

Part IV
The Part of Tens

As quickly as the web is changing, the tools used to design websites are changing as well. In this part, I've compiled lists of many useful tools, and most of them are free.

My list of the ten best resources for building HTML pages includes free code editors, file managers, editable JavaScript widgets, and the source for the wacky hipster *ipsum lorem* placeholder text used in examples throughout this book.

Here as well you'll find a guide to online resources for generating CSS, including tools for defining color schemes, generating effects, and applying gradient effects to text.

Finally, this part includes a list of ten very effective tools for handling form data — including search boxes, mail list manager software, form generators, and easy ways to collect data submitted in forms.

Enjoy an additional HTML5 and CSS3 Part of Tens List online at www. dummies.com/extras/ html5andcss3.

Code | Split | Design | Live | Live Code | Inspect | file:///Macinto

```html
1  <!doctype html>
2  <html>
3  <head>
4  <meta charset="UTF-8">
5  <title>News</title>
6  <link href=
   "all-in-one.css" rel=
   "stylesheet" type=
   "text/css">
7      <meta name="viewport"
   content=
   "width=device-width,
   initial-scale=1">
8
9  </head>
10
11 <body>
12         <input
```

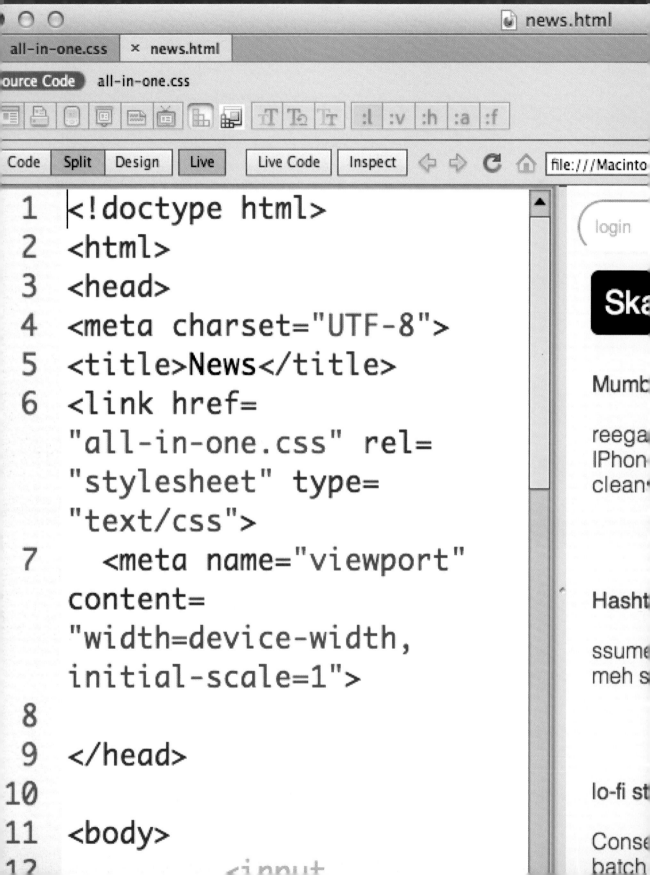

login

Ska

Mumb

reega
IPhon
clean

Hasht

ssume
meh s

lo-fi st

Conse
batch

/dkarlins/Deskto..

ard Tonx Blog

HS2.1

vick Austin authentic plaid cray
non odio Godard vero lomo ma

biente small batch, pitchfork no
arers Williamsburg ethical orga

Deep v blue bottle whatever sm
tetur mixtape sint

CHAPTER 13

Top Ten HTML5 Design Resources

In This Chapter

● Useful code editors

● Helpful online web design resources

● Deciding whether or not to invest in Adobe Dreamweaver

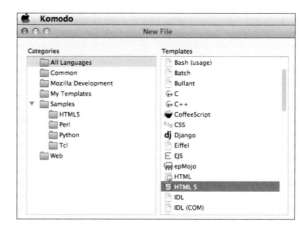

My approach in this book is to rely on HTML5 to build website content. However, that doesn't rule out using additional valuable resources, especially when some of those resources are free.

The first tool that every web designer needs is a reliable code editor with color coding and other tools to make it easy to generate and debug HTML. The first four resources discussed in this chapter are my favorite code editors. The other six resources I cite in this chapter are ones that every designer needs to bookmark.

warning

I can't emphasize this point enough: Do not use word processors (such as Google Docs, Microsoft Word, or document editing utilities included with your operating system) to create HTML files. Word processors do things like generate smart (curly) quotes (like these " ") that corrupt code.

Notepad++

www.notepad-plus-plus.org

Notepad++ is a free source code editor for HTML5, CSS3, and JavaScript, and it runs in Windows only. Figure 13-1 shows the Notepad++ interface, with open files in tabs on the top.

Notepad++ comes with a set of features that make it easy to work with and organize multiple files, catch errors as you code, and speed up coding by completing tags.

Some of the most useful tools in Notepad++ are

▶ The ability to have multiple files open in separate tabs

▶ Line numbering to simplify error tracking

▶ Auto-completion for words, functions, and parameters hinting

```
*D:\source\notepad4ever.cpp - Notepad++

Notepad_plus.cpp    notepad4ever.cpp

 1      #include <GPL.h>
 2      #include <free_software.h>
 3
 4      void notepad4ever()
 5      {
 6          while (true)
 7          {
 8              Notepad++;
 9          }
10      }
11
```

Figure 13-1

There is a growing set of plugins for Notepad++. One of the most valuable is TextFX, which includes W3C validation to check HTML and CSS files for errors.

```
http://sourceforge.net/projects/npp-plugins/files/TextFX
```

In addition to coding tools for HTML, Notepad++ supports dozens of coding languages, including

▶ C

▶ C++

▶ CSS

▶ JavaScript

▶ Objective-C

▶ PHP

▶ Python

▶ Ruby

▶ SQL

TextWrangler

```
www.barebones.com/products/textwrangler
```

For Mac users, there is TextWrangler, which also supports HTML5 and CSS3. Figure 13-2 shows the TextWranger interface with an open HTML file and other files open in additional tabs.

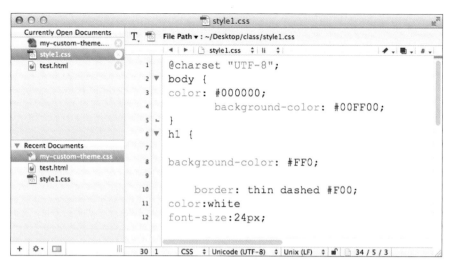

Figure 13-2

TextWrangler allows coders to work with multiple files in open tabs. It displays code in customizable fonts, with color coding to help identify syntax errors. TextWrangler is an offshoot and a simpler version of the for-fee editor BBEdit. However, TextWrangler will serve you well. And TextWrangler is free!

Features of TextWrangler include

- Search and replace
- Spell check
- File comparison (handy for identifying changes between one version of a file and another)

Komodo Edit

www.activestate.com/komodo-edit

For more advanced coders who manage more complex projects, Komodo Edit provides code hinting, organizes projects, and supports HTML5, CSS3, and server-side programming languages (Python, PHP, Ruby, and Perl) as well as JavaScript. Komodo Edit is available for Windows, Mac, and Linux. Figure 13-3 shows an HTML file open in Komodo Edit.

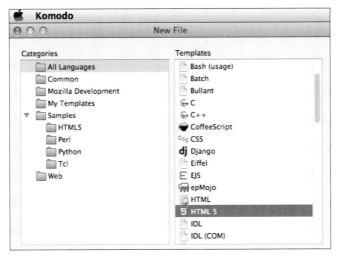

Figure 13-3

Komodo Edit is a free version of a commercial coding package Komodo IDE. Still, Komodo Edit is very powerful and will fill the needs of coders, including high-level coders.

In addition to the features noted earlier in this chapter for more basic code editors (multiple files open in tabs, find and replace, spell check, and color-coding), Komodo Edit includes more robust productivity tools, including

▶ Starter templates with basic code for HTML5 (and other) files

▶ Code hinting with pop-up boxes

▶ Automatic indenting and collapsible code sections

▶ Automatic tag closing (so when you finish an open tag, like <h1>, a close </h1> tag is created)

warning

Even though Komodo Edit is more powerful than TextWrangler or Notepad++, it's a bit less intuitive. The program organizes groups of files into projects, which can be helpful but also adds another level of structuring and organizing to working with files that might not be necessary in smaller websites.

Adobe Dreamweaver

`www.adobe.com/products/dreamweaver.html`

No discussion of HTML code editors is complete without reference to Adobe Dreamweaver. For those with the budget to manage it, Dreamweaver speeds productivity with advanced code hinting and preview environments. Figure 13-4 shows an open HTML file in Dreamweaver split view, with code on the left and a preview on the right.

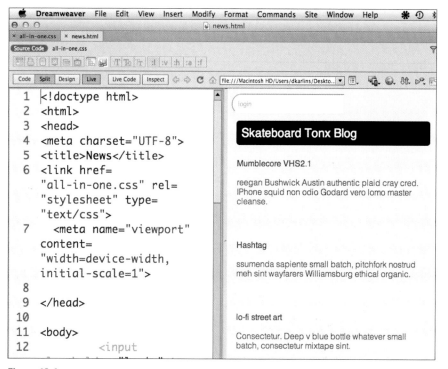

Figure 13-4

Dreamweaver provides features that other code editors don't, including

- A preview window that displays a close approximation for how pages appear in a browser
- Menu and panel options for generating HTML (as well as CSS and JavaScript)
- Templates and sample pages

I see two downsides to using Dreamweaver to build HTML pages. One is the cost. With the introduction of Creative Cloud, Adobe's new pricing model is essentially a monthly subscription as opposed to a user's ability to purchase a permanent license (like with the older Creative Suite versions). As this book goes to press, Adobe is confronting substantial protest against their new licensing policy, so check at Adobe for the latest developments. Pricing is available at www.adobe.com/products/dreamweaver.html.

The other downside is that Dreamweaver isn't an open source project. Obviously, Adobe has a vested interest in marketing other Adobe products, as is expressed in the Dreamweaver interface (which includes, for example, panels for Adobe Business Catalyst, which competes with other options for content management).

If web developers can avoid proprietary Dreamweaver features and also justify the cost, Dreamweaver provides unique productivity and design tools for creating HTML5 pages.

FileZilla

http://sourceforge.net/projects/filezilla

After HTML files have been created, web developers need tools to transfer those files from a local computer to a remote website hosting server. To do that, along with a code editor, every designer needs a reliable FTP manager. This is the File Transfer Protocol (FTP) *client* — the software — that moves files to and from a remote site. The best, and still free, FTP client is FileZilla.

When you contract for hosting, along with a URL (like mysite.com), your web host server provides you with an FTP address for your site, a login, and a password. You use that information to define an FTP connection in FileZilla. After you define a site in FileZilla, you simply drag files from your computer to your remote hosting server to make them available online, as shown in Figure 13-5.

Filename ^	Filesize	Filetype	Last modified		Filename ^		Filesize	Filetype
iphone.css	6,120	css–file	02/07/2011 14:...		audio.html		3,923	HyperText
laptop_960.css	5,906	css–file	02/07/2011 15:...		basic_fs.css		12,424	css–file
multi-screen_test.ht...	4,392	HyperText	02/07/2011 14:...		bg2.png		5,361	Portable N..
normal.css	0	css–file	02/10/2011 15:...		bike-light.jpg		12,771	JPEG Picture
on_record.mov	44,604,588	QuickTime M...	03/07/2008 13:...		busy.gif		8,632	GIF Picture
query_fullsize.css	5,919	css–file	02/10/2011 15:...		cat.html		2,605	HyperText
query_phone.css	5,906	css–file	02/09/2011 21:...		coney-island-transparency.png		182,311	Portable N..
query_tablet.css	5,913	css–file	02/10/2011 15:...		coney01.JPG		2,281,968	JPEG Picture
test.html	1,356	HyperText	05/12/2011 16:...		detail-outline.html		3,015	HyperText
testing.html	725	HyperText	02/03/2011 17:...		droid.ttf		117,072	TrueType ..
video.html	446	HyperText	05/13/2011 23:...		error.html		193	HyperText
Selected 1 file. Total size: 1,356 bytes					72 files and 56 directories. Total size: 8,248,267 bytes			
Server/Local file						Direction	Remote file	
Queued files	Failed transfers	Successful transfers					Queue: empty	

Figure 13-5

W3Schools

```
www.w3schools.com
```

Next on my Top 10 resources list is the single most useful source of online documentation for HTML coding syntax: W3Schools.

on the web

Start at `www.w3schools.com/html/html5_intro.asp`.

This handy resource is a must-have from which to grab HTML tags and parameters. Consider w3schools your one-stop shopping for HTML elements, syntax, and parameters.

As indicated in the URL, W3Schools is a *school* as well as a source of code syntax. So don't expect a consolidated introduction to HTML5 (for that, you've got this book!), but you can expect to find models, examples, and interactive code that you can use to explore specific HTML5 features, as shown in Figure 13-6.

Figure 13-6

WC3 Markup Validation Service

```
http://validator.w3.org
```

Have you ever stared at code, over and over, trying to figure out why it isn't working? Built-in tools in the recommended code editors earlier in this chapter are often helpful in pointing to the source of problems in HTML pages. When such tools are not enough, you can debug and test code using the WC3 Markup Validation Service.

You can use the WC3 Markup Validation Service to test code at a posted website by entering a URL. Or, you can copy and paste HTML into the Validate by Direct Input section at the site, and test code before posting it. Errors are listed with helpful tips on correcting them, as shown in Figure 13-7.

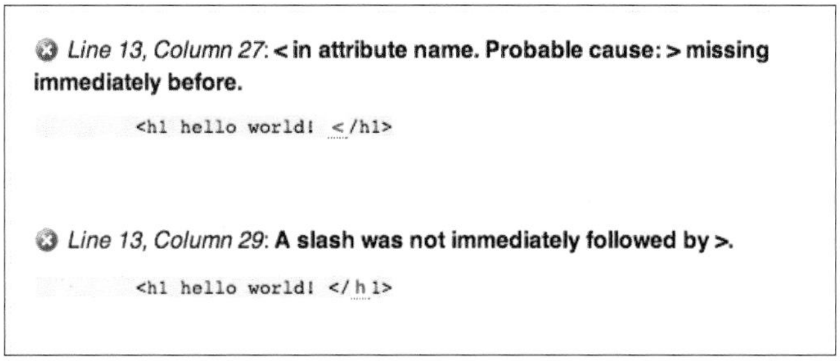
Line 13, Column 27: < in attribute name. Probable cause: > missing immediately before.
<h1 hello world! </h1>
Line 13, Column 29: A slash was not immediately followed by >.
<h1 hello world! </h 1>

Figure 13-7

AMP Express

`https://amp.ssbbartgroup.com/express`

"Accessibility" means different things in relation to websites. As I explore throughout this book, one dimension of accessibility involves making sites that work in different browsers and devices.

Another dimension to accessibility is making websites that can be accessed by people with disabilities (ranging from vision impairment to lack of hearing). The U.S. federal government has defined accessibility standards, such as Section 508 §1194.22 for Web-based Intranet and Internet Information and Applications. These standards require that websites be built in such a way that they can be read aloud by reader software, that video include captions where there is an audio track, and so on.

You can test accessibility for your site — including compliance with Section 508 §1194.22 — at AMP Express. After you sign up with AMP Express, you can submit a URL, as shown in Figure 13-8. AMP Express produces a report evaluating how the selected site stacks up to accessibility standards.

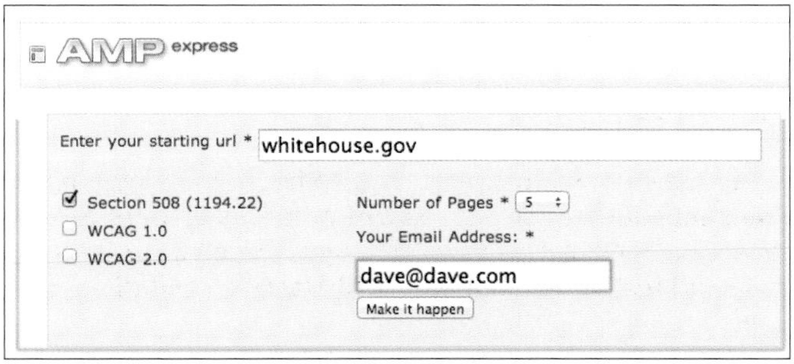
AMP express
Enter your starting url *
whitehouse.gov
Section 508 (1194.22)
WCAG 1.0
WCAG 2.0
Number of Pages *
5
Your Email Address: *
dave@dave.com
Make it happen

Figure 13-8

Hipster Ipsum

`www.hipsteripsum.me`

Building page templates often involves using *placeholder text* that will be replaced with real text when you convert HTML page templates into specific content pages. For eons, designers (first print, and now web) have used *ipsum lorem* text — nonsensical combinations of Latin words — to fill space in designs until real text is poured.

If you need some placeholder text and you've become bored with traditional *ipsum lorem* (which works fine and is generated at `www.lipsum.com`), try Hipster Ipsum text.

You tell the Hipster Ipsum site how many paragraphs of placeholder text you need as well as whether to mix in some Latin. Then Hipster Ipsum scrambles together some trendy slang and produces text like that shown in Figure 13-9.

Figure 13-9

jQuery Widget Factory

`http://jqueryui.com/widget`

JavaScript provides animation and interactivity for websites, even beyond what can be created with CSS3 and HTML5. Packages of JavaScript, editable CSS, and editable HTML make JavaScript widgets (such as like menus, tabbed pages, and slideshows) available to non-JavaScript coders.

The widget supplies (noneditable) JavaScript, along with HTML and CSS that you *can* edit to customize the content.

The jQuery Widget Factory is the most accessible source for HTML/CSS widgets that generate animated or interactive JavaScript widgets (see Figure 13-10).

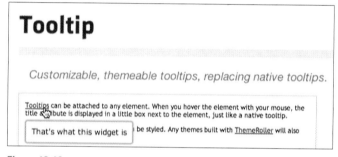

Figure 13-10

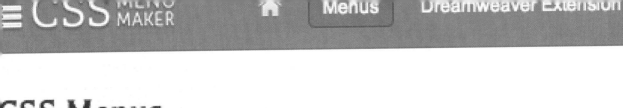

CSS Menus

Type   - Any -   ⌄   Color   - Any -   ⌄   View   12

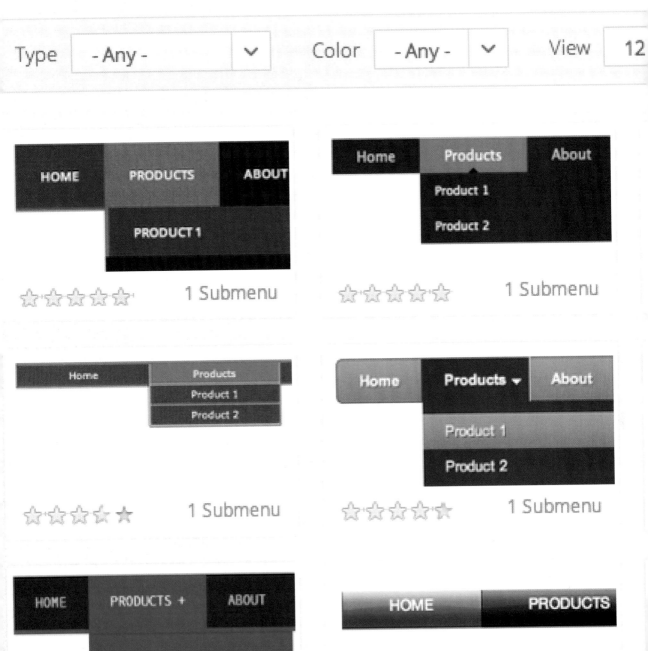

☆☆☆☆☆   1 Submenu   ☆☆☆☆☆   1 Submenu

☆☆☆☆★   1 Submenu   ☆☆☆☆☆   1 Submenu

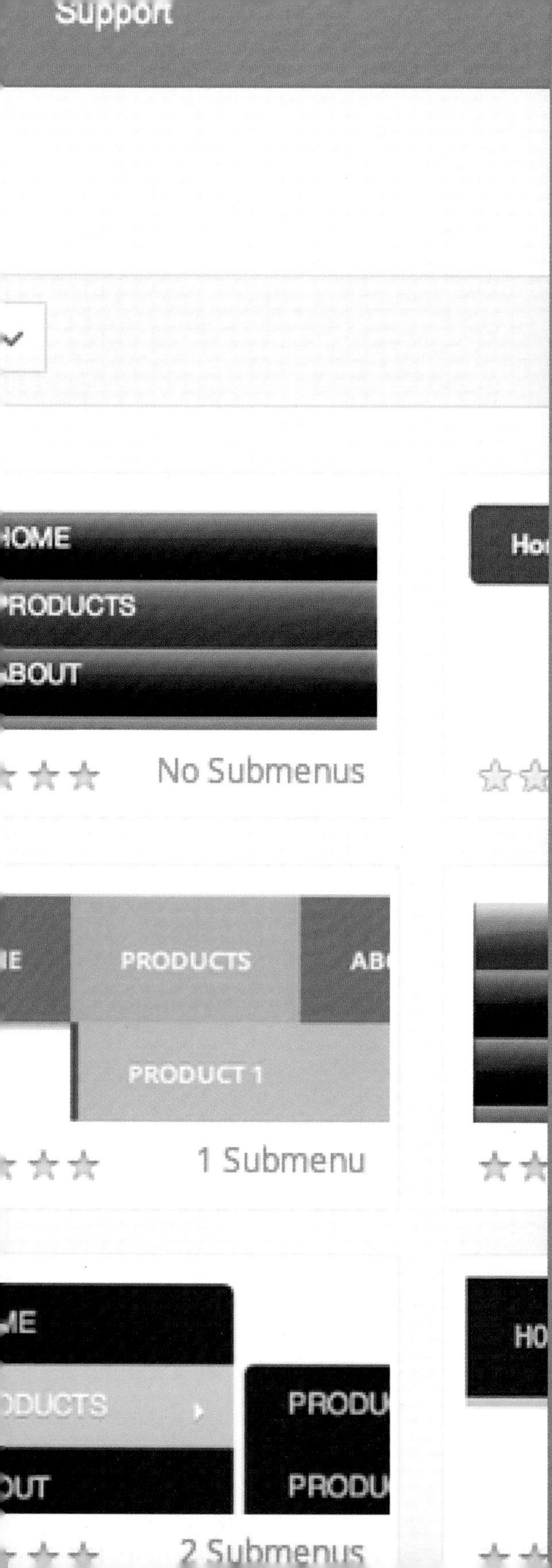

CHAPTER 14

Top Ten CSS3 Design Tools

HOME

PRODUCTS

ABOUT

★ ★ ★   No Submenus

PRODUCTS   AB

PRODUCT 1

★ ★ ★   1 Submenu

ODUCTS

OUT

★ ★ ★   2 Submenus

In This Chapter

- Helpful online tools for generating web graphics

- Useful online tools for generating web animation

- Handy online tools for generating menus

G et your money's worth out of CSS3's radically new design features. Load up your bookmarks list with the following essential design and CSS productivity resources (most of which are free).

Ultimate CSS Gradient Generator

www.colorzilla.com/gradient-editor

One of the most exciting and powerful new features in CSS3 is the ability to generate gradient blends to use as page or element backgrounds. Complex gradient blends are a big hassle to code, though. Different browsers require different syntax, and providing fallback for older browsers adds to the challenge.

The Ultimate CSS Gradient Generator creates CSS3 gradient code using an intuitive interface that looks like the gradient panels in Adobe Create Suite programs and other graphics applications; see Figure 14-1.

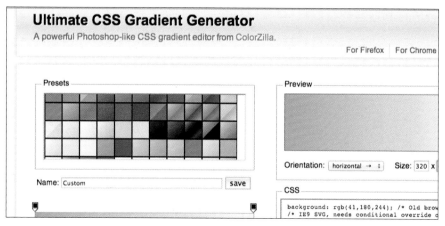

Figure 14-1

remember

You can't use the Ultimate Gradient Generator with older versions of Internet Explorer. You can create gradients that work in old versions of IE, but you'll need to go to the Ultimate Gradient Generator site in a current version of IE or a recent version of Firefox, Chrome, Safari, or Opera.

Ultimate Gradient Generator features can help you

▶ Generate horizontal, vertical, diagonal, and radial gradients.

▶ Create multistop gradients.

▶ Define opacity settings for opacity stops.

▶ Define colors in CSS hexadecimal, RGB, RGBA, HSL, or HSLA color values.

▶ Get support for full multistop gradients that work in IE9, which normally doesn't support multistop gradients.

▶ Convert gradients in images to CSS3 codes.

▶ Find dozens of preset gradients

▶ Access a preview panel with definable dimensions.

Adobe Kuler

https://kuler.adobe.com

Consciously defined color schemes — that is, sets of five main colors around which a website is designed — are underrated and essential components of creating attractive, accessible sites.

Adobe Kuler generates color schemes from colors or artwork. And you can search, get inspiration from, and edit a huge gallery of existing color schemes based on colors, or even moods, as shown in Figure 14-2.

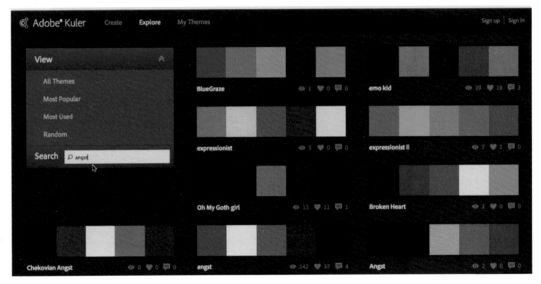

Figure 14-2

Designers versed in color theory will find tools to define color schemes based on analogous, monochromatic, triad, complimentary, compound, or shade color relationships. At the same time, the huge set of presets provides easy access to inviting color scheme sets.

The main downside in Kuler lies in limitations in exporting the color scheme to CSS color values. Users of Adobe Creative Suite products can import an Adobe Swatch Exchange (ASE) file exported from Kuler, but hand-coders have to copy and paste color values by hand into CSS style sheets.

Color Scheme Designer

http://colorschemedesigner.com

Another powerful and useful color scheme generator is the Color Scheme Designer. This online resource is particularly suited to designers conversant with color theory and terminology, and it includes tools for color-blind accessibility. Color Scheme Designer is free although it does encourage donations.

Color Scheme Designer has a cool preview feature that demonstrates how a color scheme looks applied to a page; see Figure 14-3.

Figure 14-3

And Color Scheme Designer exports color scheme values in a convenient set of non-proprietary formats, including a text file with CSS color values, or an HTML file with defined styles that integrate the generated color scheme.

CSS3 Generator

http://css3generator.com

Gradient blends may be one of the hardest things to code in CSS3, but the CSS3 Generator generates CSS3 code for everything from rounded corners to text shadows. The CSS3 effects and transforms that you can create with the CSS3 Generator include

- ▶ Text shadows
- ▶ RGBA color values
- ▶ Multiple columns
- ▶ Outlines
- ▶ Transitions (animated changes)
- ▶ Transforms (motion)

The CSS3 Generator no-frills interface is accessible and intuitive. You enter values for the effect or transform, the CSS3 Generator displays a preview, and spits out ready to copy-and-paste CSS code, as shown in Figure 14-4.

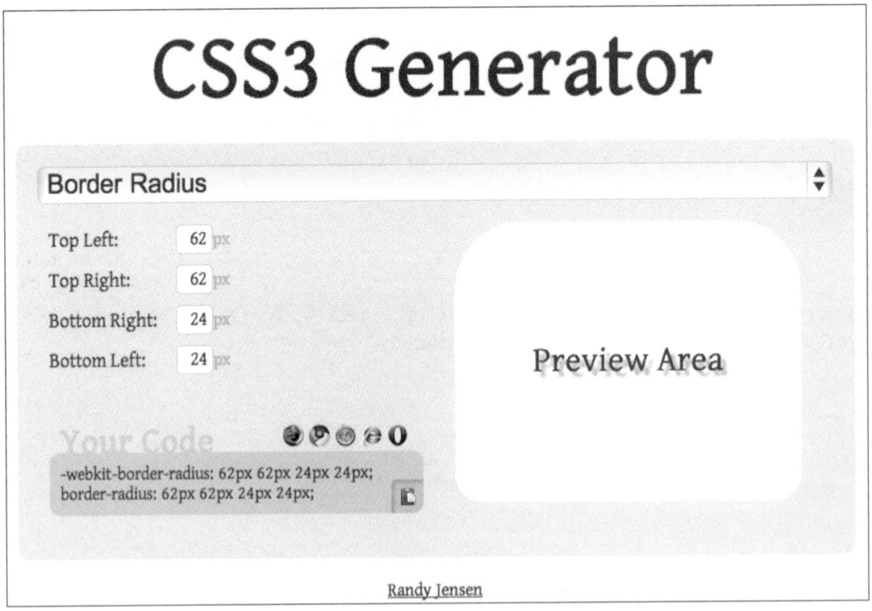

Figure 14-4

CSS3 Box Shadow Generator

`http://css3gen.com/box-shadow`

Box shadows — without any background graphic images or crudely put together individual border pieces — are one of the highlights of CSS3. If it's a box shadow you need, the CSS3 Box Shadow Generator singleimindedly churns out box shadow styles from a graphical interface, as shown in Figure 14-5.

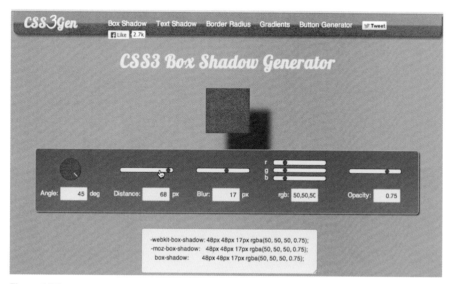

Figure 14-5

The CSS3 Box Shadow Generator is part of a suite of generators that includes resources for creating text shadows, border radii, gradients, and buttons. Output is in the form of ready to copy-and-paste CSS code that uses RGBA color values, so you can tweak opacity of the shadow on your own.

CSS 3.0 Maker

`www.css3maker.com`

Another valuable member of the CSS3-generating community is the CSS 3.0 Maker, which you can use to generate a nice set of CSS3 effects and transforms. The most valuable element of CSS 3.0 Maker, though, is the ability to generate animation using the CSS3 animate and @keyframe features. You define duration, repetition, and animation timing (such as `ease` or `ease-in`).

Transitions are defined with intuitive, interactive sliders, and then displayed in a preview pane, as shown in Figure 14-6.

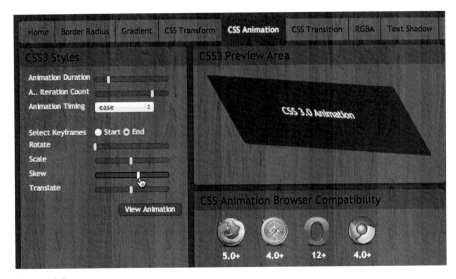

Figure 14-6

Generated code is structured into a handy, ready-to-rename class style, which can be downloaded as a zip file, or copied and pasted into a CSS style sheet.

CSS3 animation, @keyframes, and animation timing are explored in Chapter 11.

Animate.css

```
http://daneden.me/animate
```

Animate.css is another animation generator but with a personality of its own. It features preset animations, such as flash, bounce, shake, tah-dah!, swing, wobble, wiggle, and pulse — all of which have to be seen in motion to appreciated. Other animation includes bounces, fades, and rotating animation.

Animate.css is as fun to play with as it is useful for generating fun animation. Each prepackaged animation can be previewed onscreen, as shown in Figure 14-7.

Downloading the generated code from Animate.css is a bit clunkier than with similar resources. For example, there is no copy-and-paste option for moving CSS code into your style sheet file. Instead, you download a zip file that unzips into an HTML file with your defined CSS style inside the HTML <head> tag.

rotateOutUpLeft
I fight for the user.
Lightspeed
lightSpeedIn
lightSpeedOut

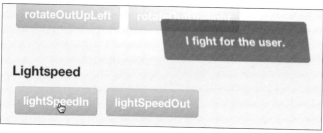

Figure 14-7

Web Designer Wall

`http://webdesignerwall.com/tutorials/css-gradient-text-effect`

The emphasis in this chapter is on graphical interface resources that generate CSS3. Closely aligned with this set of tools are online resources that provide step-by-step tutorials and downloadable demo code. In that category, gradient text effects are easy to generate and ready to apply using the tutorial/sample code at Web Designer Wall. The gradient text effects available at Web Designer Wall are uniquely specialized and provide a range of really intriguing text effects, as shown in Figure 14-8.

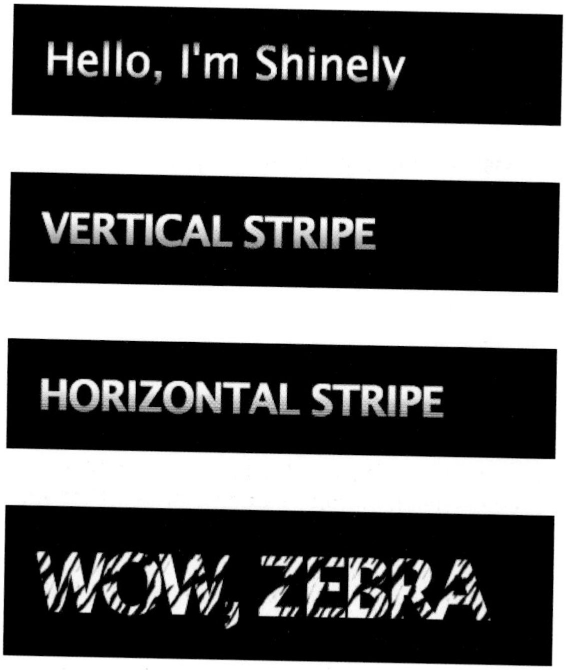

Hello, I'm Shinely
VERTICAL STRIPE
HORIZONTAL STRIPE
WOW, ZEBRA

Figure 14-8

Again, Web Designer Wall isn't quite as easy to use some click-and-generate-code style resources, but that issue is offset because no other online resource provide such a specialized and nuanced set of gradient text effects.

CSS Menu Maker

http://cssmenumaker.com

Most horizontal and vertical drop-down or flyout menus require JavaScript, which makes them a hassle to edit for coders versed in HTML and CSS3. To the rescue, a full gallery of horizontal and vertical menus built with just CSS, like those in Figure 14-9, is available at CSS Menu Maker.

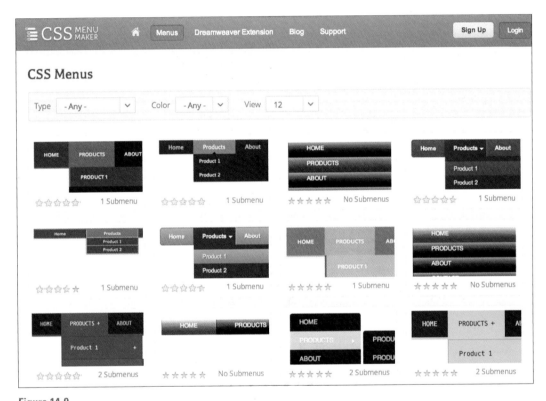

Figure 14-9

The menus at CSS Menu Maker use no JavaScript: only HTML and CSS. The site provides source code for the CSS menus that designers can download, edit, and integrate into web pages. And the site is free!

The code and files you need for a menu downloads as a zip file that includes an HTML file (with placeholder text for menu items), an external CSS file with necessary CSS, and a few tiny GIF images that supply icons for the menus. Designers with a basic grounding in HTML and CSS will find friendly instructions in the HTML file that downloads with each menu.

Notepad RT

`http://notepadrt.com`

In Chapter 13, I cover a range of HTML editors. Most of them do a nice job of editing CSS as well, but it seemed appropriate to include another editor here that does a great job with CSS3, and is free to boot.

Notepad RT has helpful syntax color-coding CSS3, including when defining new HTML5 selectors, such as `<aside>`; see Figure 14-10.

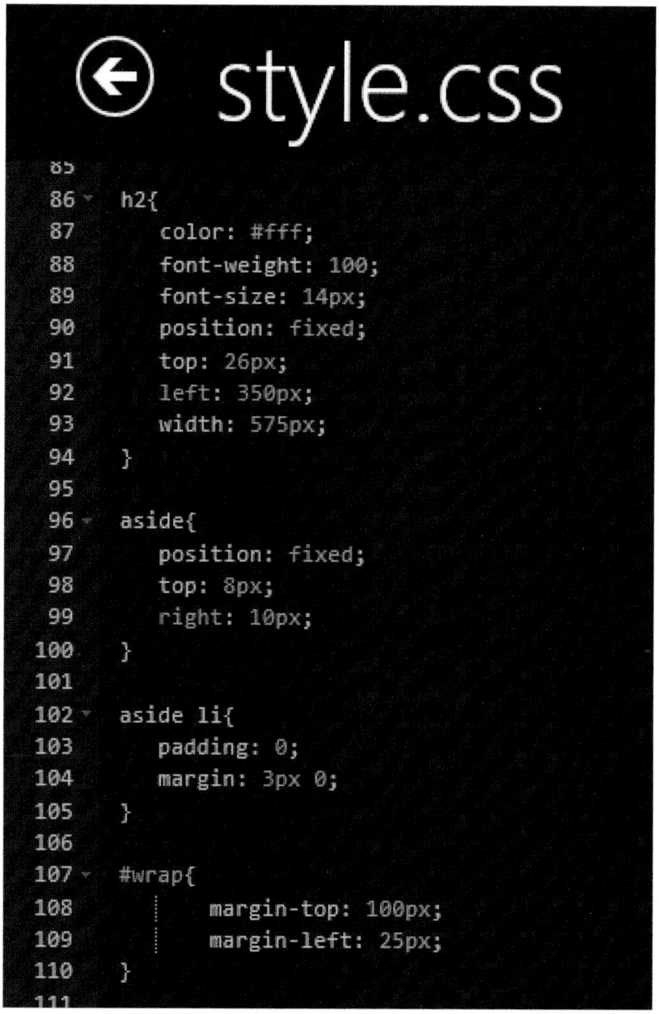

```css
85
86    h2{
87        color: #fff;
88        font-weight: 100;
89        font-size: 14px;
90        position: fixed;
91        top: 26px;
92        left: 350px;
93        width: 575px;
94    }
95
96    aside{
97        position: fixed;
98        top: 8px;
99        right: 10px;
100   }
101
102   aside li{
103       padding: 0;
104       margin: 3px 0;
105   }
106
107   #wrap{
108           margin-top: 100px;
109           margin-left: 25px;
110   }
111
```

Figure 14-10

Files can be created in-app or opened from the desktop into a full-screen editor. The editor includes many popular dark and light syntax highlighting themes to choose from. Editor windows can even be snapped next to the browser for easy debugging.

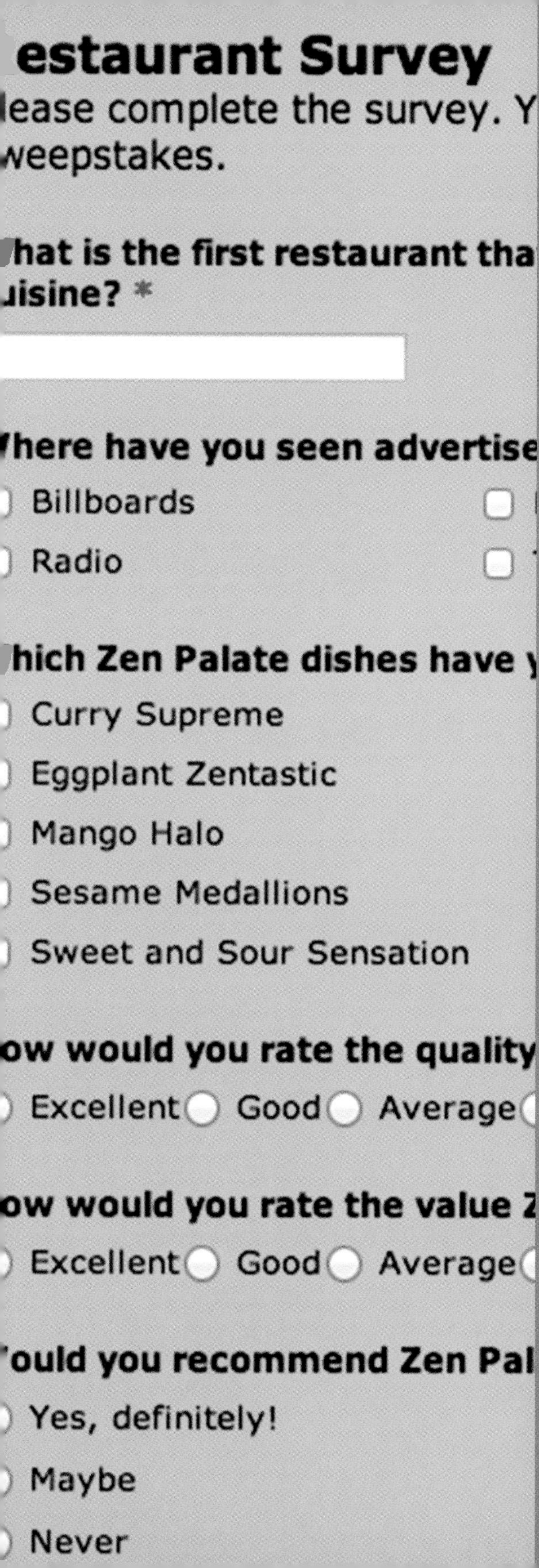

restaurant Survey

lease complete the survey. Y

weepstakes.

hat is the first restaurant tha
uisine? *

here have you seen advertise
◯ Billboards   ☐
◯ Radio   ☐

hich Zen Palate dishes have y
◯ Curry Supreme
◯ Eggplant Zentastic
◯ Mango Halo
◯ Sesame Medallions
◯ Sweet and Sour Sensation

ow would you rate the quality
◯ Excellent ◯ Good ◯ Average◯

ow would you rate the value Z
◯ Excellent ◯ Good ◯ Average◯

ould you recommend Zen Pal
◯ Yes, definitely!
◯ Maybe
◯ Never

CHAPTER 15

Top Ten Form Data Resources

In This Chapter

- Search box resources for your site

- Form design resources

- Online resources for collecting and managing form data

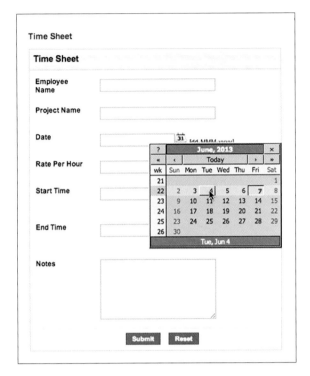

Forms are easy to design with HTML5 and CSS3, and HTML5 is loaded with new elements and parameters that make forms inviting and accessible. But where do you send form data?

Essentially, three options are available:

▶ You can contract with a back-end (server-side) database and scripting service to build resources on your server to collect and manage data. This option is expensive, relatively inflexible, and out of reach of many medium-sized enterprises.

▶ You can adapt a content management system (CMS), such as WordPress, that has some built-in form-handling tools. The downside is that you're constrained to the limited and relatively inflexible blog-style templates for building pages.

▶ The third approach takes advantages of a wealth of (mostly) free online resources that help generate forms; manage form data for search boxes, sign-up lists, and feedback forms; and collect, organize, and create reports on form input data.

This chapter discusses form management tools, ranging from search box indexers to mail list managers.

MailChimp

http://mailchimp.com

One of the most valuable resources any website has is registered or signed-up users. That user base consists of people who want to hear the message, learn about the products, or in some other way connect with the website.

MailChimp is a powerful mail list manager, and it's free for the first 500 names. With MailChimp, you generate very attractive targeted e-mailings, like the one in Figure 15-1. And MailChimp provides reports on who opens the mailings, and which links they follow. MailChimp also provides subscribers with convenient unsubscribe options, which reduce complaints and spam reports from unhappy users who find it difficult to remove themselves from a mail list.

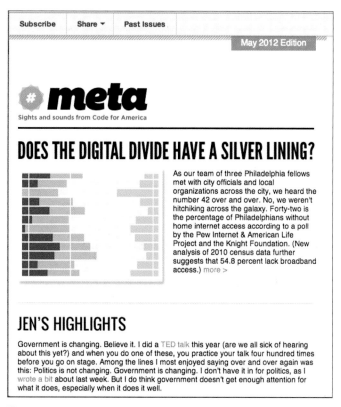

Figure 15-1

FreeFind

`www.freefind.com`

What website doesn't need a search box? Sure, they help visitors find what they're looking for at your site — and that's a good thing, right? — but search boxes and the resources associated with them also provide reports on what visitors to your site are searching for, and that information provides essential insights into how well your site is connecting with users.

The FreeFind search engine is free and easy to install. And you get help designing a form, which you can edit yourself with CSS and HTML. FreeFind sends regularly scheduled reports on what people are searching for at your site. Those reports can easily be ported into a spreadsheet (as shown in Figure 15-2), analyzed, and used to improve your site.

Day	Time of Query	Query
Sun	2/10/13 23:09	Web design
Fri	8/3/13 18:53	Robot
Wed	6/20/13 16:02	Forms
Thu	6/7/13 10:27	Adobe
Wed	5/2/13 8:07	Adobe Illustrator
Wed	4/18/13 21:17	Flash
Fri	3/16/13 18:47	Drupal
Thu	3/15/13 23:00	Books
Fri	3/2/13 16:07	HTML5 form tools
Fri	2/24/13 13:51	Adobe Illustrator
Mon	2/6/13 14:41	Flash
Mon	1/30/13 18:31	Drupal
Sat	1/21/13 0:16	Books
Thu	1/19/13 10:49	HTML5 form tools
Wed	11/2/13 6:46	DIV's
Mon	9/19/13 21:50	cs5
Thu	9/15/13 13:28	Define Flash
Sun	6/26/13 18:58	Edit queries
Sun	6/26/13 18:58	Form field
Fri	6/3/13 12:25	HTML5 article
Wed	6/1/13 13:43	Adobe Illustrator
Wed	4/27/13 13:53	Flash
Fri	4/15/13 12:09	Drupal
Fri	4/15/13 12:08	Books
Fri	4/15/13 12:08	HTML5 form tools

Figure 15-2

Google Docs

`www.docs.google.com`

Google Docs has a little-known tool for generating forms and managing form data built into the spreadsheet. When you set up an account with Google Docs, you can create a document, presentation, spreadsheet, form, or drawing. The easiest way to generate a form and manage form data is to start by creating a new spreadsheet. With that spreadsheet open, just choose Insert⇨Form from any open Google Docs spreadsheet to build a form that serves data into the spreadsheet.

Google Docs provides a friendly interface to generate a form, shown in Figure 15-3. After you complete the form, Google Docs provides a link to the form. Or — of more interest to web designers — you can generate HTML code to embed the form in your own site.

On the negative side, forms generated in Google Docs come with a message that your form is being managed by Google Docs, which is a bit of an inelegant intrusion into your site content. And porting data straight into a spreadsheet isn't the most powerful way to manage data. For a start-up, a growing online community, or an individual collecting sign-ups, Google Docs is a good entry-level resource.

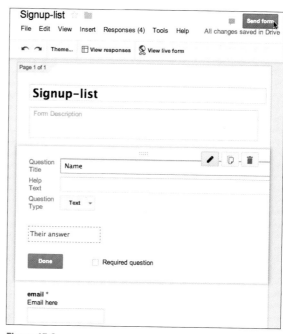

Figure 15-3

Google Custom Search Engine

`www.google.com/cse`

Speaking of Google, it also features a custom search engine that you can create for your site. Like the FreeFind search engine (listed earlier in this chapter), Google provides design templates for search boxes, like those shown in Figure 15-4.

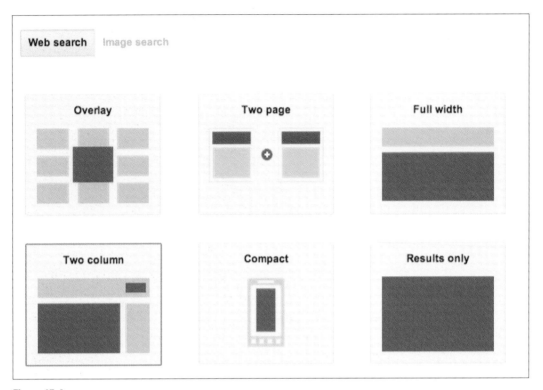

Figure 15-4

And, like the FreeFind search box generator, Google's custom search displays ads as part of the search results that appear when users search your site. You might not want that, but this is the "price" of free search tools. Both Google and FreeFind offer paid options that do not display ads.

TheSiteWizard

www.thesitewizard.com

Hosting a server-side script that manages data is actually within the reach of web designers who don't code in server-side languages (like PHP). The best tool for generating a PHP file that handles form data — without doing any coding yourself, that is — is TheSiteWizard.

TheSiteWizard generates PHP scripts that manage signup and feedback forms. Designers choose options and design a form, as well as Thank You pages and Error pages for users after they submit their form. Forms generated by TheSiteWizard are infinitely customizable. Designers can use HTML5 form tools as well as CSS3 design to make forms fit into their site's style, as shown in Figure 15-5.

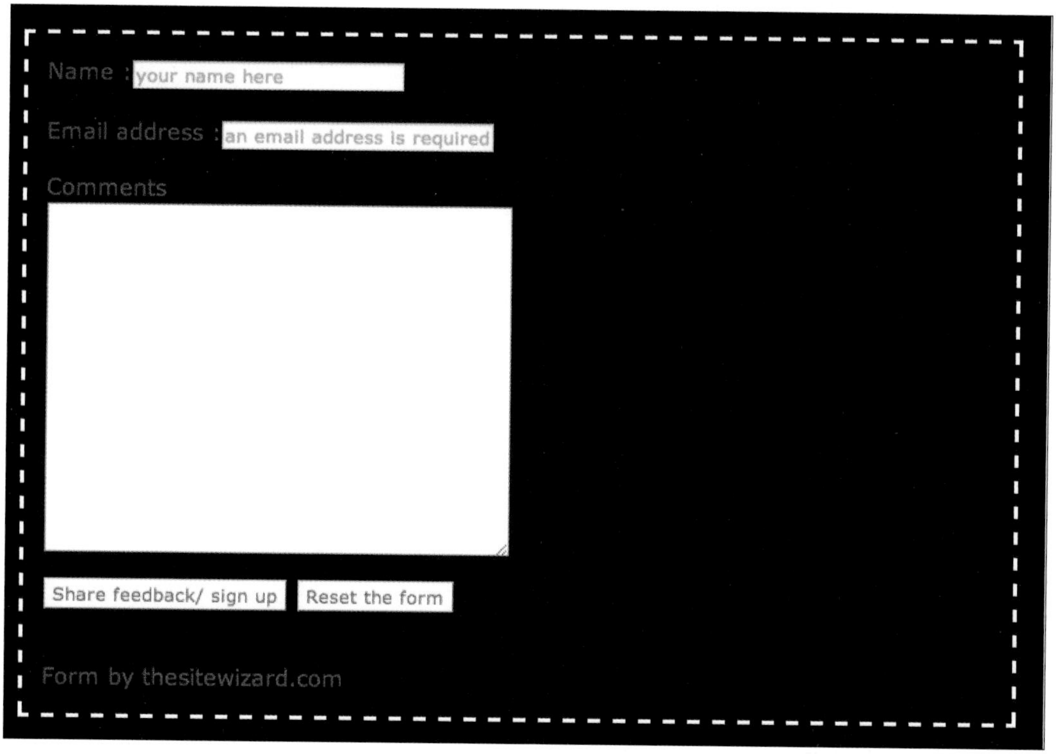

Figure 15-5

Form Tools

www.formtools.org

Form Tools is a free, open source PHP/MySQL framework for managing forms. It's more complex than the other form tools on the list, but it's more powerful as well. After registering with Form Tools, you can generate a demo and experiment with the types of forms you wish to use.

Form Tools creates quite complex and inviting forms for professional use, such as registration forms for events. These forms can be multipage, with tabs that allow a user to navigate through the form, like the one shown in Figure 15-6.

Contact Info   Guest Info   Travel and Hotel   Review   Thankyou

Contact Info

CONTACT INFO

Attendee Salutation

Please Select ⇅

Attendee First Name *

Attendee Middle Name

Attendee Last Name *

Attendee Email *

Figure 15-6

jQuery Menu Widget

```
http://api.jqueryui.com/menu
```

Not all forms require server side scripts. Sometimes form data is captured and managed right within a browser. These forms are referred to as *client-side* because the data is handled in a *client* (another word for *browser*). The most common tool for managing form data in a browser is JavaScript, and the most common client-side form is a jump navigation menu.

Figure 15-7

jQuery has a Menu Widget for client-side navigation forms that handle data in a browser. Figure 15-7 shows a navigation form generated from jQuery.

Freedback

www.freedback.com

Freedback offers an online form builder, with no HTML required. The builder isn't free, but it is discounted for nonprofits and educational institutions.

Freedback forms can be quite complex. Data is stored online and sent to you via e-mail. Figure 15-8 shows an example of Freedback's job application form.

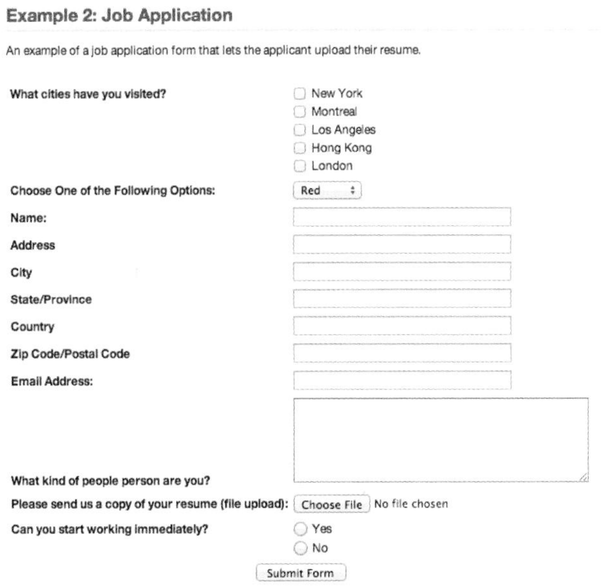

Example 2: Job Application

An example of a job application form that lets the applicant upload their resume.

What cities have you visited?
- [ ] New York
- [ ] Montreal
- [ ] Los Angeles
- [ ] Hong Kong
- [ ] London

Choose One of the Following Options: [Red ÷]

Name:

Address

City

State/Province

Country

Zip Code/Postal Code

Email Address:

What kind of people person are you?

Please send us a copy of your resume (file upload):   [Choose File] No file chosen

Can you start working immediately?
- ( ) Yes
- ( ) No

[Submit Form]

Figure 15-8

Freedback's free option allows you to generate a single form, with unlimited questions per form, unlimited submissions, spam filtering, and submission notification e-mails. Users will see an ad, though, but ad-free options start around $20 per month.

EmailMeForm

www.emailmeform.com

EmailMeForm provides forms and surveys, and forms for small sites are free. You can use EmailMeForm to create contact forms, registration forms, order forms, and online surveys. And forms can be connected with resources to collect data and payments with PayPal, Google Wallet, or Authorize.Net. Webmasters get real-time notifications when forms are submitted, and users get Thank You messages automatically.

EmailMeForm provides an impressive set of templates for specialized forms, including opinion polls, class enrollment, hotel reservations, job applications, medical appointments, and restaurant surveys (like the one shown in Figure 15-9).

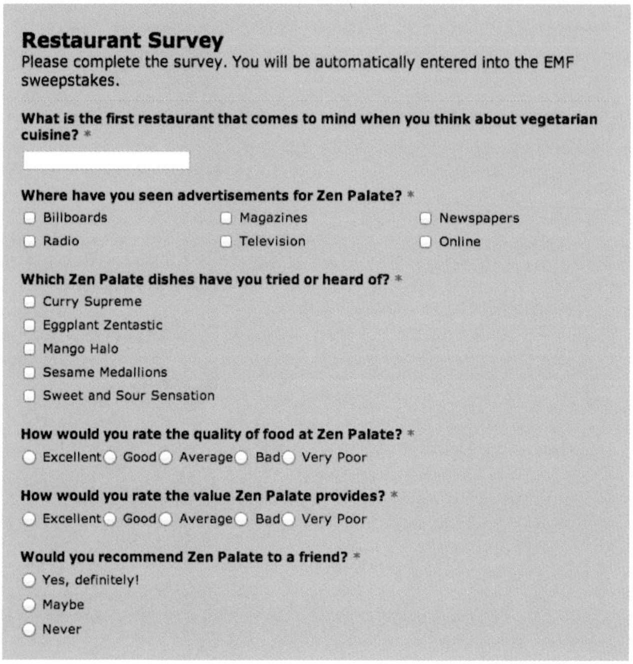

Restaurant Survey
Please complete the survey. You will be automatically entered into the EMF sweepstakes.

What is the first restaurant that comes to mind when you think about vegetarian cuisine? *

Where have you seen advertisements for Zen Palate? *
- Billboards
- Magazines
- Newspapers
- Radio
- Television
- Online

Which Zen Palate dishes have you tried or heard of? *
- Curry Supreme
- Eggplant Zentastic
- Mango Halo
- Sesame Medallions
- Sweet and Sour Sensation

How would you rate the quality of food at Zen Palate? *
Excellent Good Average Bad Very Poor

How would you rate the value Zen Palate provides? *
Excellent Good Average Bad Very Poor

Would you recommend Zen Palate to a friend? *
- Yes, definitely!
- Maybe
- Never

Figure 15-9

Zoho Creator

www.zoho.com/creator/online-form-builder

Zoho Creator is a robust, full-featured form generator and data-managing tool. Its forms are easy to build — and more importantly, are easily embedded in your website. The forms and data tools are free for personal use, but there is a fee for professional use; nonprofits can get a discount.

Zoho Creator includes tools to generate reports based on collected data including graphical data display in charts and tables, and exported into databases or spreadsheets. You're notified when a form is submitted. And like other form-generating tools, you can set *Captcha fields* (where users try to decipher cryptic text and enter it into a field to prove they are human users and not spam software).

An interesting plus is that you can include a File Upload Field in a form so users can upload resumes, photos, and other files (maximum size of 5MB).

The Zoho Creator set of form templates features professional needs, such as bug reporting, expense accounting, IT inventories, and a time sheet (shown in Figure 15-10).

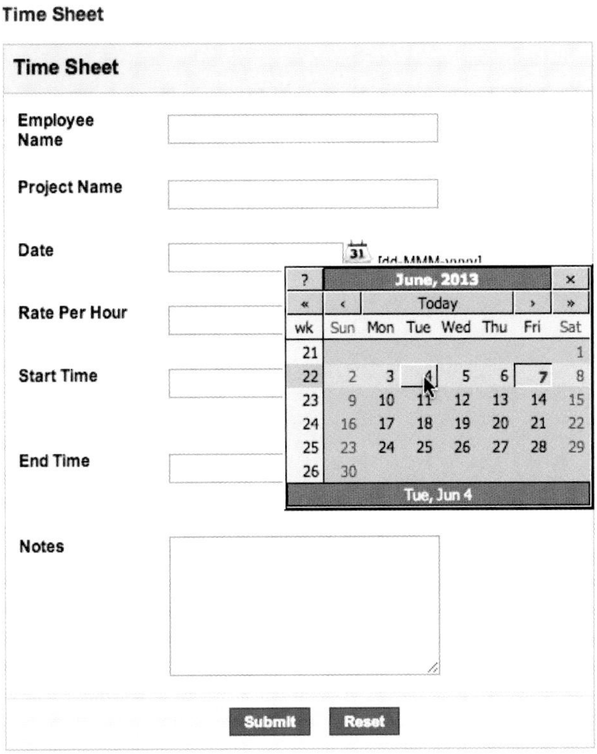

Time Sheet

Figure 15-10

PRIVACY ISSUES

Internet privacy is a hot topic these days, both in regard to government policy and the practices of sites that collect and use data. A full exploration of these issues is beyond the scope of this book, but here's a one-word basic rule of thumb: transparency. Tell users why you are collecting data. Make sure they are signing up for your e-mails and e-newsletters voluntarily. And give them easy ways to remove themselves from your list. This basic approach will promote a credible, mutually beneficial relationship with users who fill out forms at your website.

Index

About the Author

David Karlins is a web designer, an author, and a teacher. He is the author of more than 40 books on digital graphic and interactive design, including *Building Websites All-in-One For Dummies,* 2nd Edition (co-author with Doug Sahlin); *Dreamweaver CS6 Mobile and Web Development with HTML5, CSS3, and jQuery Mobile;* and *Digital Sports Photography: Take Winning Shots Every Time* (co-author with Serge Timacheff). David's articles have appeared in *Macworld*, *PCWorld*, and numerous online publications. His web design clients include a wide range of performers, performance venues, events, and retail vendors.

Author's Acknowledgments

Thanks and appreciation to the entire editorial and design team at Dummies, to my agent Margot Hutchinson at Waterside Agency, and to my students and others who contributed insights and critiques that strengthened this book — especially Richard Jørgensen.

Publisher's Acknowledgments

Executive Editor: Steve Hayes

Project Editor: Blair J. Pottenger

Senior Copy Editor: Teresa Artman

Technical Editor: Claudia Snell

Editorial Assistant: Annie Sullivan

Sr. Editorial Assistant: Cherie Case

Project Coordinator: Kristie Rees

Cover Image: ©iStockphoto.com/pagaddesign

pple & Mac

ad For Dummies,
h Edition
78-1-118-49823-1

hone 5 For Dummies,
h Edition
78-1-118-35201-4

acBook For Dummies,
h Edition
78-1-118-20920-2

S X Mountain Lion
or Dummies
78-1-118-39418-2

ogging & Social Media

acebook For Dummies,
h Edition
8-1-118-09562-1

om Blogging
or Dummies
8-1-118-03843-7

nterest For Dummies
8-1-118-32800-2

ordPress For Dummies,
h Edition
8-1-118-38318-6

siness

mmodities For Dummies,
d Edition
8-1-118-01687-9

esting For Dummies,
h Edition
8-0-470-90545-6

Personal Finance
For Dummies,
7th Edition
978-1-118-11785-9

QuickBooks 2013
For Dummies
978-1-118-35641-8

Small Business Marketing Kit
For Dummies,
3rd Edition
978-1-118-31183-7

Careers

Job Interviews
For Dummies,
4th Edition
978-1-118-11290-8

Job Searching with
Social Media
For Dummies
978-0-470-93072-4

Personal Branding
For Dummies
978-1-118-11792-7

Resumes For Dummies,
6th Edition
978-0-470-87361-8

Success as a Mediator
For Dummies
978-1-118-07862-4

Diet & Nutrition

Belly Fat Diet For Dummies
978-1-118-34585-6

Eating Clean For Dummies
978-1-118-00013-7

Nutrition For Dummies,
5th Edition
978-0-470-93231-5

Digital Photography

Digital Photography
For Dummies,
7th Edition
978-1-118-09203-3

Digital SLR Cameras &
Photography For Dummies,
4th Edition
978-1-118-14489-3

Photoshop Elements 11
For Dummies
978-1-118-40821-6

Gardening

Herb Gardening
For Dummies,
2nd Edition
978-0-470-61778-6

Vegetable Gardening
For Dummies,
2nd Edition
978-0-470-49870-5

Health

Anti-Inflammation Diet
For Dummies
978-1-118-02381-5

Diabetes For Dummies,
3rd Edition
978-0-470-27086-8

Living Paleo For Dummies
978-1-118-29405-5

Hobbies

Beekeeping
For Dummies
978-0-470-43065-1

eBay For Dummies,
7th Edition
978-1-118-09806-6

Raising Chickens
For Dummies
978-0-470-46544-8

Wine For Dummies,
5th Edition
978-1-118-28872-6

Writing Young Adult Fiction
For Dummies
978-0-470-94954-2

Language &
Foreign Language

500 Spanish Verbs
For Dummies
978-1-118-02382-2

English Grammar
For Dummies,
2nd Edition
978-0-470-54664-2

French All-in One
For Dummies
978-1-118-22815-9

German Essentials
For Dummies
978-1-118-18422-6

Italian For Dummies,
2nd Edition
978-1-118-00465-4

Available in print and e-book formats.

Math & Science

Algebra I For Dummies,
2nd Edition
978-0-470-55964-2

Anatomy and Physiology
For Dummies,
2nd Edition
978-0-470-92326-9

Astronomy For Dummies,
3rd Edition
978-1-118-37697-3

Biology For Dummies,
2nd Edition
978-0-470-59875-7

Chemistry For Dummies,
2nd Edition
978-1-1180-0730-3

Pre-Algebra Essentials
For Dummies
978-0-470-61838-7

Microsoft Office

Excel 2013 For Dummies
978-1-118-51012-4

Office 2013 All-in-One
For Dummies
978-1-118-51636-2

PowerPoint 2013
For Dummies
978-1-118-50253-2

Word 2013 For Dummies
978-1-118-49123-2

Music

Blues Harmonica
For Dummies
978-1-118-25269-7

Guitar For Dummies,
3rd Edition
978-1-118-11554-1

iPod & iTunes
For Dummies,
10th Edition
978-1-118-50864-0

Programming

Android Application
Development For
Dummies, 2nd Edition
978-1-118-38710-8

iOS 6 Application
Development For Dummies
978-1-118-50880-0

Java For Dummies,
5th Edition
978-0-470-37173-2

Religion & Inspiration

The Bible For Dummies
978-0-7645-5296-0

Buddhism For Dummies,
2nd Edition
978-1-118-02379-2

Catholicism For Dummies,
2nd Edition
978-1-118-07778-8

Self-Help & Relationships

Bipolar Disorder
For Dummies,
2nd Edition
978-1-118-33882-7

Meditation For Dummies,
3rd Edition
978-1-118-29144-3

Seniors

Computers For Seniors
For Dummies,
3rd Edition
978-1-118-11553-4

iPad For Seniors
For Dummies,
5th Edition
978-1-118-49708-1

Social Security
For Dummies
978-1-118-20573-0

Smartphones & Tablets

Android Phones
For Dummies
978-1-118-16952-0

Kindle Fire HD
For Dummies
978-1-118-42223-6

NOOK HD For Dummies,
Portable Edition
978-1-118-39498-4

Surface For Dummies
978-1-118-49634-3

Test Prep

ACT For Dummies,
5th Edition
978-1-118-01259-8

ASVAB For Dummies,
3rd Edition
978-0-470-63760-9

GRE For Dummies,
7th Edition
978-0-470-88921-3

Officer Candidate Tests,
For Dummies
978-0-470-59876-4

Physician's Assistant Exam
For Dummies
978-1-118-11556-5

Series 7 Exam
For Dummies
978-0-470-09932-2

Windows 8

Windows 8 For Dummies
978-1-118-13461-0

Windows 8 For Dummies,
Book + DVD Bundle
978-1-118-27167-4

Windows 8 All-in-One
For Dummies
978-1-118-11920-4

Available in print and e-book formats.

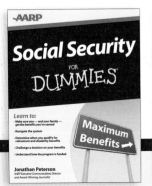

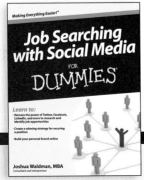

Take Dummies with you everywhere you go!

Whether you're excited about e-books, want more from the web, must have your mobile apps, or swept up in social media, Dummies makes everything easier .

Visit Us

Like Us

Follow Us

Watch Us

Join Us

Pin Us

Circle Us

Shop Us

Dummies products make life easier

- DIY
- Consumer Electronics
- Crafts
- Software
- Cookware
- Hobbies
- Videos
- Music
- Games
- and More!

For more information, go to **Dummies.com®** and search the store by category.

A Wiley Bra

Dummies is a registered trademark of John Wiley & Sons, Inc.